TROUBLED LIVES

LOTTE AND JOSEPH HAMBURGER

Troubled Lives:
John and Sarah Austin

UNIVERSITY OF TORONTO PRESS
TORONTO BUFFALO LONDON

© University of Toronto Press 1985
Toronto Buffalo London
Printed in Canada
ISBN 0-8020-2521-8

Canadian Cataloguing in Publication Data

Hamburger, Lotte, 1924–
  Troubled lives
  Includes bibliographical references and index.
  ISBN 0-8020-2521-8
  1. Austin, John, 1790–1859. 2. Austin, Sarah,
  1793–1867. 3. Lawyers – England – Biography.
  4. Authors, English – 19th century – Biography –
  Marriage. I. Hamburger, Joseph, 1922– II. Title.
  K230.A8624 1985   340'.1092'4   C84-099337-4

To Annette, Jeffrey, Philip, and their grandmother, Kate,
who accepted the Austins' presence with good humour.

It is too painful to think that she is a woman, with a woman's destiny before her – a woman spinning in young ignorance a light web of folly and vain hopes which may one day close round her and press upon her, a rancorous poisoned garment, changing all at once ... into a life of deep human anguish.

George Eliot *Adam Bede*

Contents

Preface

John and Sarah Austin were part of the Victorian intelligentsia, members of what their friend James Stephen called 'the Order of the Quill.' John Austin (1790-1859) was a major figure in English legal thought and a founder of what came to be known as the Austinian theory of jurisprudence, and Sarah Austin (1793-1867) was well known in her own day for her literary work, especially for her translations of important German works. Both Austins had close friendships with Bentham, James Mill, John Stuart Mill, Grote, Senior, Thomas and Jane Welsh Carlyle, Guizot, and Sydney Smith – a circle so illustrious that it has overshadowed the Austins themselves, and neither has been the subject of a full-scale biography. The nearest approach to an account of Sarah Austin is a Victorian volume of family letters, connected by minimal narrative, *Three Generations of English Women* (1888, 1893), that was published by Janet Ross, Sarah Austin's granddaughter.

For all of John Austin's importance to legal philosophy, the most basic facts surrounding his life and work have remained obscure, partly because he became a recluse and partly because his wife, after his death, determined that it should be so. When she was criticized for failing to include sufficient factual details about her husband's life in her preface to his work, she retorted that it contained all the public needed to know – she was writing the history of his book not of the man. She feared that the life of the man would belittle him, and hence she was reserved and even secretive about many of the details of his career. While Sarah Austin was far more widely known than her husband during her lifetime, and her name recurs in many reminiscences of the period, the personality and accomplishments of the woman who could draw to herself an astonishing number of gifted men and women have also remained elusive.

Sarah Austin made a name for herself as a writer in literary and political journals and, above all, as a translator, especially of German, at a time when knowledge of German ideas and literature in Britain was still very limited. In this account we consider her literary work and political writing, but the emphasis is on the part she played as woman and wife. Fortune smiled on Sarah at birth – endowed her with vitality, beauty, and intellectual ability, and granted her a happy youth – and then turned its back. At about nineteen she fell in love with a brilliant, learned, but flawed man, and soon enough found herself enmeshed in a tragic marriage in which she shared what she called her husband's 'troubled life' and became his fellow sufferer. She had set out on marriage with the idea of being a 'helpmate' to her husband, an enlightened idea at the turn of the century when she was growing up, but eventually she seems to have been entrapped by this notion, and her life certainly put it to a severe test. Finally she managed to rescue something from her unfortunate situation, yet she paid a heavy price and did not emerge unmarred from her struggle. Thus there are no heroines or heroes in this account, which presents a supremely gifted but temperamentally ill-matched couple and their marriage and, incidentally, one more example of an unusual nineteenth-century alliance.

John Austin impressed a small group of contemporaries by his highly original ideas and strong opinions, but he failed to live up to his promise and published so little that he regarded himself as a failure, and he died an embittered man with no apprehension that his name would live. Only after his death when his complete work on jurisprudence was published did he become a major figure in legal philosophy. Posthumously the Austinian theory of law acquired its great influence, and it continues to provoke interest and controversy among scholars – the very word 'Austinian' has become part of the language. Austin's work established the study of jurisprudence in Britain: he was the catalyst that set others on the path of examining fundamental legal notions. One can 'find thoughts distinctly traceable to him far away among people who never heard of him,' Walter Bagehot noted. Among lawyers his admirers included James Fitzjames Stephen and A.V. Dicey, and even those who were critical of his work, such as Henry Sumner Maine, have emphasized its significance. He was, as Professor Hart pointed out, the progenitor of a long line of distinguished jurists. Thus the Austinian school has dominated the field, and while it has not lacked critics, as Hart put it, 'never, since his death, has it been ignored.'

Books and articles on Austin's jurisprudence abound, but his work on the larger questions of political theory has been all but ignored. Here we emphasize and reconstruct his speculations about the best institutions of government, not only for their intrinsic interest but for the influence they ultimately exercised on his views of jurisprudence. Austin as a political theorist abandoned the formal and definitional approach of his juris-prudence, and his speculations about government and politics were adventurous and striking and at times were expressed in vivid language that recalls the Austin who was judged glorious in talk. Three stages of Austin's changing political ideas are depicted: his early Benthamite radi-calism, which preceded his jurisprudence; his political theory with its novel ideas about the principle of utility, authority, science, and élites, that accompanied his jurisprudence during the middle of his life; and his post-1848 conservatism. This final transformation of his beliefs was im-portant because it led him to doubt the political theory he had ex-pounded in the *Province of Jurisprudence* as well as the principle of utility, which was a fundamental part of his jurisprudential system. His conser-vatism ultimately led to a recantation of parts of his jurisprudence, so that at the end of his life he had affinities with the historical school.

John and Sarah Austin are presented here in a dual portrait. The interwoven character of their lives makes this appropriate, for a biogra-phy of one of them without the other would have been a distortion. It was due to Sarah Austin's effort, after her husband's death, that his entire work on law was finally presented to the public. Without her determina-tion his name might well have remained obscure. She was also the essential witness and recorder of their existence; without her letters, this story could not have been told. An understanding of his life is enhanced by examining hers, and her life is incomprehensible without considering his, for it was shaped – probably misshaped – by her efforts to gain him recognition.

John Stuart Mill is a ubiquitous figure in this book. Both personally and intellectually he was closely connected with the Austins. For a time he was almost like a son – he played with their daughter, went on holidays with them, shared intimacies. He also studied with John Austin and owed him an intellectual debt so great that, despite a quarrel with Sarah Austin, he never turned his back on his former mentor. Mill observed much of the grief in the Austins' lives, and his testimony is an important part of this book.

Our interpretation of the personal side of the Austins' lives has been shaped by new evidence – mainly manuscript letters, many of them Sarah Austin's. These letters introduced us to a more tragic and complicated woman than we had encountered in her granddaughter Janet Ross' compilation of family letters – *Three Generations of English Women*, a volume that has been most useful, since many of the letters she printed were subsequently lost in World War II. Janet Ross's volume also posed a challenge, for it presented only selected parts of her grandmother's life. By omitting so much that was 'private' or too strong politically or judgmental, she flattened Sarah Austin's character till she seemed insubstantial. Yet Sarah's strong personality is inexplicable without considering her personal life, especially her marriage, and her outspoken opinions, which were often 'against the tide.' Ross further diluted the image of her grandmother by putting the emphasis on the eminent friends with whom she corresponded – nearly half the letters in the collection were in fact to Sarah and not from her, and those from her were predominantly written after 1848, that is, after she was fifty-five years old. It was the old, resigned, conventional, and very conservative woman that spoke in them. Janet Ross found the late eighteenth-century provincial Unitarian moral earnestness and intellectual seriousness that had shaped her grandparents' attitudes unacceptable. The Austin story with its themes of disappointed hopes, strong moral beliefs, intellectualism, and extremes of opinion on both sides of the political spectrum was obscured for a more socially acceptable portrait.

In our account of the Austins' private life, we chose to retain the immediacy (and in Sarah Austin's case, especially the clarity and pungency) of the original voices at the cost of having to tolerate frequent quotation marks. Also, we decided, with no disrespect to our chief characters, to forgo perfect symmetry in the use of their names. We thus varied our usage according to the nature of the subject matter and context and aimed to avoid clumsiness in the flow of the narrative.

This is a work of joint authorship, but each of us has written different parts. Although each has contributed something to every chapter, Lotte Hamburger is mainly responsible for chapters 1, 3, 4, 6, and 7, and Joseph Hamburger for chapters 2, 5, 8, 9, and 10.

Acknowledgments

We would like to express our gratitude to the following persons and institutions for allowing us to publish passages from manuscripts in their custody: Badische Landesbibliothek, Karlsruhe; Bayerische Staatsbibliothek, München; Biblioteca Labronica, F.D. Guerrazzi, Livorno; Mrs Georgiana Blakiston; Bodleian Library, Oxford; the Trustees of the Bowood Manuscript Collection; British Library; British Library of Political and Economic Science; the Syndics of Cambridge University Library; Sir Andrew Duff-Gordon; Durham University Library; Freies Deutsches Hochstift, Frankfurt am Main; Dr Albert Ganado; Houghton Library, Harvard University; Historical Society of Pennsylvania, Philadelphia; Lord Howard of Henderskelfe; Huntington Library, San Marino, California; Institut de France; Local History Library, Norwich; Longmans Group Ltd; Manchester College, Oxford; John Murray, Publishers; the Trustees of the National Library of Scotland; National Library of Wales; Nationale Forschungs und Gedenkstätten der Klassischen Deutschen Literatur, Weimar; Public Record Office, and the Controller of H.M. Stationery Office, London; Director, Royal Botanic Gardens, Kew; Sächsische Landesbibliothek, Dresden; St Bride Printing Library, London, and Taylor and Francis Ltd; Mme Gruner Schlumberger, Val Richer (Guizot Papers); Staatsbibliothek, Preussischer Kulturbesitz, Berlin, früher Preussische Staatsbibliothek; Staats und Universitätsbibliothek, Hamburg; the Master and Fellows of Trinity College, Cambridge; Universitätsbibliothek Bonn, Autographensammlung; University College, London; Department of Special Collections, University Research Library, University of California at Los Angeles; University of Iowa Library; University of Michigan Library; University of South Carolina Library; Victoria and Albert Museum; Mr Gordon Waterfield; Dr Williams's Trust, London; and Yale University Library, including the Osborn Collection.

Our work on the Austins introduced us to some remarkably generous persons. We feel special gratitude to Mrs John Austin of Grove Farm, Suffolk, and her late husband for showing us Austin family memorabilia and offering us the kindest hospitality. We also feel particularly indebted to Mr and Mrs Noel Blakiston for their warm-hearted hospitality and for letting us see some significant Sarah Austin letters. We would also like to thank Ann Robson and Jack Robson of the University of Toronto for reading the manuscript and giving us the benefit of their encyclopaedic knowledge and in other ways for smoothing our 'scabrous road' – to borrow a phrase of John Austin's. Mr and Mrs Gordon Waterfield were the kindest of hosts, shared with us such family letters as they still possess, let us examine Sarah Austin's commonplace book, and showed us family memorabilia. Dr Paul Xuereb of the University of Malta was another of our generous helpers, not least in locating two scarce lithographs portraying the Austins' entry to Valletta in 1836.

We would like to record our gratitude to several other persons who answered specific inquiries or offered other assistance: Robert Balay, Yale University Library; Alan Bell, National Library of Scotland; Kevin Bridson, formerly librarian at the Linnean Society of London; William Brock, University of Leicester; Rev. M.R. Buckley, formerly rector of the Weybridge Parish Church; Nigil Cross, Royal Literary Fund; Jeanne Fahnestock, for information about the *Athenaeum*; Dr Walter Ganado; Brian Hayes, for permitting us to see his unpublished dissertation on Norwich politics; Esther Houghton, Wellesley Index of Victorian Periodicals; A.D.E. Lewis, University College, London; Wallace Morfey, historian of the Ipswich School; *New Statesman and Nation*, for access to its marked file of the *Athenaeum*; H.O. Pappe, University of Sussex; Stephen Parks, curator of the Osborn collection, Beinecke Library, Yale University; Jeffrey Sammons, Yale University; Richard Sanders, editor of the *Collected Letters of Jane and Thomas Carlyle*; Barbara Smith, Manchester College Library; Mr and Mrs J. Speak, for showing us Nutfield House, Weybridge; R.K. Webb, Institute of Advanced Studies, who sent us an illuminating essay on Unitarianism in all its complex varieties; the curator, Staatliche Museen, Preussischer Kulturbesitz, Berlin (for photographs of the Hensel portraits of Sarah Austin); and Marius Zerafa, director of the Museums Department, Malta, for providing a photograph of the lithograph showing John Austin's entry into Valletta.

Research on John Austin has been generously supported by grants from the A. Whitney Griswold Faculty Research Fund of the Council on the Humanities and the Concilium on International and Area Studies at Yale University. The National Endowment for the Humanities and the Earhart Foundation generously supported research in which John Austin's jurisprudence and political theory had an important place.

Sally Taylor, aged fifteen or sixteen. Drawing by Amelia Opie
From Janet Ross *Three Generations of English Women* (London 1888)

Sarah Austin, 1835. Drawing by Weld Taylor, after H.P. Briggs
From Lewis Melville *The Berry Papers* (London 1914)

Sarah Austin, 1840, by John Linnell
Photograph by courtesy of the National Portrait Gallery, London. Location of portrait unknown.

Sarah Austin, 1843, by Wilhelm Hensel
Reproduced by permission of the Nationalgalerie, Staatliche Museen, Preussischer Kulturbesitz, Berlin

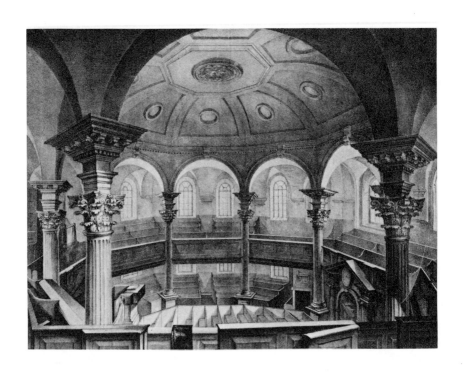

The Octagon Chapel, Norwich

From John Taylor *The History of the Octagon Chapel, Norwich* ... (Hackney 1848).
By permission of the British Library

John Austin and George Cornewall Lewis being welcomed in Valletta,
26 October 1836. From a lithograph in the Museum of Fine Arts,
Valletta

Hermann von Pückler-Muskau, by Franz Krüger

Hermann von Pückler-Muskau. Lithograph by Friedrich Jentzen, c. 1824, from a portrait by Franz Krüger

TROUBLED LIVES

1

'Worthy of being a wife'

WHEN SARAH TAYLOR ANNOUNCED HER ENGAGEMENT to John Austin in 1814, it created quite a stir in some Norwich circles. The triumphs of 'Sally' Taylor had been tea-table gossip for some time.[1] The youngest of seven children, endowed with striking beauty and abundant mental gifts, she was, after some incautious entanglements, making a choice that surprised nearly everyone. Her friends found it incongruous that this exceedingly lively, flirtatious twenty-one-year-old-girl should prefer the sombre, austere John Austin to all her other admirers. He was undoubtedly a man of compelling intelligence; admittedly he was handsome – slender, on the tall side, with large, deep-set hazel eyes and the erect carriage of a former military man. That his hair had gone white, though he was only twenty-four years old, gave a distinctive look to an already emphatic personality. Temperamentally, however, they seemed strangely matched. Sarah was self-confident, 'dazzling, attractive, imposing,' with an impulsive, warm manner and a love of society in which she could display her charm and intelligence. Austin, on the other hand, was diffident yet proud, often appearing arrogant and icy; his occasional vehemence, dogmatism, and arresting eloquence in conversation alternated with a despondence and lassitude that bordered on melancholia. Many who met him were struck by his original and strong mind: according to the poet Henry Taylor, 'one could not see him at all without knowing something of the intellect which lay hidden in him.'[2] Yet while John Austin awed some of his contemporaries, he does not appear to have attracted many close friends in his youth.

Sarah's family had doubts: initially her parents were strongly opposed to the engagement.[3] The precise nature of their objections is a matter of speculation, but there are hints that indicate some of the obstacles. They had known about young Austin for some time, for he had met Sarah in 1812 when she was nineteen years old and he had just left the army aged twenty-two. (Their introduction may well have been through John Austin's sister Anne Austin, who was Sarah's friend and became the wife of John Rising Staff, a Norwich solicitor and later the town clerk of Norwich, whose family was on terms of friendship with Sarah's parents.)[4] The army was not a career esteemed by the Taylors. The same year Sarah met John, her mother, Susanna Taylor, expressed the hope that the young boy cousins of the Taylors would be anything but soldiers and sailors: 'Let them be chemists and mechanics, or carpenters and masons, anything but destroyers of mankind. This is not very chivalrous, but I hope it is something better.' A military career was also suspect because it was incompatible with the development of that vigorous and early use of the mental faculties that she saw as the foundation of later discipline, enjoyment, and achievement. To spend one's youth in the army was to waste one of the most precious periods of life.[5]

John Austin, however, had done just that. Apparently in a fit of anti-Napoleonic enthusiasm, he joined the army just three weeks before his seventeenth birthday. On 12 February 1807, with the name Jonathan, not John, he was commissioned an ensign in the 44th (East Essex) Regiment. He stayed in the army for five years, in spite of increasing disillusionment. His choice to enlist certainly appears to have been singularly inappropriate to his temperament. A young man who could write in his diary 'My own happiness is commensurate with and inseparable from the progress I make in the acquisition of knowledge' was obviously unlikely to find the military life congenial.[6] And the army experience left him with an unfortunate residue of bitterness and self-dissatisfaction.

His army career began commendably enough. He joined the 2nd Battalion at Fort George in Guernsey, and early the following year when he was recommended for a vacant lieutenancy, his commanding officer described him as 'a remarkably fine young man, and a very good attentive Officer.'[7] Soon after this, however, the chance roulette of army postings played him false, and instead of finding himself absorbed in the life of purposefulness that he seems to have hoped for, he found that for the greater part of five years he was chained to an existence of anxious stagnation. Whereas the regiment he had joined was to take part in the Peninsular campaign, John Austin was transferred to the 1st Battalion, with which he spent the next three years in Sicily, defending the island against an invasion by Napoleon's forces that never took place.[8] Even his commanding general was to describe this war of waiting as 'a long tedious term of watchful duty.' During much of this period Austin was detached to a grenadier battalion at Faro point – above Homer's Charybdis – with Scylla just two-and-a-half miles away on the mainland, where Murat's soldiers were poised for invasion.[9] In spite of brief periods of tense anticipation and one attempt to harass the enemy, in which he probably took part, this war of nerves created opportunities for an aimless, mindless, and dissipated existence.[10]

Boredom in this inactive army increased even more when, in August 1811, Lieutenant Austin's battalion returned to its garrison in Malta. The extent of his lapses from his own standard of conduct can be guessed from the magnitude of his self-disgust: 'The last day of December has irresistably forced upon my attention the conduct of 1811. The retrospect has hardly given rise to one single feeling of self-satisfaction. During that period, the waste of money, of time and of health has been enormous; and indolence – always the prominent vice of my character – has within the last nine months assumed over me an empire I almost despair of shaking.'[11] In his diary he continued to record 'lethargy of the faculties' and 'listlessness of indolence and ennui.' To counter such feelings he read – Locke's *Essay Concerning Human Understanding*, Dugald Stewart's 'Essay on the Beautiful,' and Mitford's *History of Greece* – but he also described a debauch, a row, impertinent conduct in the presence of a general, and confinement to quarters for an unnamed offence.[12]

John Austin regretted entering the army, and he came to disdain army life even more than Susanna Taylor did.[13] Although he now felt that the army was entirely the wrong career for him, he was undecided about an alternative, and here he showed the vacillation that appears to have made the Taylors nervous. He postponed his decision by arranging a six-month leave of absence from 1 March 1812. A day later he received a distraught letter from his father, Jonathan Austin, pleading with him to resign his commission because his younger brother Joseph had died from yellow fever while serving on a warship off the island of Java. His father also offered him support while he settled into a new profession. Lieutenant Austin thus returned home, but he hesitated until his leave had all but expired to submit his letter of resignation.[14]

The Taylors also noted his hesitancy about beginning a new life once he returned to his home in Ipswich. It is not clear what he was doing during the two years between leaving the army in 1812 and beginning his legal studies. In his diary he had constantly reproached himself for dilatoriness, but almost two years of indecision about the next step followed. There thus appears to have been some ground for Susanna Taylor seeking reassurance about his present and future purposefulness. 'His engagement as you observe will quicken his exertion,' was a friend's response to her anxieties[15]. John was clearly worthy of Sarah on grounds of character, but the Taylors appear to have discerned beneath his forceful manner and elevated ideas a diffident, indecisive, and overly sensitive constitution ill-fitted to his ambition. There were also more obvious obstacles. When in 1814 he asked for Sarah's hand he had just begun reading law and still had three years to take dinners before he could be called to the bar at the Inner Temple. With no independent income and the prospect of years of study, which would be followed by the hazards of trying to make a name at the bar, it hardly seemed the auspicious moment for him to take on another commitment, especially as dependence on his father was clearly irksome to a man of his pride.

The Taylors were particularly sensitive to the vicissitude of fortune in the autumn of 1814, since the young physician husband of Sarah's only sister, Susan Reeve, had just died, leaving his widow with two small children to rear. Susan, for the time being, was once more living with her parents. Mrs Taylor, torn by the conflicting emotions in her house, tried to find comfort in the girls' closeness and drew for her friend Anna Letitia Barbauld 'a touching picture ... of the two dear sisters, whose situation is so different, whose hearts are so much in unison.' Sarah's hopes provided some distraction to the stoical Susan, who wrote to a brother, 'How I long to talk ... about Sally's affair. Does it not seem as if it was to be a comfort in time of need to us. I mean, by furnishing a matter of deep interest?' Yet Mrs Taylor remained uneasy about endorsing her younger daughter's attachment. Married life brought 'too many cares and responsibilities to be entered upon without trembling and anxiety,' and the situation recalled to her how reluctantly she had consented to Susan's ill-starred early marriage. She had been eager not to have Sarah's affections engaged till she was older. 'The marriage of children has been one of my greatest trials,' she lamented to one of her unmarried sons. Law was by no means a certain livelihood, she feared, yet business also was beset by such uncertainties 'that a woman may marry with favourable prospects – and soon be surrounded by helpless children without adequate means of support.' Seeking to still her nagging worries, she argued that 'in a profession like the law if a man does establish himself he [was] subject to fewer vicissitudes.' Whatever the future might bring, this parting from her youngest child would be no small sacrifice; the painful thought was only alleviated by recalling that she was being asked to reconcile herself to a very long engagement with marriage as a distant prospect.[16]

Yet even Mrs Taylor conceded that there were some things that spoke in favour of this engagement. Mr Taylor was sixty-four and she would soon be sixty. The position of single girls was fraught with difficulties. Evidently thinking of Sarah, she noted that 'independence of mind and such a degree of confidence in their own powers as prevents their being a burthen to others is unwillingly allowed them.' It was unfortunate that Sarah, who did not disguise her self-confidence and cleverness, was criticized for being so independent. 'People like feeble helpless beings till they find how troublesome they may become,' noted Mrs Taylor, who had a keen interest in the new ideas about women that were being broached at the turn of the century when Sarah was growing up. She admitted that her daughter's high spirits and vanity at times led her into 'scrapes and difficulties,' but initially she was content merely to reprimand gently. 'The experience you have had,' she told Sarah at the age of eighteen, 'is considerable for your age; by a more rigid plan with you I might have spared both you and myself some pain, but you would have known much less of the human heart.'[17] As Sarah, however, proceeded to break more hearts and to acquire a reputation for irresponsible flirtatiousness, the family's concern about her 'indiscretions' increased. We do not know the details about her transgressions or how much pressure was brought on her to mend her ways, but one of her brothers who was informed about her flirtatiousness appears to have been censorious, and Thomas Madge, the minister, seems to have thought her incorrigible. Her mother evidently came to feel that linking her with 'a man of honour and feeling' would settle her and put to rest the gossip the family so deplored. 'Seeing therefore that girls are despised if they are insipid, and if they are entertaining in constant danger of being misrepresented, it may be the wisest way to escape from these evils if it can be done without encountering greater and to accept a proposal which settles the mind as to its future destination.' A steady connection with a man of dignity and solidity such as John Austin would avoid all ambiguity.[18]

John Taylor, Sarah's father, was moved by arguments of a different kind. The Taylors were one of the most prominent dissenting families in Norwich, known for their talent and energy and their many contributions to the commercial and civic life of this manufacturing cathedral city. Norwich was gradually losing some of its old prosperity and intellectual eminence, but until recently it had been one of the most important cities of the kingdom; its wool manufacturing wealth and cosmopolitan spirit stimulated by a large immigrant population were reflected in a thriving cultural life. The Taylors and their numerous relatives, including the Martineaus (Sarah and Harriet Martineau were first cousins), the Rigbys, and the Reeves, had positions of considerable influence in the city. They prided themselves on their 'middle station' in life and on the fact that their influence and prestige depended not on riches and rank but on their industry and talent. They also had reason to be proud of their family's staunch nonconformity and stand for liberty of conscience. No young Taylor was allowed to forget his distinguished ancestors, their part in the struggle for toleration since the seventeenth century, their triumph over legal proscription, and their long tradition of public service on the side of liberal principles in religion and politics.

Family, religious, and civic pride mingled and strengthened each other and had a tangible symbol in the beautiful light-filled Octagon Chapel where the Taylors and their Unitarian neighbours congregated every Sunday. Sarah's father recalled how as a very young child he had stood in awe next to his grandfather, the well-known minister and scholar Dr John Taylor, while he laid the foundation stone of the eight-sided, many-windowed structure with its rich interior of wainscoting and its ornamental ceiling, which remains one of the most exquisitely graceful eighteenth-century interiors surviving in Norwich.[19] John Taylor's maternal ancestors had been resident in Norwich for more than two centuries, and the achievements of the family in all its branches were interwoven with the history of the city; despite the Test Acts, various family members had been mayors, aldermen, and sheriffs; and they had also achieved prominence in business, medical, professional, and literary life. The Taylors' position as one of the three leading dissenting families in Norwich and their reputation for talent and solidity was such that Sarah's father understandably felt little urgency about seeing his younger daughter settled; he also thought it his duty to point to the economic realities that might blight the young couple's expectations, and it appears he cautioned Sarah, as he later did her brother Arthur, that when the ways and means of supporting a family had to be considered, speculative accounting based on hopes hardly sufficed. What was to feed the young couple while their fortunes materialized[20]?

John Taylor's own financial anxieties illustrated the uncertainties of fortune even in an established business. He had for decades been one of the leading wool and yarn factors in Norwich. The business had been founded by Sarah's grandfather, Richard Taylor, one of nine children, who had been encouraged to expand his wool combing business and go into the weaving trade by his father, the learned eighteenth-century minister of the Octagon, who with the paternal solicitude characteristic of the Taylors had relinquished his pleasant study with its warming fireplace so that his son could convert it to a warping room.[21] Yet in spite of a hopeful start, this Richard Taylor died comparatively young, and, while his eldest son was trained in his grandfather's footsteps in the ministry, his second son, Sarah's father, had to leave school at twelve to help his widowed mother and then to train by apprenticeship in Norwich and London for what became a flourishing enterprise at a time when Norwich was at the height of its wool manufacturing prosperity. Sarah's father became one of the wool aristocrats of the city. He could recall the time when the demand for Norwich goods was so great that 'the great fairs of Frankfort, and Leipsic, and of Salerno, were thronged with purchasers,' and the weavers were so busy at their looms at all hours that the city and the villages twenty miles around seemed as if illuminated at night.[22]

Yet during Sarah's youth it was becoming evident that the industrial revolution was leaving Norwich behind. As her father explained, 'The ingenuity of the mechanic invented a new mode of spinning by machinery which deprived thousands of hands of that employment and laid the Axe at the Root of our Occupation.' With steam replacing hand looms, spinning and weaving migrated from Norwich to Yorkshire. John Taylor, an extraordinarily capable entrepreneur, wisely diversified early by investing a substantial portion of his capital in the printing business (which later became very successful and developed a new printing machine) conducted by his sons Richard and Arthur, to whom he lent £6000;[23] but when Sarah asked for his assent to her engagement his circumspect outlook may in part have reflected his changing business prospects. The slow death of his trade, which eventually could no longer be taken over as planned by Sarah's brother Edward, cast a shadow well before the mid-twenties when he dissolved the firm and summed up what had been an economic and personal trial for him and for Norwich: 'Othello's occupation gone!' he mourned: 'There was a time when mine was thought an important branch in our Manufactory and my advice and assistance sometimes called for; now I am not wanted, but am indeed a Cypher.'[24] Since his trade was in a decline, he seems to have been doubly reluctant to see Sarah commit herself to a long engagement – least of all to a scholarly young man who was untried and whose prospects were so uncertain.

There was more to recommend the engagement to the Austin family. Whereas the Taylors played a prominent part in Norwich civic and cultural life and had a formidable lineage of distinguished ancestors, the Austins were respectable but obscure. The contrast between the two families is reflected in the fact that the Austin family's history in the seventeenth and eighteenth centuries is as unrecorded as that of the Taylors is well documented. Little is known of John Austin's mother, Anne; she was the daughter of a yeoman farmer, 'well-educated and gently nurtured,' deeply religious, and inclined to be melancholic. Austin's father, Jonathan, was a Suffolk miller and corn merchant with mills at Creeting and Ipswich in Suffolk and Longford in Essex, who became exceedingly prosperous through circumstances similar to those that had contributed to the decline of John Taylor's worsted business. The war against France, which denied the European markets to English wool merchants, made it possible for Jonathan Austin to amass a fortune by taking government contracts. It would appear that he was the first in his family to enjoy considerable wealth. He was also an ambitious, strong-minded character who had received little education himself but with his wife's encouragement was determined, as he became more affluent, to offer better opportunities to his seven children. Late in life he had his portrait painted by John Linnell, and in it he looks straight out at the world – a stocky, determined figure holding a gnarled walking stick. Perhaps the stick was symbolic of an aspect of his character, for Henry Reeve, Sarah's nephew, also spoke of Jonathan Austin's 'sturdy sense and vigour';[25] unfortunately the two sons, John and Charles Austin, who by their achievements did most to keep his name alive, did not inherit his physical vigour.

In spite of his minimal formal education Jonathan Austin was said to have had a very precise mind and a dislike of exaggeration, which perhaps led him to value good schooling. Three of the five Austin boys went to Ipswich School, and John could have been one of them, for he had knowledge of ancient languages; but since Sarah never mentioned where he went to school, he may have been educated at home by tutors. Charles Austin attended Bury St Edmunds before going on to a brilliant career at Jesus College, Cambridge. Little is known of George Austin except that he was a philologist, an 'insatiable reader,' and for many years an expatriate at Freiburg. Alfred Austin became assistant poor law commissioner and then secretary to the Board of Works. The traditional upward path of the services was chosen by the two oldest sons, John and Joseph; two of the younger sons studied for the bar, as John Austin eventually did also. The success of the father's influence can be gauged from the fact that his sons not only became highly educated but also had strongly developed intellectual interests. Their good reputation is corroborated by Mrs Taylor, who had high standards and declared that the Austin brothers were all to be admired.[26] The two daughters also seem to have been well instructed; Anne Staff would not have been Sarah's friend if she had been anything less, and Charlotte Austin, the unmarried sister, was known to be very well read and cultivated. John Austin as a young man claimed that his father endorsed education merely as a means for enrichment, but in spite of the father's ambitions, three of the brothers had an inclination to retire from active life quite early. Charles Austin, having made a great name and fortune as a barrister that even the most ambitious father would have been proud of, retired to a squire's life and a grand mansion in Suffolk before he was fifty. According to Sarah, he now devoted his life to doing all manner of sweet nothings. George Austin retired for many years to a scholarly life in Germany, and John Austin showed a preference for scholarship from the time he left the army. Jonathan Austin, who respected and liked Sarah, may have encouraged his son's engagement plans not merely because the Taylors were a family of substance but also because he saw the engagement as a spur to prod his oldest son into sustained, purposeful effort.[27]

It was Jonathan Austin's offer to contribute £300 annually once John and Sarah were married that eased the way for John Taylor to give his assent and to promise £100 annually on his part. A marriage settlement had been arranged. Sarah's oldest brother announced that the affair was settled: 'Our sister Sally has engaged the affection of a young man who from what is said of him seems worthy of her ... I must say I am anxious to become a little better acquainted with one whom we may call our brother.' As Mrs Taylor explained, 'Opposition from his parents would have occasioned great difficulties, but their generous affectionate conduct entitled them to liberality and decision on our part.' Mr Taylor, benevolent and ruminative, became reconciled to Sarah's match, though not without misgivings and warnings about the financial and emotional risks that lay ahead, and that it was as well to consider before marriage what would follow thereafter. Then he appears to have acquiesced much in the spirit in which he reluctantly consented to the marriage of one of his sons: 'Every human Soul wants a very close union with another Being, to whom it can without the least reserve unbosom itself.'[28]

The weeks of suspense and anxiety over, Sarah wrote to a cousin: 'I assure you that my heart and my judgment are equally satisfied with the man of my choice ... he is all and more than I ever imagined, ... he loves me dearly, and finally ... I am the happiest girl in the world.' She was proud 'to marry solely for passionate love,' and ready to dedicate herself to a new life. Meanwhile, as she bravely determined to face the long wait, it was evident that she was sustained by her belief in John Austin's elevated character and talent, and by her conviction that he would distinguish himself. She felt she had kept her promise to her mother never to seek an alliance with 'a weak man [or] an unprincipled man or one who had not a reasonable chance of maintaining her.'[29]

Those who had doubtfully shaken their heads over the seeming disparities of temperament would have been more incredulous had they been permitted a glimpse of John's extraordinary letter of proposal. In what must be one of the unlikeliest of such letters ever written and accepted, John Austin, in a painfully stilted, legalistic, and naïve document – something between a draft of a contract and a confession – catalogued the reasons against his suit. 'Primo,' there was the long wait till they could afford to marry and live off his earnings – a wait, according to his calculations, of between nine and twelve years. 'Secundo ... it is also very probable that my profession may never bring me into one shilling,' and the pain of failure, should it occur, would be 'enhanced and aggravated by the unworthy spectacle of my protracted dependence.' 'Tertio,' there was the possibility that he might, out of caprice or disgust with poverty, 'damn [him]self to wealth and contempt in the arms of age and ugliness and folly.' Only in the occasional sentence did he permit himself an approach to romance, as when he acknowledged that her 'very heartstrings [had] inextricably entwined themselves with [his] fidelity and honour.' He was not going to stoop to conquer, and as Sarah acknowledged later, her 'destiny [was] distinctly put before her.'[30]

On her side he asked for a self-examination. She was to look into her past conduct, not so much for 'those slight stains' upon her reputation which would wear away under 'a more guarded deportment' and his '*protecting* attachment,' but to determine by an 'ordeal of self examination' whether her soul was 'really worthy to hold communion' with his. He also wished to know whether she was 'that volatile, vain and flirting thing, hackneyed in the ways of coquetry, and submitting its light and worthless affection to the tampering of every specious cox-comb; – or [whether she had] really *nerve* enough for the deep-toned, steady, and consistent enthusiasm, upon which both [his] pride and [his] tenderness might securely rely.' Proud, cautious, and demanding, even in love, John Austin was not going to link his name with a young woman, however entrancing, if she would – wittingly or not – enmesh him in turmoil or the indignity of being thrown over. As he advised his friend Nassau Senior, who had been jilted, it was worth seeking 'the well-weighed and devoted attachment of some more estimable woman' – someone who had 'mind and heart enough to estimate at its right value the love of a man of sense and honour.' In his own suit he offered 'conditional proposals,' as in the negotiation of a treaty. His training in legal chambers and his temperament inclined him to a pedantic and definitional exactitude. He acknowledged: 'The habit of drawing [i.e, drafting] will in no short time give me so exclusive and intolerant taste ... for perspicuity and precision, that I shall hardly venture on sending a letter of much purpose, even to you, unless it be laboured with accuracy and circumspection which are requisite in a deed of conveyance.'[31]

How did Sarah react to this strange, joyless document, which combined chastisement with an appeal for heroic affection in the face of a catalogue of obstacles? The present-day reader might be inclined to take it as a testimony of Austin's youthful earnestness and wish for candour in a situation usually obscured by gallant sentiments. Sarah, aware of both his pride and his uncertainties, and conscious of their mutual love, might well have dismissed the conditions without too much heart-searching. In fact, the reverse seems to have been the case: both of them could not have been more in earnest.

Sarah revealed that there was nothing light-hearted in her acceptance of the conditions. She wrote to her brother Richard to reassure him that this time she was serious. Indeed, she echoed Austin's letter with a fervour of resolution that foreshadowed what was to come.

> You will imagine that I should not have dared to accept the sacred and weighty deposit of the tranquillity and dignity of such a man as he is, if I had not felt myself incapable of trifling with it, and resolute in my determination to exert the most vigilant selfcommand and the most severe selfexamination to prevent my ever unintentionally or for a moment wounding feelings it is equally my duty and my interest (to say nothing of my inclination) to consult.[32]

To a cousin she wrote with 'the overflowing of a full heart' of her love – 'a love which I firmly believe will do more for the elevation and improvement of my character than anything in the world could.' She was as eager as her suitor to correct her imperfections. His moral rigour and earnestness appealed to her own idealism, and his evident intention to make a mark in the London intellectual world put her in awe of him. He stood out in the circle of young men she knew by virtue of his talent, his austerity, by the demands he made on himself and others, and by his prospects for intellectual eminence. Dazzled, in love, and bent on purging herself of vanity and superficiality, and with her imagination aflame with the promise of a marriage of high purpose, Sarah marvelled that she, who had been repeatedly warned about the flighty impression she created, had won a man of such 'dignity and solidity' of character. She felt hardly worthy of him. Writing to one of her brothers, she said: 'I cannot help thinking that when you [meet] him you will wonder at his choice. I do most mig[htily].'[33] Her beauty and love of social success did not preclude a yearning for moral and intellectual elevation that Austin now promised to satisfy.

Love and a wish for moral regeneration and purposefulness had triumphed. The carefully cultivated conscience fostered by her upbring- ing and John Austin's influence now brought about a complete transfor- mation in the image she presented to the world. Her sister noted this change as the two of them lived together during the ordeal of disposing of Susan's deceased husband's belongings. Sarah confessed to her during this sad companionship that she found 'herself so happy ... as to make her almost ashamed it should be so,' and Susan commented, 'There is a kind of happiness arising from a quiet conscience that will take possession of the mind under the saddest dispensations, and *that peace* I firmly believe she has found.' Outsiders who had known her previously were also amazed at the transformation, and once more there was astonished gossip among the young nonconformist intellectuals who asked whether this was indeed the demise of the old 'Sally.' William Johnson Fox, who later became a well-known Unitarian clergyman, and who was acquainted with Sarah's brother Richard, wrote from Norwich:

I have seen Sally T[aylor], but 'oh, how changed!' – from the extreme of display and flirtation – from all that was dazzling, attractive, and imposing, she has become the most demure, reserved, and decorous creature in existence. Mr. A[ustin] has wrought miracles, for which he is blessed by the ladies, and cursed by the gentlemen, and wondered at by all. The majority say, 'tis unnatural, and cannot last. Some abuse the *weakness* which makes her, they say, the complete slave of her lover; others praise the *strength of mind* by which she has so totally transformed her manners and habits.[34]

Little did Fox know that Austin was asking for far more than miraculous changes in demeanour. The long proposal letter contained another theme. It also revealed John Austin's expectation of emotional support. He asked Sarah 'to brace [herself] up to that fortitude of affection which would wipe the damps of anguish from [his] forehead,' and he looked to her to urge him on to 'heroic industry,' and to prop and 'sustain the weakness of a spirit that must cling to sympathy for support.'

The engagement letter in part recalls the mood in which as a twenty-one-year-old army officer he had confided to his diary how his high moral and intellectual ambition, spurred by his consciousness of his 'plebian fortunes' and his 'fears of never emerging from obscurity,' might be undermined by his indolence and melancholy.[35] Sarah, with her abundant energy, initiative, and strength of will, would, he hoped, save him from all such corroding doubts.

With hindsight this letter is an extraordinarily revealing document. Did she wonder at the time that there was no forward-looking anticipation of happiness in his anxious, introspective, self-regarding letter, and that the most he hoped for was the emotional support of a 'high-minded woman' who would spur him to exertion? Retrospectively, when after his death she reread his letters, the shadows they cast seemed long: 'All his love-letters, during our five years engagement, speak, not of the happiness he hopes to enjoy or to give, but of his reliance on me as his prop and comforter.' Significantly, she added later, 'And this tempted me.'[36]

Sarah's transformed manner startled her friends, but her sister, who was her confidante at this time, hinted that John was more suitable for Sarah than outsiders realized. Susan forecast that her sister's indiscretions would indeed end, that a new reign of seriousness would prevail: 'You have no idea how strict the hero's notions are.' She was surprised – even amused – by the severe tone of the proposal letter: 'I want to see the man, and yet I dread it. He must be very terrific, but I do think he's the man for Sally.'[37] Was Susan merely demonstrating sisterly loyalty, or did she see deeper affinities and compatibility of values?

The paradox of the pleasure-loving girl falling in love with a moral perfectionist can be reconciled – partially at least – by recalling Sarah's and John's backgrounds. John Austin's high moral and intellectual aspirations, though not his severity, blended well with the tone that prevailed in her family. The compatibility of values derived in large part from a shared religious background. While Sarah had worshipped in the company of her numerous relatives in the Octagon Chapel, John had joined his family in their weekly attendance at the Unitarian Chapel in St Nicholas Street, Ipswich – another fine, many-windowed old meeting house that still stands. Though John Austin for a time became an unbeliever, he had a Unitarian upbringing and his moral outlook parallelled Sarah's.[38] Unconventional as the engagement letter was, its earnest tone and call for self-scrutiny, improvement, and sacrifice in order to achieve worthy ends were familiar to Sarah. He asked her to turn over a new leaf and to purge herself of common vanity, to uplift him by her faith and support, and she had been raised to be susceptible to such an appeal. As she made her resolution to be worthy of both her fiancé's and her family's expectations, she humbly wrote to her brother Richard in order to allay his concern: 'The more deeply I feel my present (or I will trust in a great degree past) imperfections, the most anxiously I shall labour at their correction. Be my success what it may, I am sure you and John have contributed no little to it. I believe my best proofs of my gratitude lie in my actions, therefore I will make no professions.'[39] John Austin's censoriousness was not shared by her parents, but his moral perfectionism was in tune with their outlook on life.

A committed Unitarianism gave substance to Sarah's family life. Her eighteenth-century great grandfather, Dr John Taylor, from whom the branches of the family were descended, was a learned theologian who had carried his congregation from a severe Presbyterianism to an undogmatic Unitarianism. This pious man, whose influence was still perceptible in the Taylor family, had very liberal notions about religion and was a major figure in the history of dissent. Storms of controversy had greeted his rationalistic approach to the study of the scriptures and his deviation from Presbyterian orthodoxy. His work on the doctrine of original sin has been described as 'undermining the root ideas of the Calvinistic system both in England and in the American colonies.' He had also been a great classical scholar and an indefatigable labourer on an important nine-volume Hebrew concordance of the Old Testament. The letter in which he announced the conclusion of this labour of love reveals the spirit that animated his work: 'This Day I have corrected ye last Sheet of my Concordance, which hath been near 5 years in printing, and in w[hi]ch I have been exercised, more or less, for near two and twenty years. May the remaining part of my Life, be still useful, and subservient to the Interests of true Religion, which it is my Desire and Delight to promote.'[40] The example he had set of an open-minded approach to religion and a dedication to scholarship survived among the Taylors, as did his sense of responsibility to the community.

Sarah's father bore his grandfather's name and revered his memory. He had to content himself with becoming an influential man of business rather than pursuing theological learning, but he strove to add cultivation of mind to his more worldly talents, and he identified with the ideals of his illustrious ancestor. His devotion to the congregation, of which he was deacon for forty-eight years, is still evident in his painstakingly compiled, handwritten manuscript history of the Octagon Chapel and its ministers.

In keeping with his creed, God was approached in a spirit of thanks and joy rather than confession and lamentation; and John Taylor, who had a fine voice and a talent for music and poetry, composed a number of melodies and hymns. He was also an active figure in municipal affairs and a believer in his grandfather's lesson that 'nature has so linked mankind together, that every one is accountable for his character to his neighbour.' Thus he supported many public causes and lent his counsel and money generously, for example to the ever-impecunious William Godwin. He saw himself as guardian of his family's tradition of uprightness, learning, and responsibility and never failed to impress on the Taylor children that they should be worthy of the name they had inherited.'[41]

By example and precept Sarah's parents guided their seven children to a belief in the importance of moral values, and they tied the bond to family firmly with unstinting affection and family pride. Mrs Taylor unceasingly supported and guided her children, but she was also sensitive to their susceptibilities. She wrote of Sarah and Susan, 'With all due deference to their discretion, I am often in a fright least they should not conduct themselves so as to obtain the credit I wish them but don't tell them so for I would not discourage them.' Mr Taylor's letters also convey a picture of a remarkably engaging, astute man – far-seeing in business, simple in his enjoyments, elevated in his principles, yet down-to-earth in his worldly advice. He took his grandfather's tract written on the birth of his first grandchild to heart. Parents were 'to light the understanding of [their] children, to excite them to proper action, to moderate and direct their passion, and to do all [they] can to set them unto the right way of life.'[42] The Taylors adhered to this precept of early moral and intellectual discipline, and they stimulated each of their seven children to develop well-directed energy. Sarah's brothers all came to be men of some distinction in their fields, which included mining and marine engineering, printing, and music. Sarah's sister after her husband's death dedicated her life to raising her son, Henry Reeve, who became an influential man of letters. Undeniably the Taylor children had native talent, but they also had family values that fostered and directed it to a remarkable degree.

An atmosphere of energy and striving was cultivated in the household. 'Our present Happiness is dependent upon our own active endeavour,' is how an earlier young Taylor had put it, and this emphasis on industry still prevailed. 'Usefulness' was an oft-used word, and 'By their fruits ye shall know them' was a favourite Sunday text. Religion sanctioned 'a rule of life'; it had a practical tendency and aimed to 'ally itself with morality, and condescend to human uses.' There was a moral purpose to existence, and it could be best achieved by a life of duty, responsibility, and useful activity. The spirit of dutiful endeavour prevailed during the anguish of pain and even in the face of death. When John Taylor was struggling to survive a kidney-stone obstruction, he prayed that he might live so that he could continue to serve his family and society, remembering 'that the best preparation for death is a life lived to the last with useful deeds, performed under a constant sense of God's divine science and man's accountableness.' Sarah's moral ideas were deeply etched by this background, which was to influence her no matter how much she distanced herself from Norwich or her parents' Unitarianism.[43]

Mrs Taylor was no mere bystander to Sarah's education. She saw herself as an ever-watchful guardian of her daughters' development. The example she set of a cultivated woman of great strength of character who managed to combine extensive domestic duties (for she worked alongside her servants) with literary interests and friendships was not lost on her daughters. She was an embodiment of Sarah's great-grandfather's lesson that 'the conscience can never be comfortably settled when the mind is not well instructed in knowledge and duty.' Any dissenting minister who visited Norwich enjoyed her hospitality and conversation, as did many others with intellectual interests, including barristers on the Norfolk circuit, such as Henry Crabb Robinson and James Mackintosh. One such contemporary has recorded: 'She was one of the most agreable women I ever knew – full of information, the mind cultivated in a considerable degree, of very cheerful disposition, and promoting cheerfulness all around her.' Family duties came first for Mrs Taylor, but she liked nothing better than to converse with the scholar Dr Parr or to indulge in 'feasts of reason' with the famous botanist James Edward Smith, founder of the Linnean Society, and among her close friends were clever literary women such as Anna Letitia Barbauld, Amelia Opie, and Lucy Aikin. To judge by her children's wide intellectual interests, her enthusiasm for mental exertion must have been infectious. Even tutoring her daughters was a pleasure to relish; on reading Latin with Sarah's sister she commented how it filled her mind: 'Life is either a dull round of eating, drinking, and sleeping, or a spark of ethereal fire just kindled.' The improvement of one's mind was one of the more noble occupations of a rational person. There was no mistaking Mrs Taylor's motherly admonitions. Her letters to her daughters were filled with an affectionate but relentless didacticism on her two favourite themes – the imperative need for the highest moral standards and the pleasures and compensations of intellectual improvement. Sarah was fourteen years old when her mother wrote, 'Even at your early age, the great points of moral conduct must be understood, and I think I may safely trust that they will in no instance be deviated from by you either in thought, word, or deed.' At the end of one of her own long homilies even Mrs Taylor once sighed: 'If all my moralising can but give you right views and feelings.'[44]

Mrs Taylor's admonitions, although uncommonly insistent, were conventional enough for her day, but the unusual part of her regimen was her passionate determination that her daughters' education should not take second place to that of her five sons. She scorned the superficialities that passed for a girl's education. Intellectual curiosity, respect for learning, and belief in enlightenment were part of the Unitarian ethos, with its emphasis on rational private judgment in all matters, even religion, and the Taylors gave their girls an education that was exceptionally thorough even by Unitarian standards. As Harriet Martineau later recalled (and in this respect the Taylor and Martineau households were similar), the parents 'pinched themselves in luxuries to provide their girls as well as their boys with masters and schooling'; and they brought the children up 'to an industry like their own: the boys in study and business; the girls in study and household cares.'[45]

A well-furnished mind, Mrs Taylor never tired of telling her daughter, was a lifelong guard against tedium and vapidness; and it could also be a resource against want: 'Besides the intrinsic pleasure to be derived from solid knowledge, a woman ought to consider it as her best resource against poverty.' The fate of some of Sarah's schoolmates and acquaintances illustrated the oft-repeated theme of the vital importance of education and self-dependence: 'A well educated young woman may always provide for herself, while girls that are but half instructed have too much cultivation for one sort of life and too little for another.' Mrs Taylor saw to it that Sarah was given a thorough education that included Latin, mathematics, philosophy, and political economy and did not exclude the development of discipline and pride that came from mental drill similar to that given to Sarah's brothers.[46]

Sarah never mentioned attending school, and she seems to have been instructed at home by her mother, such brothers as were still in Norwich, and visiting tutors, and in small groups that followed courses of reading and study. Mrs Taylor shared Anna Letitia Barbauld's opinion that the intellectual development of a young girl had to be parallelled by domestic and emotional training given by her mother. In Sarah's case the scheme was successful, for we have descriptions of her wide reading and lively interests as a girl of thirteen. In a letter to 'darling Dick,' an older brother whom she was undoubtedly eager to impress, she told him that she was reading Caesar in Latin and *Davila*; furthermore, she wrote: 'I have begun to read Gil Blas from which I anticipate a high treat. The style is rich in idiom and those odd and droll expressions which make French so good a colloquial language. In English I am reading one of the books which foreigners esteem an ornament to our tongue. I mean Clarissa. I must say I think it rather a laborious task.' She also wrote that she had been much entertained by attending a course of lectures on Mnemonics, which succeeded in 'converting the driest parts of learning, dates, numbers etc., into a play or a Xmas game.' Late in life she recalled how such mental stimulus had gone along with domestic training. She had been expected to 'go to market, to direct the management of food, to judge of quantity and quality of the various articles of domestic consumption; to know how every thing in the house is cleaned, repaired, kept in order; to cut and make clothes; to direct the washing, to wash and iron fine linen, lace, etc. ... All of wh[ich] we were taught to do, and made to do, and I don't think we are more ignorant and unlearned than our neighbours.'[47]

Far-sightedness led Sarah's mother to encourage her daughters to learn not only the more conventional languages, such as Latin, French, and Italian, but also German. To make German part of a young girl's curriculum was a bold move. Some decades later a desire to master this language became less unusual, but in the early years of the century the study of German literature was confined to comparatively few persons, many of them from the provinces. William Taylor of Norwich (a family friend and not a relative), an enthusiast for spreading knowledge of German ideas and one of the first to write in English on Herder and Lessing, was looked upon by many as an eccentric. He 'was quite as much wondered at for knowing German, as a person would now be for a profound acquaintance with Russ[ian].' Edgar Taylor, a barrister cousin and a translator of Grimm's fairy tales, who in 1825 collaborated with Sarah in her first acknowledged translation, may also have influenced Mrs Taylor to encourage the learning of German. The groundwork Sarah acquired in languages is indicated by her reading during the studious, self-disciplined five years of her engagement between 1814 and 1819. She read not only Tacitus and Cicero but Goethe's drama Iphigenie in Tauris, some of Bentham's works in their French editions, and Machiavelli in Italian.

Sarah's youth was by no means tarnished by such study. Rational pleasures – sociability, travel, music – were all part of her parents' scheme of education. Sarah had the opportunity to visit her numerous family in Bath, Yarmouth, Diss, and other provincial cities. She had great vitality, was an excellent rider and swimmer, and took fencing lessons with John. The old and the young in her family had much zest for life and relished all sorts of simple enjoyments, such as games, singing, sailing up the river Wensum, and large convivial gatherings.

> My youth [Lucy Aikin explained] was spent among the disciples or fellow-labourers of Price and Priestley, the descendants of Dr. John Taylor ... Amongst these there was no rigorism. Dancing, cards, the theatre, were all held lawful in moderation; in manners, the Free Dissenters, as they were called, came much nearer the Church than their own stricter brethren, yet in doctrine no sect departed so far from the Establishment.[48]

Fearing that the horizon of a small city would be narrowing, Mrs Taylor sent Sarah to London when she was fourteen to visit Anna Letitia Barbauld, with whom she read Boileau and Pope and who exposed her to the theatre, opera, and metropolitan conversation and stimulated her to aspire to a life with a larger circumference than was likely in Norwich. When she was sixteen and eighteen she was again sent to London. It was no coincidence that none of the Taylor children remained in Norwich.

Sarah's education led her to set her sights not only beyond Norwich but also beyond the conventional notion of wifehood. She was born in 1793, a year after Mary Wollstonecraft published a *A Vindication of the Rights of Woman*, and novel ideas about women's education and roles were being debated throughout her youth. Her family in particular was exposed to these winds of change through personal acquaintance with some of the initiators of them. Mr Taylor had been William Godwin's schoolfellow for a time, and Mrs Taylor's intimates, Amelia Opie and Anna Letitia Barbauld, knew Mary Wollstonecraft well and discussed her impassioned plea for wider horizons for women. It is thus not surprising that Mrs Taylor impressed on her daughters the advantages of intellectual companionship in marriage or that Sarah, who had received a better education than most of the men of her day, was drawn to a plan of life that seemed to her more noble than that aspired to by the run-of-the-mill of her contemporaries. In her recollections of her Norwich childhood Harriet Martineau recalled the admiration with which Mary Wollstone-craft was regarded, and Sarah absorbed some of her ideas, or at least an echo of them. Among Wollstonecraft's ideas was one, by no means new but to which she gave emphasis, that a woman should prepare herself to be more than merely serviceable or pleasing to her husband. She should aim to be a companion to him – friendship was the sublimest of the affections; 'the woman who strengthens her body and exercises her mind will, by managing her family and practising various virtues, become the friend, and not the humble dependent of her husband.' Influenced by such ideas of a marriage of companionship, Sarah regarded herself as one who would be the partner, intellectual equal, the friend, and helper of a husband who would make a name for himself by serving society. It appears also that John Austin shared and encouraged such ideas. One is bound to speculate about this when one notes that some of his early letters to Sarah after their marriage were signed John Austin, husband and friend.'[49]

In regarding herself as a companion to her husband in all his endeavours, Sarah was also following her mother's advice. Mrs Taylor had impressed on her that in marriage it was 'impossible to be happy without each party [being able to] say of the other, I have found a companion, for to sit down every day with a person who only interrupts the enjoyment which may always be derived from reading and thinking is a great aggravation instead of an abatement of the evils of life.' When Mrs Taylor explained the engagement to one of Sarah's brothers she once more stressed such intellectual compatibility: 'It was a vigorous mind that Sally always seemed to lay the greatest stress upon in her calculation of [a man's] qualities, and I expected if such a mind was found with an unblemished character it would determine her choice.' Austin in his proposal of marriage asked for emotional support, but he also held out to Sarah the prospect of a marriage that offered the gratifications of shared intellectual values and communion of ideas. In the engagement letter he had, in his stilted manner, asked if she could 'determine sedulously to form [her]self to that enlarged yet feminine reason, which could at once enter into [his] most comprehensive views.'[50] Sarah, imbued with a belief in discipline and self-culture, and by no means without intellectual ambition herself, was eager to collaborate in a life of principle dedicated to a struggle for worthy causes. Both of them aimed at a life beyond dull insignificance.

The groundwork for establishing an intellectual companionship began very early in the engagement, which became something of an intellectual apprenticeship for her. John Austin seems to have taken over from Mrs Taylor as Sarah's tutor. 'I shall desire to talk with you on all subjects which engage my attention,' he wrote, as he begged her to read the same books he was studying. Under his influence she now read modern and ancient authors – the list (which included works by Blackstone, Hume, Helvetius, and Tacitus) over the five years of their engagement would have done credit to the most dedicated student of philosophy of law or politics. She waited for his letters, 'full of love and of reason, of wise and high-minded advice,' exhorting her to study and to prepare herself to share his interests.[51]

Such a course of reading as a preparation for communion in married life was not altogether unique. Soon Sarah was to meet other women who had gone through a similar tutelage during their engagement. While her fianc remained in London and continued his legal studies, Sarah now passed 'five years feeding only on love, and severe study, in order to become worthy of being a wife.'[52] In recalling this period later she did not mention that the intellectual partnership for which she prepared was committed to a specific political-philosophic outlook. During the years of their engagement John was strengthening that interest in legal philosophy and politics that was to be the dominant passion of his life. Sarah came well prepared to share such interests. She had acquired from her family not only intellectual interests and moral earnestness but liberal sympathies, an impulse to useful action, and a strong taste for politics. John now fed an appetite that had been stimulated by the commitments of her parents and by some of her brothers, who were deeply involved in Norwich politics; she was a more congenial partner for John than many realized. Her family's moral heritage and political outlook were not to be cast off in marriage.

John Austin was called to the bar in 1818. On qualifying he seems to have taken a position as a conveyancer, a line of work with very limited prospects, but a year later Sarah's father agreed that the time had come for her to give 'her hand and Heart to the Man of her choice.' She had 'wisely taken ample time to prove the sincerity of his affection, his temper, and all those qualities of the Mind and Heart, which the married State demands to make it what it should be.' After a five-year engagement he apparently did not care to recall John Austin's earlier assurance that he would not marry until he was established. Austin, it was said, 'deserved her by his talents, his virtues, his love, and his constancy.' And there was Mrs Barbauld's advice: 'Two or three years indeed to mature their affection and prove their constancy, I will allow them, but I hope it will not be longer. I own I am a friend to young people venturing a little.'[53]

The summer of Sarah's marriage coincided with the last of those great family gatherings held at five- to seven-year intervals in order to rivet 'the golden chain of ... family love so fast as to secure almost the impossibility of its ever being broken.' Now in July 1819, sixty-four Taylors and Martineaus, the largest number ever to come to such a gathering, assembled in a concert room in Norwich to be addressed by Sarah's uncle, the Rev. Philip Taylor. It seems fitting that Sarah, who had so entirely imbibed the family lessons, should as a farewell to them partake in this great affirmation of the principles by which she had been raised. Thus once more she heard about her 'venerated ancestors' and their devoted attachment to the sacred cause of truth and civil and religious liberty. Once more she listened to the evocation of family virtues – the respectability and uprightness of the 'male and female relatives, who now stand distinguished in society by their professional talents, their virtue, and their usefulness'; and she again heard the exhortations to 'that long train of well-educated youth, who daily spring toward manhood, and will soon occupy their destined stations in active life.'[54] Although this was to be the last such reunion, the prophecy of a continuing chain of talented family members was fulfilled; however, the era of the Taylors of Norwich was closing.

Melancholy was woven into the letters written by Sarah's parents that summer. The meeting recalled the previous reunion in 1814, which had been shadowed by the death of Susan's husband. Mrs Taylor owned herself not much in the humour for merrymaking, although she was determined to put on the best appearance she could. She also grieved in anticipation about parting with what a friend called 'so dear a daughter, so sweet a companion and friend.'[55] Mr Taylor's mood echoed his wife's: 'I believe *my* loss does not excite so much commiseration as it deserves,' he wrote to his son Richard. Without Sarah he would be 'most frequently alone, tho' in Company,' for he would be left with his book, since 'almost constant somnolency ... irresistibly comes over your Mother in the Evenings.'[56]

There were no honeymoon plans since there was a need to economize. John and Sarah were to go off quietly to their lodgings in London and later to return to Norwich to pack their belongings. As the couple prepared for the wedding, Richard Taylor in London received a letter from his father announcing the arrival of 'Sister Austin' – a 'name which it will require some little time to familiarize your tongue with.' In keeping with the family's mood, he added, 'She quits tomorrow the paternal Roofs, and from this time becomes the partner in other pursuits, Pleasures and Pains than were found here: I pray Heaven her change may not be for the worse, but for the better!' The letter recalls an earlier one from Sarah's oldest brother announcing her engagement: 'I hope and trust it may end in her comfort and happiness, and I have not a doubt but that if she become a wife, she will be indeed an excellent one.'[57] At the end of August 1819 the marriage took place in the church of St George's, Colegate. The Octagon Chapel was close by, but marriage services could not be performed in Nonconformist chapels, and Sarah and John, not inappropriately, were married in an Anglican church where elaborate monuments and mural tablets commemorated her eighteenth-century ancestors' achievement and worth. The values of these ancestors, after all, had helped mould her character and ambitions. On leaving the church, Sarah could have seen her sister Susan standing behind a door weeping. As the London coach departed from Norwich, an elaborately worked, magnificently ornate gold watch was, according to family legend, thrown into Sarah's lap by a disappointed suitor – perhaps a reminder in years to come that she might have chosen differently.[58]

2

A political odyssey

THE AUSTINS MOVED TO LONDON at a time of great political excitement. The Peterloo riot had taken place a week or so before their marriage, and the public was profoundly disturbed by the news that eleven persons had been killed and countless others injured when the mounted yeomanry rode through a Manchester crowd assembled to hear the radical orator Henry Hunt. The country had been restive for some time, but the Peterloo affair set off waves of fear and anger that sparked further radical agitation, and within a year additional sympathy for the radical cause was generated by the queen's trial and press prosecutions of writers and booksellers such as Richard Carlile. The agitation of public opinion swirled around the Austins during their first years as a married couple and seems to have sharpened their taste for politics. They had been drawn to radical politics before they came to London, but now their political inclinations were fired by national events and given substance and a philosophic framework by their association with Jeremy Bentham and James Mill, which began soon after their marriage.

Early family influences had nourished the Austins' political sympathies. As Sarah Austin put it many years later, they were 'brought up in the intensest Whiggery,' which was her way of making their early radicalism appear respectable. In the same spirit she also recalled that her husband had been 'reared in ultra-Liberal opinions,' and she noted that, like his brother Charles, he was inclined to radicalism even before coming under the influence of Bentham and James Mill. John Austin's experiences in the army may also have encouraged his political views, for he resented officers who enjoyed promotion and authority undeservedly, and he admired the system of promotion by merit, which he associated with the army in democratic America.[1] Whatever the roots of his outlook, his political leanings were evident in the books that he recommended to his fianceé during their long engagement. At his behest her reading included Bacon's entire works and several books and pamphlets by Bentham, including the *Plan of Parliamentary Reform* in 1817, *Defence of Usury* and *Church of Englandism* in 1818, and *Judicial Establishments* and *Introduction to the Rationale of Evidence* in 1819. John Stuart Mill, corroborating Sarah's account of her husband's early politics, pointed out that John Austin shared many opinions with the radical James Mill, not as a disciple, but as a result of his independent reading and reflection.[2]

The Taylor family was unmistakably radical, and its radicalism went beyond the Foxite sympathies of many of its Norwich neighbours. Its politics could be traced to religion, for as Dissenters, they were, in John Stuart Mill's phrase, among the disqualified classes and therefore were 'natural Radicals'; this was a connection recognized by Burke, from another point of view, who spoke of Unitarians as 'hot men' and therefore dangerous.[3] In keeping with Mill's characterization, the Taylors, as one of the leading Unitarian families in Norwich, led the movement there for the abolition of dissenters' civil disabilities, and later Sarah's eldest brother, Richard, promoted dissenters' interests in the City of London Council and through the Non-Con[formist] Club, where he was joined by John Bowring, William Johnson Fox, and Joseph Parkes. Although members of the family held local office, like other Dissenters, they were angered by the exclusionary laws which, if enforced, would have denied them their positions of influence and dignity. The family was proud of its tradition of support for liberal causes. John Taylor made quite a name for himself as a composer of political songs for elections and other events, including the celebrations of Charles James Fox's birthdays. His 'Trumpet of Liberty,' which upheld the rights of mankind and called for a new era of liberty, was first performed to celebrate the centenary of the English revolution of 1688-9, and it became a great favourite in Norwich. Like others in his circle, he welcomed the French Revolution, and Susanna Taylor, known as the 'Madame Roland' of Norwich, celebrated the fall of the Bastille by dancing around a tree of liberty. John Taylor also contributed to *The Cabinet*, a short-lived radical journal published at Norwich in 1795 but discontinued because it was regarded as dangerous. It printed arguments from Godwin's *Political Justice* and Mary Wollstonecraft's *A Vindication of the Rights of Woman* and called for reform while castigating Pitt's ministerial despotism.'[4]

The political outlook in the Taylor household was reflected in the activities of some of Sarah's brothers, who were active in the reform movement during the post-Waterloo years, and this in a city reputed to be a centre of reform agitation. Philip Taylor, before moving to Marseilles where he founded a marine engineering firm that still exists, had good credentials as a radical. As he recalled with pride forty years later, he had worn the tricolour cockade to signify his sympathy with the principles of the French Revolution. He emphasized his sympathy with the working classes, which were, he said, 'generally treated like an inferior race of animals by the rich; for *mere money* in England produces the vilest of all aristocratical feelings and conduct.' The squirarchy and the clergy were condemned as 'petty tyrants' who evaded their responsibilities. Although his antagonism against the established classes was powerful, the extent of his radicalism was tempered by an insistence that radical goals could be reached without pillage or more than a brief interruption of social tranquillity. From France in 1830 he wrote to his brother Richard, 'O, how I wish you and E[dward] had come here, just for the revolution!'[5]

Edward Taylor, another brother, was in the thick of local politics during the years of Sarah's youth and engagement. He was in the worsted business with his father, and only in middle age did he achieve prominence as Gresham Professor of Music in London, a vocalist, and a translator of German and Italian songs. Honoured by his friends as a leader in the Norwich radical movement, he was castigated by his opponents as a demagogue on too familiar terms with the local 'democratic cabals.' His blunt manner and 'majestic voice,' which he later used – much to Sarah's distress – as a public singer, added to his popularity. After his election as sheriff in 1819, he thanked a crowd for having demonstrated a preference for a friend of radical reform. As this was just after the Peterloo meeting, he also complained about the 'merciless soldiery' and that the laws had been 'outraged and trodden underfoot, – not by the people but by the magistrates, whose duty it was to protect them.' Should his listeners ever wish to petition for the redress of grievances, he told them, he would be there, 'not indeed to let loose the soldiers upon you, but to raise my feeble voice in order to obtain a redress of those grievances which I, in common with you all,feel that we labour under.' Edward Taylor was in touch with radicals of national importance, such as Cartwright, Burdett, and Cobbett. Apparently he was victimized by an informer and mentioned in Parliament as a 'dangerous man' but was able to avoid prosecution through intervention by well-placed friends.[6]

John Austin's radical outlook made the Taylor brothers politically congenial to him, and when he came to London he was above all eager to meet the notable radical Jeremy Bentham. Even before meeting him,

Austin was his 'enthusiastic admirer, almost a worshipper.' It is not clear how they were introduced, but it may have been through Peregrine Bingham, a friend of Austin's at Lincoln's Inn and at this time already one of Bentham's disciples. The meeting took place in 1819, after Austin had been called to the bar in Trinity term, 1818, and shortly before his marriage. Soon after the meeting Austin humbly offered to sacrifice worldly opportunities to Bentham's cause. Indeed, his letter offering allegiance to Bentham was much more impassioned than the unpromising letter offering marriage to Sarah. 'I have long revered you,' he wrote to Bentham, and added, 'My deep conviction of the importance of your doctrines has long inflamed me with an earnest desire to see them widely diffused and generally embraced ... I shall not be the least zealous amongst those preachers of the gospel who (as I hope) are daily increasing in numbers and in faith ... I shall feel no violent desire for any other object than that of disseminating your doctrines.' His young wife, he assured Bentham, would fully support him in his devotion, and he added, 'I am truly your disciple.'[7]

It is doubtful that John Austin ever had a strong wish to practise law, unlike his brother Charles, who, although radical in politics as a young man, devoted himself to making a great fortune as a barrister. From the beginning John was convinced of 'the absurdity of the system,' a view that made it difficult to be a practitioner. In this he followed Bentham, who condemned lawyers for 'insincerity and dishonesty' and as 'indiscriminate defender[s] of right and wrong.' Austin regarded the legal profession as 'venal and fee-gathering,' and he did not blanch at calling it disgusting. In a transparently autobiographical observation Austin noted that some of those who have studied the science of jurisprudence 'have conceived a disgust of practice.'[8] He began in 1819 as a conveyancer, and he was identified in the Law List as an equity draftsman until the late 1820s. He also travelled on the Norfolk circuit, but by his own account he held only one brief, which was given up, he claimed, because he thought his case unsound. His real interests were politics and legal philosophy, and he steeped himself in these subjects, quitting the bar in 1825. His theoretical bent is evident in the announcement he made to the other students early in his law training – that his goal was 'to study and elucidate the principles of law.'[9]

With such a goal Austin was easily drawn into Bentham's circle. Sarah and he moved into a house near Bentham's in Westminster, and this also made them neighbours of the Mills. Thus the Austins joined the group of devotees and disciples that surrounded the elderly but still vigorous legal philosopher. Not all their activities involved what Austin called the 'gymnastic of the mind,' for we have a description of Bentham's coach house converted into a gymnasium where one could see 'the stern vigour of John Austin balancing on the bars,' while Bentham's amanuensis scrambled on a trapeze and young Mill swung from the beam. Sarah meanwhile fostered the friendship with Bentham, with whom she developed a playful relationship. She made herself useful to him and was eager to please, and he was flattered by the attentions of this intelligent, attractive young woman who had read and understood quite a few of his books. She genuinely appreciated his 'benign heart' and his wish to 'cheerfullize existence.' (She apologized for using this word, which was one of Bentham's inventions.)[10] But it was with the Mills that the greater intimacy was struck. Although seventeen years younger than James Mill, Austin, like so many others, such as Ricardo and Grote, developed a close friendship with him, and this association soon brought him a much wider circle of acquaintances, mainly among radical lawyers and journalists, some of whom later achieved prominence in Parliament.

An especially intimate relationship developed with John Stuart Mill. He became like an adopted son in the Austin household. He went on holidays with them, and Lucy, the Austins' daughter, called him Bun Don (for brother John) and *Brüderchen*. Young Mill enjoyed a warm, affectionate relationship with Sarah, but, in view of its consequences for Mill's intellectual development, his close connection with John was even more significant. John Austin tutored him in Roman law, Blackstone, and Bentham, and became something of an intellectual guide to Mill, who was becoming restless under his father's influence. Mill later recalled Austin's somewhat paternal demeanour: 'He took a sincere and kind interest in me, far beyond what could have been expected towards a mere youth from a man of his age, standing, and what seemed austerity of character.'

This close relationship, which continued throughout their lives in spite of political disagreements in later years and a falling-out between Mill and Sarah Austin, allowed John Austin to exercise a remarkable intellectual influence on Mill. The first of the two occasions when he provoked a fundamental shift in Mill's thinking occurred in the early 1820s when he was tutoring him. Of course Mill was already radically inclined, but Austin appears to have been responsible for interpreting Bentham's teaching in such a way as to turn Mill into a doctrinaire Benthamite, one, as Mill put it, who had 'a creed, a doctrine, a philosophy; in one among the best senses of the word, a religion.'[11] The personal bonds between them were strengthened during this early period by their like-minded radical politics.

One distinguishing characteristic of the Benthamite radicals that Austin and Mill shared in the early 1820s was an extreme dogmatism. According to Henry Crabb Robinson, Austin already had 'pugnacious habits' while a law student and was vehement and dogmatic about his beliefs, and Austin himself admitted that his attachment to Bentham's doctrines was 'violent.'[12] The fundamental assumption of this dogmatically held doctrine was a belief that the aristocracy used Parliament and other institutions such as the courts, the church, and the army to promote its own interests, which, because they were the interests of a class, were sinister. Consequently, while the aristocracy pursued its own interests, those of the entire populace were sacrificed, and the people were exploited. Since they both represented the aristocracy, Whigs and Tories were regarded as equally guilty. Underlying this analysis was the implication, which Austin kept inconspicuous but did not entirely conceal, that a democratic suffrage, or something close to it, was the only effective device for preventing the domination of Parliament by sinister interests. The groundwork of this radical doctrine had appeared in Bentham's *Plan of Parliamentary Reform* (1817), which was among the books that Sarah was made to read during her engagement, and it reappeared in many of the pamphlets and articles written by the Benthamite radicals during these years when the Austins were settling into London life. It was especially evident in the *Westminster Review*, the journal established by Bentham in 1824 for the propagation of his radical doctrine.

Austin's first publication – a thorough radical attack on the aristocracy – appeared in the fourth number of this journal, in 1824. The subject of his article was an analysis of the law of primogeniture, which naturally lent itself to a discussion of aristocracy itself. Using vituperative and contemptuous language, Austin attacked the Whig *Edinburgh Review*, thereby imitating James Mill and John Stuart Mill, for whom such aggressiveness was a hallmark of Benthamite radicalism. The *Edinburgh Review* (specifically the economist James Ramsay McCulloch, whose article Austin was discussing, although he did not name the author) was guilty of inconsistency, sophistic thinking, and historical blunders; indeed, McCulloch 'reduced himself to absurdity.' Austin first criticized primogeniture on economic grounds, but in the end it was 'aristocratical ascendancy and aristocratical misgovernment' that was condemned. Not only did primogeniture lead to the concentration of landed wealth in a small class, but it also led to exploitation of the people, for the younger sons and other relations, excluded from their fathers' estates, would have to be provided with incomes at public expense: 'To maintain the custom of primogeniture amongst the governing class, the people could be taxed and pillaged with little moderation ... Offices, which had survived the ends for which they were created, would be kept alive at the public charge, because the emoluments of such useless offices would yield a convenient provision for the younger children of the aristocracy.' This indictment reflected the spirit of *The Black Book*, a radical document first published in 1820, as well as Benthamite radicalism. This outlook led Austin to observe that 'colonies useless to the mother country would be retained at an enormous cost, that governments and other appointments might be ready for the same interesting class,' and that consequently there were 'larger establishments of all sorts than are needed by the community' and 'unnecessary and wasteful wars,' all because 'the few are instinctively led to pursue their own narrow interests at the expense of the many.'

Austin favoured the democratic suffrage implied by this analysis, but he was circumspect in expressing his views, perhaps because frequent attempts were made at that time to enforce the law of seditious libel. He therefore described a hypothetical country by 'throwing out a few vague conjectures, the creatures, perhaps, of imagination, rather than of reason and experience.' In a country with virtual representation, he wrote, the 'aristocracy would be thoroughly despotic,' while in a country in which the people were '*really* represented' (for example, the United States of America) they were protected from pillage by a body of *real* representatives.' What was wanted was a country 'where the *people reign*' and where primogeniture did not exist.

These views on aristocracy and democracy were accompanied by others that were also typical of the radical outlook. France before the Revolution was described as misgoverned and corrupt, and the Revolution was 'the Grand and Necessary Reform,' which regrettably 'was not accomplished with greater discrimination and forbearance.' Yet 'no reasonable man can wonder that a nation thus pillaged and insulted was provoked to break its chains on the heads of its hateful oppressors.' So favourable was his judgment of the Revolution that Austin insisted that the prime movers were not so much revolutionaries as reformers whose struggle led to the establishment of 'better institutions.' He not only justified the French revolutionaries, but in surprisingly violent language he also defended the idea of revolution. Should such a crisis occur again, he said, 'the obstinate and malignant enemies of the general happiness ... must be smitten with the sword of justice, or encountered in the field of battle.'

In keeping with this judgment of the French Revolution, Austin at this time called Burke one of 'the tools of the oligarchy' who was guilty of 'traducing the mass of mankind' and deserving of punishment 'for libel on the people.' Tradition and justification of the past were ridiculed. Common law was a chaos that arose in 'savage and stupid ages'; to be 'the slaves of custom' was to be 'in the infancy of reason.' Each generation in a progression was wiser and better than its predecessor. 'The silly or designing cant ... about the wisdom and virtue of ancestors ... is belied by all the evidence which discloses the character of our forefathers.'[13] As expressions of radicalism during the early 1820s these views were not novel; but in the light of Austin's politics in later life, and even in contrast to his opinions only a few years later when he was lecturing on jurisprudence, they are remarkable.

AN EVENT IN 1826 led to a transformation of John Austin's life and opinions – he was made Professor of Jurisprudence and the Law of Nations in the new University of London. The university had been taking shape for some years, and several of Austin's friends, including James Mill and George Grote, were among those who founded the institution and served on its governing council. When Austin accepted the appointment he gave up his meagre law work because now he could look forward to a modest but secure income and an opportunity to pursue his legal studies. Since the university was not expected to open until 1828, he decided to prepare his lectures at Bonn, perhaps because the faculty there included five professors of jurisprudence.

The year or so spent at Bonn was agreeable, and the Austins probably found this period more to their liking than any of their later sojourns in other Continental cities. Now that they enjoyed a prospect of John's continuous employment, anxieties about the future could be put aside. Bonn was inexpensive and attractive. The town was intimate – one could walk from the Kölner gate to the Coblenz gate in about ten minutes – and they found that the unhurried pace of living contrasted pleasantly with London's more rapid tempo. Within the town there was a beautiful Gothic Münster with extensive orchards that reached to the Rhine. Although there was some manufacturing – wine-making and charcoal production – life was dominated by the university, with its nine hundred students and its faculty of about seventy. It was here in the world of books and scholars that the Austins found an agreeable niche.[14]

Austin was attracted to the orderly routines of the *Gelehrte*, and as he prepared his lectures he adopted some of their habits. Typically, he worked from eight to noon and from late afternoon well into the evening;

the hours in between were occupied more casually with walking and dinner. Four times a week he met with a tutor, a young doctor of law, who read legal works with him and also helped with his German. Only towards the end of his stay in Bonn did he think his German sufficiently good for him to attend lectures. He worked 'with unvarying cheerfulness and satisfaction,' and perhaps this as much as the attractive surroundings made Sarah look back on these as their 'pleasant days in dear Germany.'[15]

In Bonn Austin laid the foundations for the work that made him famous as a major contributor to the analytical school of jurisprudence. He wished to establish jurisprudence as a science, and he now embarked on what he called his 'long and scabrous road' as an expositor of this new branch of knowledge.[16] He continued to devote himself to this task for about six years after returning from Germany, and during this period (1828-34) he presented his lectures as Professor of Jurisprudence in the newly established University of London and also published the general, introductory lectures as *The Province of Jurisprudence Determined* (1832). These and some additional lectures (which were included in a posthumous publication under the title *Lectures on Jurisprudence or the Philosophy of Positive Law*) constitute the bulk of Austin's writings and are the basis of his extraordinary reputation as a major spokesman for legal positivism and as the foremost exponent of the analytical school of jurisprudence.

Ostensibly the lectures were concerned only with jurisprudence, and this aspect of them has attracted considerable scholarly attention. Here Austin carefully defined law and distinguished it from morality as he identified the basic concepts that were to be found in all systems of law. These included sovereignty, command, sanction, habitual obedience, independent political society, and positive morality. There was, however, much more than jurisprudence in Austin's lectures (and in his *Province of Jurisprudence Determined*). In addition to explaining the central concepts of jurisprudence and the boundaries that separated it from other sciences, Austin presented the results of his speculations in the field of political philosophy. These speculations were not logically dependent on the jurisprudence, and most of those interested in Austin have ignored them. Yet, although Austin is mainly known for his work on jurisprudence, his political ideas were far from ephemeral. His first and last publications were political, and arguably his political philosophy was in competition with his specifically jurisprudential ideas for his attention.

The political themes in the lectures were introduced when Austin distinguished between jurisprudence, which was concerned with law as it existed, and other sciences, such as political economy, legislation, and politics, which, according to Austin, were ethically oriented and concerned with discovering the principles that promoted general happiness. The interest in happiness led Austin to engage in lengthy disquisitions to justify the use of the principle of utility as the best way of determining what promoted happiness. These inquiries set the stage for his specifically political speculations. Having persuaded himself that there was a valid intellectual foundation for the ethically oriented sciences, he went on to speculate about the kind of political institutions that would establish the laws and policies generated by these sciences. In the course of doing this, Austin ceased to be a radical, but in his political speculations he continued to ask the questions for which previously answers had been provided by Benthamite radicalism. Thus he still sought to discover how good government was to be achieved by asking who should rule, how rulers should be selected, and why subjects should obey, but while at Bonn he discovered different answers to these questions.

Who should have authority to legislate, and how should they be chosen? The Benthamite radicals gave unambiguous answers to these questions: legislators should be elected by a democratic suffrage, and the best legislators were responsive to the people's wishes. Austin now rejected this and adopted the diametrically opposite view that political authority should be given to those most capable of making wise policy, that is, to those intellectually qualified by virtue of their superior knowledge of economics, ethics, and political science.

Austin's new confidence in rule by an intellectual élite was based on his belief that the ethical choices in legislation could be made scientifically. As an admirer of Bacon, the greatest of scientific visionaries, he was optimistic about the possibility of establishing scientific knowledge of ethics. He was impressed with the achievements of the natural sciences and the progress of political economy – as early as 1813 he 'professed to be a political economist and was vehement in the assertion of Malthus's principles' – and he anticipated the successful development of political and other moral sciences. By applying the principle of utility all these sciences would discover ways of improving human life. In the future science would determine whether actions were benevolent and useful or mischievous and pernicious. The result would be a utilitarian science of ethics, including the sciences of law and morality, economics, and political science. Austin did not seem troubled by the difficulties of such an enterprise; he declared, 'There is no peculiar uncertainty in the *subject* or *matter* of these sciences,' and, quoting Locke, he looked forward to the time when 'ethics would rank with the sciences which are *capable of demonstration.*'[17]

Scientific ethics, Austin argued, could be established, but it would be understood by only a few, just as only a few understood the conclusions of natural sciences. Thus there was a need to defer to the authority of those with scientific knowledge, which arose from the complexity of political and economic matters and the long time required to discover knowledge about them. Experience was too limited and time too short for each person to investigate the complex issues in legislation, political economy, morality, and political science (all branches of science that Austin mentioned). Each of these branches of knowledge could be established as a science, so that sufficient reasons might be given for each of the rules that form a body of law or morality; but 'no single mind could have found the whole of those rules, nor could any single mind compass the whole of their proofs.' Everyone had limited knowledge, but the multitude were especially dependent on guidance from experts. Even in ideal circumstances, most persons would have to accept the conclusions of the experts 'on *authority*, testimony, or trust.'[18]

Having made a claim for the authority of a scientific élite, Austin faced the problem of explaining how the multitude of laymen would be induced to accept this authority. Two conditions were specified: those who possessed authority had to agree among themselves, and they had to be free of selfish motives that might bias their conclusions. These conditions prevailed in the mathematical and physical sciences; we commonly trusted the conclusions in these fields because 'the adepts in these sciences and arts mostly agree in their results, and lie under no temptation to cheat the ignorant with error.' Although he had no evidence for the belief that the earth moves around the sun, yet he believed it to be true because it was 'perfectly rational, though it rests upon mere authority.' Unhappily the situation was quite different with ethics and the related sciences of legislation, politics, and political economy. Here the inquirers 'have rarely been impartial, and, therefore, have differed in their results.' They were 'advocates rather than inquirers'; instead of honestly drawing inferences according to evidence and logic, most of them have hunted for arguments in favour of *given* conclusions.' Consequently those claiming expertise disagreed, and the multitude, faced with 'varying and hostile opinions,' experienced 'invincible doubt.' This condition would be remedied by the maturing of the moral and social sciences. Eventually the experts in these fields would 'dispel the obscurity by which the science [of ethics] is clouded, and would clear it from most of its uncertainties ... As the jar of *their* conclusions gradually subsided, a body of doctrine and authority to which the *multitude* might trust would emerge from the existing chaos.'[19]

This understanding of authority meant that the citizen would have a passive, acquiescent role, but trust in authority was not to be blind, for it was not to arise from tradition or religious belief or communal bonds, but was to be based on understanding: the multitude was to be 'docile to the voice of reason.' A modicum of understanding was all that was possible in a populace necessarily composed of laymen, but at least ordinary people could 'clearly apprehend the *leading principles*' of political and economic sciences, with the consequence that 'all the more momentous of the derivative practical truths would find access to their understandings and expel the antagonist errors.' Thus the multitude would recognize and trust 'the statements and reasonings of their instructed and judicious friends,' and they would reject 'the lies and fallacies of those who would use them to sinister purposes' and 'the equally pernicious nonsense of their weak and ignorant well-wishers.' Austin looked forward to the people's being armed with knowledge of leading principles, and 'though most or many of their opinions would still be taken from *authority*, the authority to which they would trust might satisfy the most scrupulous reason.' To Austin this line of reasoning led to a 'most cheering truth.'[20]

The readiness with which the populace might accept the authority of the instructed was exemplified by political economy, which Austin called 'the inestimable science,' itself interwoven with morals, politics, and legislation. The broad 'leading principles' of this science could be mastered by the multitude, whereas the nicer points would remain inaccessible, and thus public opinion on such points would always have to rely on authority. It is curious that Austin, who was aware of machine breaking and rick burning, as well as opposition to Malthusian doctrine and private property, entirely failed to anticipate the vigorous resistance to policies supported by political economists during the ensuing decades. He returned from Bonn supremely confident that the populace could acquire sufficient knowledge to sustain a reasoned trust in the authority of the instructed in all branches of moral and political science.[21]

Since John Austin's views presupposed a populace with at least a modicum of knowledge, he favoured universal education such as he had found in Germany. On this issue, however, Sarah Austin's rather than his voice is heard. The need for national primary education was one of the first issues on which she stepped forward to expound ideas that she and John shared. This became a favourite cause, on which she wrote journal articles which helped her to become known, but the political position that underlay her views owed a great deal to her husband's new approach to politics.

Sarah Austin's interest in the details of educational practices began

with a chance meeting with Victor Cousin in Bonn in 1827. Her
enthusiasm for Cousin's teaching led her to publish in 1834 a translation
of his *Report on the State of Public Instruction in Prussia*, which extolled the
idea of national education, and although she complained that 'this dry
laborious work never brought me one atom of either honour or profit,' it
did bring her some notoriety, for in her preface to the translation she
defended unpopular opinions, including universal and therefore compulsory education and a measure of state control of the curriculum.[22] In
1835 she also elaborated her views in a long article that was published as a
small volume in 1839.

Sarah's rationale for state-sponsored, compulsory education on the
Prussian model shows how much she shared John Austin's new views on
the relation of the governed to those who govern. Yet because support for
national education principally came from radicals, the élitist justification
for her position was largely ignored, and she continued to be regarded as
a radical, although she denied this to Cousin and others: 'I am not a
Radical, far from it.'[23] In fact, she defended national education because it
allowed for the creation of intelligent, informed loyalty to authority.

Such authority was needed, she argued, because of moral and social
disintegration – and here she supplemented Austin's argument for
authority. She was keenly aware that the conditions for sustaining
traditional authorities had been undermined. Her reading of the Factory
and Poor Law Commissioners' reports, which described the social and
intellectual conditions of the working classes, persuaded her that society
was threatened by moral anarchy. Society, she said, 'is no longer a calm
current, but a tossing sea. Reverence for tradition, for authority, is gone.
In such a state of things, who can deny the absolute necessity for national
education?'[24]

This state of things was only aggravated by reformers who argued that
education was the way to advancement and that 'knowledge is power.'
Such arguments stimulated expectations which would inevitably be
disappointed; they would make men act 'above their station, disgust them
with labour, make them ambitious, envious, dissatisfied.' Furthermore,
such ideas would lead to class conflict and disorder – there would be
'illusions pregnant with disappointment and suffering, the causeless
antipathies ... [and] the violences and the crimes.' Thus she ridiculed the
ideals of the Society for the Diffusion of Useful Knowledge (although
earlier, in 1824, she had written for it) and the Mechanics Institutes, both
greatly favoured by radicals, when she cast doubts on the usefulness of the
diffusion of technical arts and general information. Instead, believing

that 'the people must be instructed, guided – in short, governed,' she recommended the kind of education that would promote love of labour, moderation in desires, and a belief in order, and thus acceptance of authority.[25]

Since the authority which Sarah Austin wished to uphold was partly moral in character, she, like her husband, recommended a curriculum that included moral teaching, and in contrast to many rationalists in the education reform movement, they would both have allowed religious instruction.[26] Her words echoed his: the combination of moral and religious with secular education 'would embrace all the most important parts of ethical science.' To overcome sectarian fears about the substance of religious teaching, she proposed a common secular curriculum with each religious group determining the particular religious teaching in its schools.[27] The overall aim was to instil thoughts and feelings that would dispose the multitude to give respect to authority.

The aim of Sarah Austin's education program was a society in which class conflict would be mitigated and democratic pressure reduced: 'Whenever education shall have done its work – whenever the people shall be sufficiently enlightened to see all that the business of legislation demands – then, and not before, will they cease to struggle for a power they will see it is impossible they could wield; then ... will the grand conflict that now agitates the world cease.'[28] No longer was there anything democratic or radical in her views – they mirrored Austin's new élitist theory.

AUSTIN'S NEW IDEAS could hardly have differed more from his previous Benthamite radicalism, and a comparison of his new ideas with those he had abandoned will show how much change had taken place. This is not to say that he became a conservative, a change that was yet to come in the 1840s and especially after 1848. At this time he was anti-radical but not conservative. However, Austin's rejection of Benthamite radicalism did not prevent him from continuing to be a utilitarian and from upholding many of Bentham's ideas about law and jurisprudence. From the Benthamite point of view, on the other hand, Austin's new ideas provided for a continuation of aristocratic government – the only difference being that he wanted an aristocracy of intellect instead of an aristocracy based on lineage and property.

Austin now disagreed with the Benthamite radicals about the correct perception of the political landscape. The Benthamites thought the most important conflict was between the aristocracy and the people, and they emphasized the role of 'the People' as the body for which a radical party would provide leadership and representation. Austinian analysis, however, aiming to be literal and realistic, saw through radical rhetoric to what was regarded as the purest reality, and there it alway found, regardless of forms of government, a relationship between sovereign and subject which made it difficult to consider radical rhetoric about 'the People' as having any place in a precise account of what really takes place. Thus Austin criticized those who believed that 'the power of the sovereign flows from the people, or the people is the fountain of sovereign power.'[29] He was unmistakably rejecting Benthamite radicalism, including his own views as presented in the *Westminster Review* as recently as 1824.

Austin's severe doubts about radicalism also arose from his estimate of the populace. Whereas in 1826 he thought 'most men ... habitually prudent,' in his lectures he referred to 'the rabble, great and small' and spoke of 'the dull taste of the stupid and infuriate majority.'[30] The low estimate he had of the populace at this time was referred to by Brougham, who recalled that 'for public opinion [Austin] had little respect.'[31] Whereas earlier Austin shared the Benthamite belief that sinister interests were to be found among the aristocratic few and never resided in the people, in the lectures he announced that 'the guides of the multitude [are] moved by sinister interests, or by prejudices which are the offspring of such interests.'[32] Of course, to say this was to condemn popular radical leaders.

Austin's new ideas challenged radicalism on other fronts. Benthamite radicals held that those who enjoyed authority could not be trusted, and that consequently their authority had to be circumscribed by carefully designed constitutional checks. The assumption was that all persons pursued their own selfish interests, and that office-holders, even if democratically elected, would use their authority to serve themselves. The Benthamites justified universal suffrage and frequent elections as obstacles to the sinister exploitation of authority by those in public office. Although critical of traditional Whig constitutionalism, they proposed their own kind of constitutional checks. Austin, on the other hand, developed an entirely different perspective on constitutional limitations, and in his analysis, which gave the central place to a strictly legal definition of sovereignty, they had a greatly diminished significance. Strong, unchallenged authority, he argued, was inherently a part of the sovereign state's existence. Although constitutionalism invoked moral ideas in order to limit legal authority, in reality it could not diminish such authority, for sovereign power, as he understood it, 'is incapable of *legal* limitation.'

Thus, he said, 'every supreme government is legally *despotic*,' and consequently 'the current distinction between free and despotic governments ... is expressed in terms which are extremely inappropriate and absurd.' He ridiculed the notion of limited monarchy, which 'involves a contradiction in terms' if it is suggested that the king's power is legally limited.[33] Of course, Austin recognized that beliefs about constitutional limitations in fact did exist – for him they were part of positive morality and (to use his words) not part of law strictly so called – but his concentration on law as it existed (in his sense of the word) and his definition of the boundaries of jurisprudence had the consequence of reducing the significance of constitutional checks. Although in the example of limited monarchy he criticized a prominent part of the British constitutional tradition, the ground of his criticism also put him into disagreement with the Benthamite radicals.

There was another consideration that led Austin to depreciate the idea of constitutional limitations, including those advocated in Benthamite radicalism. Since science could discover how to maximize general happiness, Austin argued, sovereign authority guided by such a science ought not to be limited by constitutional checks. Such checks Austin called positive morality. They originated in opinion, moral beliefs, and tradition; they did not have legal status, and they were binding only to the extent that morality and opinion were felt to be compelling. The constitutional limitations and norms of constitutionality that were known to Austin originated in a pre-scientific age, and he argued that it would be undesirable to allow such norms to check the laws made in the light of the science of legislation. He would have opposed constitutional limitations, however, even if they originated in scientific positive morality. If they were justified by the same science of ethics that was also the source of positive law, it would be pointless to have them serve as checks on positive law, for constitutionalism had meaning only when it invoked standards that were independent from and 'higher' than the laws that it judged.[34] Thus his lack of sympathy for the very idea of constitutional limits reflected an understanding of sovereignty and the state both as they existed and as they could exist ideally.

The ideas developed at Bonn created another cleavage between Austin and the Benthamite radicals. In the lectures he included in his explanation of the principle of utility a theological position which assumed the existence of a deity and the necessity of explaining God's relation to human actions. Apart from this, his defence of the theory of utility was unobjectionable to the other Benthamites; but Austin's theological context for the theory was, from their point of view, unnecessary. His position, which was somewhat conventional and reminiscent of Paley, was presented without a hint of irony.[35] He argued that since God in his goodness intended human happiness but did not make clear how it could be achieved, it was necessary to observe the tendencies of human action, including the sum of its probable consequences, to determine 'the probable effect of our conduct on that *general happiness* or *good* which is the object of the Divine Lawgiver in all his laws and commandments.' The principle of utility filled a gap left by God's uncommunicativeness: 'We may infer the laws which he has given, but has not expressed or revealed.'[36] These views may not have reflected Austin's personal religious outlook, for he was said to have embraced Bentham's irreligion, and he was part of a circle of unbelievers (as Henry Reeve called them when recollecting the talk in Austin's drawing room in 1831) whose conversation typically turned 'on the want of evidence of a superintending Deity and Providence in the affairs of the World.'[37] On the other hand, his intelligent and thoughtful fourteen-year-old daughter reported in 1835 that her father was 'not an atheist but he reasons about religion as to its utility in regulating the conduct and regards Christianity as the best and highest morality.'[38] At the very least, Austin's position in the lectures reflected a willingness to comply with conventional piety, and in this he differed from the other Benthamites, whose circumspect allusions to religion did not conceal their disbelief.[39]

The differences between Austin and the Benthamite radicals did not end here. Whereas radicalism visualized intense political and class conflict and justified the goals and the program of one party in that conflict, Austin now believed that conflict of any kind was undesirable and unnecessary. In his favoured regime contention and division were to be avoided, and broad agreement if not perfect harmony was to prevail. He went so far with this line of argument as to have regretted that the Reformation had taken place and to have thought that it had 'on the whole, been an evil to mankind,' for it popularized theological questions, made the multitude quarrelsome, and 'produced sectarianism, with all its concomitant evils of hatreds, divisions, persecutions, etc.' Such considerations led Austin to speak appreciatively of the medieval church and to wish for a 'truly Catholic and comprehensive church ... which views every man as a Christian, as the state views every man as a subject.'[40] But he was searching less for a common religious outlook than for shared values and a common point of view which were to come from a general acceptance of scientific ethics. There would be unanimity regarding this science among those in authority, and that unanimity, along with education in the 'leading principles' of scientific ethics, would lead to agreement within the populace and to trust in authority and therefore to agreement between rulers and ruled.

The goal of harmony was linked with the principle of utility. This principle, rightly understood, facilitated the achievement of harmony, for Austin assumed that if antagonists consulted it, they would inevitably reach a compromise on their differences. Thus he called it 'the healing principle of utility.' He used the hypothetical example of conflict between a government and a rebellious opposition. If each party consulted the principle of utility, they would compare the benefit of reaching their goals with the cost of doing so. Thus, if the government considered the cost of repression, it would make concessions to the rebellious opposition, and if the opposition considered the cost of civil war, it would settle for less than all it was seeking. Each would 'compare the worth of its object with the cost of a violent pursuit' and judge the cost too high. The result would be moves away from the extremes and towards compromise if not perfect agreement.

The failure to use the healing principle of utility was traced to abstract standards and doctrinairism. Thus if a beleaguered government insisted on defending 'the sacred rights of sovereigns,' or if the rebellious opposition insisted on establishing 'the rights of man,' neither would be disposed to compromise. Using the example of the conflict with the American colonies, Austin explained that Parliament had the legal right to tax the colonies, but 'the stupid and infuriate majority who rushed into that odious war, could perceive and discourse of nothing but the *sovereignty* of the mother country, and her so called *right* to tax her colonial subjects.' Burke, with his conciliatory policy, was regarded as a spokesman for the principle of utility. He recognized that it was not the interest of England to insist upon her sovereignty. The revenue that would have been gained was not large; the relief from taxation at home was trifling; resources were in danger of being squandered; and the colonial subjects were to be driven to rebellion. These considerations would have led to a policy of conciliation if the 'dominant opinions and sentiments [in England] had been fashioned on the principle of utility.'

> But arguments drawn from utility were not to the dull taste of the ... majority. The rabble, great and small, would hear of nothing but their *right* ... Mr. Burke would have taught them better: would have purged their muddled brains ... with the healing principle of utility. He asked them what they would get, if the project of coercion should succeed; and implored them to compare the advantage with the hazard and the cost.

Had they 'seized the scope of his arguments,' Austin claimed, the needless and disastrous war would not have occurred.[41]

Austin's defence of conciliation, compromise, and harmony and his deep dislike of division and conflict meant that he could no longer look favourably on political beliefs that were sectarian, utopian, or doctrinaire, and therefore the strategy adopted by Bentham's and James Mill's disciples during the 1820s and 1830s became anathema to him. The Benthamite radicals welcomed and promoted conflict between those representing the people and all other politicians representing the aristocracy. Their tactics of party realignment required that they become an extremist party indifferent to the conciliation of differences called for by Austin's understanding of utility as a 'healing principle.' Moreover, they tended to be doctrinaire. According to Macaulay, James Mill was the leader of a sect and an advocate of 'Utopian democracy,' and Austin, despite his friendship with Mill, appears to have come to similar conclusions. Furthermore, the political language of the radicals included examples of what Austin called jargon, 'unmeaning abstractions,' and 'senseless fictions,' which contributed to factional opposition and divisiveness. Parties which use such jargon, he said, 'must inevitably push to their objects through thick and thin, though their object be straws or feathers as weighed in the balance of utility.' Since the Benthamite radicals were eager for conflict, they exemplified the kind of divisive, extremist group he now condemned. Their greatest concern was to alter the form of government, and Austin must have had them in mind when he noted that 'for such verbal differences between forms of supreme government has the peace of mankind been frequently troubled by ignorant and headlong fanatics.'[42]

WHEN THE AUSTINS RETURNED from Germany in 1828 it was evident that dramatic changes had occurred in their outlook. John Stuart Mill reported that Austin's 'personal disposition was much softened; he was less militant and polemic,' and Mill added, 'in politics ... he acquired an indifference, bordering on contempt, for the progress of popular institutions.'[43] In his lectures Austin noted that those who distinguished between free and despotic governments were 'lovers of democracy'; but by avoiding this distinction and calling it 'extremely inappropriate and absurd,' Austin separated himself from those, such as the Benthamite radicals, who were lovers of democracy. Like Mill, he approved of the Reform Bill, although without great hopes for benefits from it, and he and Mill, unlike all the others who had been part of the Benthamite radical group in the 1820s, did not work to promote its passage. The other Benthamites could hardly have been in doubt about where Austin stood, especially those who attended his lectures; and Sarah reported, 'I excite horror among my Radical friends for not believing that all salvation comes of certain organic forms of government.' These differences led to a cooling of friendships with some of the Benthamite radicals. Sarah recalled that they were 'all vehement and undoubting – all, but one – my husband, with whom they almost quarrelled for his doubts.'[44] Relationships did not become acrimonious, but neither were they particularly intimate.

With Bentham, however, relations became strained. According to Sarah, Austin 'used vainly to represent to [Bentham] that the ignorance and wrong-headedness of the people were fully as dangerous to good government as the "sinister interests" of the governing classes. Upon this point they were always at issue.' Bentham, now over eighty, had become accustomed to flattery rather than discussion, and as their disagreements became more evident, it 'gradually ended in Mr. Austin seeing less and less of him.' Sarah spoke about this as causing both of them great pain, as they were extremely attached to 'the dear old man.'[45] Perhaps their disagreements explain why Bentham, who might have been expected to leave his books on jurisprudence to Austin, left them instead to Edwin Chadwick.[46] Although in the lectures Austin spoke of Bentham with great respect, in the end it was Bentham's flaws that survived in his memory. When faced by Auguste Comte in an irritable mood, Austin described him thus: 'Like Mr. Bentham (of whom he constantly reminds me), he is so wedded to his own devices and so full of presumptuous contempt for all which has been done by others.'[47] Years later, when asked whether her husband had been one of Bentham's disciples, Sarah recalled not his early commitment to all Bentham's ideas but his mixed judgment during this middle period: 'In politics and philosophy, *certainly not*, though in both he found much to admire in his writings; but it was as a Jurist, or rather as the most original and inventive of all writers on Law, that he looked up to him with profound veneration.'[48]

Although Austin's relations with most Benthamites became somewhat distant, his relationship with John Stuart Mill – that ubiquitous figure in Austin's life – remained close. Once again, as in the early 1820s, Austin had a formative influence on Mill's thought. For by 1831 Mill, like Austin, had ceased to be a Benthamite radical and rather suddenly adopted a belief in the importance of giving authority to a scientific élite to which the multitude would defer. Mill's published expression of this belief first appeared in the *Examiner* during the early months of 1831 under the title 'The Spirit of the Age.' These ideas left a permanent residue in his political thinking, but after a brief period when they held a central place, they were combined with his old but now qualified belief in the need for democratic checks on authority. Yet the principle that there was a need for deference to the authority of the instructed remained with him, and it was evident in such places as his essay on Coleridge, where he attached great significance to a clerisy, and his *Considerations on Representative Government*, where this belief was reflected in his provision for the Legislative Commission. Austin appears to have suggested the idea for this body, for he recommended a Permanent Commission of Legislation with features similar to the one proposed by Mill.[49]

Mill's ideas on the authority of the 'instructed Few' (as he called the intellectual élite in various essays published during the 1830s) is usually traced to the influence of the St Simonians, whose terminology he adopted and whose influence he acknowledged in his *Autobiography*. There is much to indicate, however, that Austin played a part in shaping Mill's beliefs on this subject.[50] Mill attended Austin's lectures on jurisprudence during two of the first three sessions, and his approval of Austin's ideas about the need for deference to a scientific élite was evident in his 1832 review of *The Province of Jurisprudence Determined*.[51]

In the light of this influence one can discern in Mill's admiration and wish to be helpful to Austin a sense of intellectual indebtedness. He tried to find employment for Austin at a time when it was most needed for both psychological and financial reasons; he consulted Austin about James Mill's epitaph; he sent Austin sheets of his *Logic* before it was published, hoping that Austin would review the work; and in 1848 he presented Austin with one of the few copies of his *Principles of Political Economy* that included the flattering dedication to Harriet Taylor. Mill's appreciation of Austin continued long after he became estranged from Sarah, and his gratitude to him even outlived their political disagreements, which became evident in 1848. Thus after Austin's death Mill wrote (not to Sarah but to her granddaughter Janet) that 'few have contributed more [than Austin] by their individual influence and their conversation to the formation and the growth of a number of the most active minds of this generation.' Austin, he said, was 'one of the men whom I most valued, and to whom I have been morally and intellectually most indebted,' and he added, 'I have always regarded my early knowledge of [Austin] as one of the fortunate circumstances of my life.'[52] It also should be noted that during the years after the Austins returned from Bonn, Mill, who suffered from depression during his 'mental crisis,' might have felt a bond of sympathy with John Austin, for whom depressed moods were chronic. The old Benthamite friends easily recognized the drastic change in the Austins' political outlook and especially the turning away from a belief in democracy, but the cause of the change was mysterious. There is no evidence that a specifically German intellectual influence was at work. In that part of his writings on jurisprudence which was written at Bonn or soon after his return (including the lectures that make up *The Province of Jurisprudence Determined*), most of John Austin's references to German authors are critical. Although he admired German literature and respected German scholarship, he regretted 'the proneness of German philosophy to vague and misty abstraction.' He thought German writers (Kant, Krug, Politz) and the Austrian Gentz guilty of defending the 'false and absurd' hypothesis of an original covenant. Their self-contradictory arguments were but 'a taste or sample of the high ideal philosophy which the Germans oppose exultingly to the philosophy of Bacon and Locke: to the earthy, grovelling, *empirical* philosophy, which deigns to scrutinize facts, or stoops to observation and induction.'[53] In his discussion of the original covenant Austin focused on recent German writing, and he was unembarrassed by the association of that doctrine with two of his great intellectual heroes, Hobbes and Locke. Austin's comments did not mean that he was unaffected by German writing on philosophy and jurisprudence, but that this influence, such as it was, minimally affected only the most general context and a few subordinate parts of his theory of law, but barely touched the main features of Austinian theory.[54]

It was not so much the influence of German ideas as the example of German institutions that contributed to the changes in Austin's political outlook. There were striking parallels between his new ideas and certain features of German society. As Mill noted, it was not only German literature, but also 'German character and state of society [that] had made a very perceptible change in [Austin's] views of life.'[55]

In Germany the Austins found rule by a small bureaucracy under a monarch and what they regarded as good government yet without democracy. According to Benthamite radicalism, this was inconceivable. From Bonn Sarah reported with admiration 'the absence of all that we know (to our cost) under the name of *patronage*,' and on her return she wrote admiringly about 'the high character of the functionaries of government and administration, from the highest to the lowest.' Unlike in England, where there was patronage, nepotism, and corruption, in Germany there were 'no oligarchical interests to consult, [and] men are appointed to offices for which they have given evidence of fitness.'[56] Austin pointed to Prussia as a country 'whose administrators, for practical skill, are at least on a level with those of any country in Europe.'[57] His previous admiration for the meritocratic system in the army of the American democracy was seemingly forgotten; in Germany he had an opportunity of observing appointment for merit in a regime that was anything but a democracy.

Germany's good government was also evident in its system of national education, whereas such a thing did not exist in England. The German states, Sarah Austin admiringly reported, saw to it 'that every one of its subjects not only *may* but *shall* and *must*, be instructed'; they regarded education as a government's 'most sacred duty towards its subjects,' and did not leave people to shift for themselves or to depend on charity for instruction – 'the "despotic" Government of Prussia would be careful not to insult its subjects with such a suggestion.'[58]

These reflections – on the quality of officials, the absence of patronage, and the emphasis on education of the people – nourished doubts that the democratic recipe recommended by radicalism was the necessary or even the best means for achieving good government. As Mill put it, Austin 'thought that there was more practical good government, and ... infinitely more care for the education and mental improvement of all ranks of the people, under the Prussian monarchy, than under the English representative government.' Mill also reported that Austin held 'that the real security for good government is "un peuple éclairé," which is not always the fruit of popular institutions, and which if it could be had without them, would do their work better than they.'[59]

The example of Germany did more than stimulate doubts about radicalism; it was also a source of ideas that found their way into Austin's new outlook. Most notably, Austin's belief in authority for those who possessed scientific knowledge seems to have received great impetus in Germany. His high expectations for moral and political science derived in part from Bacon and Hobbes, but the 'reverence for intellectual rank' and the appointment of intellectually eminent persons to high office in Germany may have persuaded him that it was possible to establish a scientific élite in positions of authority. 'The picture of the life of a man of letters, in one of the "despotic" states of Germany,' Sarah Austin said, 'is fitted to excite some reflections not altogether favourable to "popular institutions," in those who live in a country where government and people are too much occupied in scrambling for supremacy, to care about arts or letters.' Sarah, it is true, was worried that government in Germany might divert men of knowledge from scrutinizing political matters too closely –

'Governments can always command the time, talents, and pens of the vast body of *gelehrte* into any frivolous unprofitable channel they will' – and she suspected that this explained German pedantry. Such impulses, however, were checked by public opinion, which insistently called for governmental deference to learning:

> Genius, learning, and liberal thought have a far other field, and a very different hold over the hearts and minds of men of all ranks in Germany, than here; – that the employment of such men as Goethe, Herder, the Humbolds [sic], Niebuhr, Ancillon, and many others distinguished in art, philosophy, and letters, as active functionaries of the state, is one of the tributes which the Governments of the enlightened part of Germany pay to merit, and is completely in harmony with the tone of public opinion.

If this could be achieved in Germany, the Austins reasoned, why not elsewhere?[60]

Another political phenomenon observed in Germany was the strong attachment of the people to the government, which was one of the things Austin called for in the *Province of Jurisprudence*. He and Sarah were impressed with the support enjoyed by the Prussian government. Sarah pointed to 'the universal confidence' which the bureaucracy inspired, and she noticed the contrast of England, where government was supposed to have been based on consent, but where in fact (Sarah could say in 1833) 'a considerable portion of its subjects [were] in a state continually bordering on revolt.' She also wrote from Germany to describe 'the great attachment of the people of all classes to their King.'[61] Such observations suggested that the people did not have to be unrelenting in their suspicion of authority, as recommended by radicalism, but that they could accept and even support it.

These new themes in John Austin's political thought – the importance of a competent bureaucracy, national education, and belief in the authority of those who were best qualified – did not arise from a drastic change in his understanding of the practical problems requiring solutions. He still wished to eliminate ignorance, nepotism, and corruption, as he had before he went to Germany as a Benthamite radical. The problem continued to be that of providing good government, but after his visit to Germany he adopted a different remedy. Instead of a democratic suffrage he looked to an educated people that would accept guidance from a trained bureaucracy which included those qualified by their knowledge of economic and political science.

The Austins were greatly moved by their experiences in Germany, and their fondness for the country was increased by their belief that life there was in sharp contrast to life in England. It was not only the failure of England to appreciate men of letters, to provide adequate education for the people, and to eliminate corruption in public life. There was also in England an unattractive emphasis on individual advancement and competitive struggle. It was a country where 'everything is impatiently pushed forward to answer the ends of immediate gain,' whereas in Germany, Sarah noted, 'one does not see the strife and the struggle, the carking care, the soul-consuming efforts to get and to spend that are the pride and the curse of England.' Austin saw things the same way after his sojourn in Bonn. Mill reported that he returned with 'a strong distaste for the general meanness of English life, the absence of enlarged thoughts and unselfish desires, the low objects on which the faculties of all classes of the English are intent.'[62] It was not that they were uncritical of Germany – Sarah, especially, complained about the prejudice against women, the censorship, and the pedantry – but on balance they found it attractive.

Personal considerations had some part in this judgment. It was an intellectually fruitful period for John Austin. While organizing his thoughts about law, he developed new ideas, and whereas some important features of his jurisprudence were derivative from Hobbes and Bentham, he was not imitative, and some of his new political ideas were genuinely original.[63] Furthermore, at this time Austin discovered great confidence in his own capacity to see clearly and write precisely; he thought 'his special vocation was that of untying intellectual knots' and that he ha a capacity to bring to his own arguments the 'dint of dry reason.'[64] By using these skills he developed a distinctive way of analysing legal and political thought. He disdained the 'mischievous and detestable abuse of articulate language,' and in his work he frequently complained about 'verbal ambiguities,' 'muddy speculation,' 'confusion of ideas' (by Fichte and Godwin) and 'double logical error' (by Bentham and various German writers), 'impenetrable obscurity' (of Blackstone and Hale), and the use of a term (by Locke and Bentham) that was 'pregnant with confusion and perplexity.' Austin's aspiration was to follow Locke by achieving 'that matchless power of precise and just thinking, with that religious regard for general utility and truth, which marked the incomparable man who emancipated human reason from the yoke of mystery and jargon.'[65] Austin succeeded, in the opinion of John Stuart Mill, who said, 'He uses no word by which something is not added to the sense.'[66] Although quite often he was diffident, Austin seems to have enjoyed moments of productive self-confidence in Germany.

There were other circumstances that help explain the Austins' satisfaction with the German interlude. For Sarah there was a touch of nostalgia, as she was continually reminded of her childhood in Norwich and the customs and sayings she had heard her parents recollecting from their own youth. For once they could live within their narrow means, and they also had the prospect of the professorship in London. Also it was flattering to be fêted by the most distinguished persons at Bonn, including Schlegel and Niebuhr.[67] They had found an agreeable niche, as John Austin revealed in his observation that 'no life would suit me so well as that of a German professor.' And Sarah reported that the position of the illustrious and revered teachers in German universities seemed to him 'the most enviable in the world.' Indeed, Austin confessed that he had 'found in the works of [Germany's] philosophers, her historians, and her scholars, exhaustless mines of knowledge and instruction, and exhaustless sources of pleasure or consolation.'[68] It is no wonder that on their return Mill thought Austin had acquired 'a kind of German religion' and Sarah described herself as *verdeutscht*.[69]

Following his return from Bonn Austin depreciated party politics and showed no interest in them, and in so far as he took a part in practical affairs he confined himself to the role of technical expert. Some years later there were two occasions for doing this, first as a member of the Criminal Law Commission from 1833 to 1836, and later (1836-40) as one of the two commissioners who conducted an inquiry into the laws and constitution of Malta. Both involved drafting and codification. In the first he was disappointed, and he resigned from the Criminal Law Commission because it went about its task of consolidating the criminal law in too piecemeal a fashion and thus denied him an opportunity to codify. After his resignation he began work as an 'unauthorized individual' and intended to write a complete draft of a criminal code.[70] When he was in Malta he drafted many laws and regulations, notably a law concerning the press and libel. Codification and drafting exemplified the solid legislative and administrative improvements which Austin thought far preferable to constitutional reforms.

John Austin's new political ideas, especially his scientific élitism, separated him from most of the parties and ideas that could be found in the political arena. Not only was he critical of Benthamite radicalism, he also opposed Chartism and socialism,[71] and he criticized the advocates of *laissez-faire* (but not the less extreme proponents of free trade). Yet, at the opposite extreme, he unsparingly criticized protectionism, and thus we may assume that he had no affinity with the large part of the Tory party that defended it. In addition, he could not have been comfortable as a Whig, despite the occasional professions of attachment to the Whig party made on his behalf by his wife. His scepticism about constitutional reform would have made him critical of those Whigs who leaned to radicalism, and, more important, his severe criticism of such notions as limited monarchy, consent, and mixed government, as well as his critique of vague and emotional rhetoric about liberty, were implicitly critical of Whiggism. When complaining that liberty 'has been erected into an idol, and extolled with extravagant praise by doting and fanatical worshippers,' he appears to have had traditional Whig rhetoric in mind.[72] Indeed, Austin's literalness prevented him from sharing the values and myths of the British constitution. Both his science of jurisprudence and his new political outlook ran counter to all traditional ideas of constitutionality.

His new outlook put him into something like domestic exile even before he went into actual exile on the Continent, first in 1835 and again in 1841. His idiosyncratic views were partly a matter of his eccentricity – Sarah's nephew Henry Reeve described 'his predilection for perverse judgments and paradoxical opinions' – and they were also in keeping with his secluded, isolated manner of living. They were carried so far that during his middle years (c. 1828-47, aet. 38-57) one cannot associate him with either a liberal or a conservative outlook. He had been a radical but now criticized much in radicalism, and yet he retained his wish for improvement, his distaste for many aspects of English life, and his opposition to what he continued to call sinister interests. On the other hand, although he was to become quite conservative, this did not occur until later, mainly in reaction to the events of 1848. In the lectures, although he revealed his disapproval of revolution, he had not yet reached the state of mind that led him to say that the French Revolution should not have occurred.[73] Nor during this middle period of his life did he hesitate to criticize the constitution, which was highly favoured by conservatives, whatever their party. Hardly a neutral, during this middle period Austin stood alone and cannot be classified easily, making him, as Bagehot said of himself, 'between sizes in politics,' or, one might even say, outsize in politics. This lack of affinity with any of the conventional political positions is perhaps what Mill had in mind when he described Austin as 'the man most without prejudices, conservative or revolutionary, religious or anti-religious, that one can find in all England.'[74]

3

'If I sink, he falls'

AFTER THE BONN INTERLUDE John Austin took up his professorship, but his earlier difficulties were to haunt his new endeavours. He was thirty-eight years old and not settled in a profession. The uncertainties of his career had dominated the first decade of his married life; it was imperative that he now avoid another false start. It had seemed entirely appropriate that he should have left the army, for a life in the law promised to be so much better suited to his intellectual inclinations. During the years in chambers his superior intelligence had not gone unnoticed, and there were those who forecast a brilliant future for him; but the bar had not suited him any better than the army. While his younger brother Charles was later to display dazzling talent as a barrister and leave approximately £140,000 on his death, Austin had difficulty getting a brief.

Sarah Austin said that not long after their marriage it became evident to her that he would not succeed at the Bar – that he was too self-distrusting, nervous, lacking in agility and audacity, and unable to keep up with the pace of the confrontational life of a barrister. Yet she did not explain that his attempts to establish himself in one branch of the law or another continued for six years. Summing up this period she said that his 'habits of mind were fatal to success in business.' The one account we have of his conduct as a barrister illustrates the characteristics that were to spoil his chances for success in many of his worldly encounters. Henry Crabb Robinson has left a record of an incident at Norwich.

It was in the City Court. He was the 4th barrister in the Hall and therefore according to a rule recently laid down by the bar that two counsel must be employed in every appeal – he was entitled to a brief. I called to him 'Here Austin is a brief for you.' If a thunder bolt had fallen he could not have stood more aghast. I put the brief into his hand & pointed out the very common question he had to ask. But he could not utter a word. I put the question for him. A very easy one. Now this has happened to many an able, even eminent man before. And I should have thought nothing of it. But when the Attorney offered him his fee, he rejected it with indignation as if he had been insulted. And then I said to [my]self – there is no help for him.[1]

Certain aspects of this performance – the diffidence, the self-defeating pride that caused him to reject the fee, and the awkward abruptness of manner – reflected flaws in Austin's demeanour that he was aware of himself. He had after all asked Sarah in his engagement letter to 'soften [his] technical asperities.' Right from the start of his career, his nervous excitability and hauteur made those who came in contact with him uneasy, and it is no wonder that he took up conveyancing, a branch of the profession known to be suited to timid or retiring persons who were 'averse from, or disqualified for, the stirring and exciting scenes of warfare in the Courts.'[2] Little is known about those first disillusioning years when Austin struggled to establish himself. Sarah later did not dwell on his lack of success at the bar, saying that it was not his real vocation, but she did not disguise that the drawn out decision to change course once more was agonizing for them both. When he finally gave up in 1825, the experience left him with a bitter taste of failure; but a more grievous one lay ahead.

The university offer seemed to open an ideal vista, and he began his new career as a professor with high hopes. His health, which had been very uncertain, improved and most of the time he prepared with much cheerfulness. Sarah's spirits also rose: to Harriet Grote she wrote, 'I believe with all my heart ... that you will rejoice to see his excellencies come to view and my anxieties cease.' From Bonn, where Austin went to prepare his course of lectures, he wrote reassuringly about his progress to Grote, who was on the council of the university. For the first time since he completed his studies for the bar everything seemed to promise well. There was, however, a flaw in his method of preparation that reduced his chances of success. He postponed writing the lectures for the first part of the course until two or three months before the opening of the university because he feared he might be tempted 'to polish the expression at the expense of more important objects – just ideas, and clear, compact management.'[3] Since Austin's tendency to reformulate and redefine his ideas was known to be near obsessional, this approach seemed eminently reasonable. Later it became evident that he may also have delayed writing the lectures because of the agony that such work cost him. Once he was back in London, under the pressure of the approaching first lecture, the tension and anxiety mounted; his nerves began to undermine his health, and he succumbed to one of his frequent bouts of disabling illness.

When the university opened in November 1828 John Austin felt unable to commence. In a letter to the council that bristled with defensiveness and pride, he explained that he would not be ready for a considerable time: 'When I am ready, I will give you notice; and if the Counsel [sic] should then accept my services, I will deliver my intended course.' He mentioned his elaborate preparatory work, the recent illness which had slowed down his work on the lectures, and his determination not to appear before the public 'until the matter which I have prepared is completely written out.' As an extenuating circumstance he pointed to 'the extent and the intricacy' of his subject, 'the laborious research and exact discrimination' which it required, and the disadvantage of working without a model. Characteristically, he elaborated on the moral dimension of his predicament – a dilemma that can hardly have been of interest to the university. 'If I had not exerted myself to the best of my ability, I should reproach myself severely with this partial breach of my engagement. As the case stands, I am acquitted by my own conscience, and I shall not be much affected by the censure of others.'[4] Ultimately the delay was for a whole year.

In May of the following year Austin wrote to the university that he was better and that the lectures could be announced for the ensuing session. Yet at the last moment he once more postponed the first class, although this time only for a week: 'So much of my future success will depend upon the effect of the first few lectures, that I shall esteem this short respite a great favour.'[5] His first lecture on 16 November 1829 was anything but promising. Henry Crabb Robinson heard it and noticed the same debilitating stage fright that he had witnessed when Austin was given the brief at Norwich: 'I heard him deliver an inaugural lecture, but in so great terror that the hearers could not attend to the matter of his lecture from anxiety for the lecturer.'[6] Henry Cole, a friend of John Stuart Mill and the future organizer of the Great Exhibition of 1851, also heard the opening lecture and recorded his impression: 'Attended Mr. Austin's introductory lecture upon Jurisprudence in which he endeavoured to show the difficulty of an introductory lecture on that subject which he certainly did. His manner was peculiarly studied – his delivery distinc[t] – his language well chosen – and he evinced a thoroug[h] knowledge of his subject.'[7] Cole evidently appreciated some of Austin's qualities, but he was more impressed with the ponderous manner which failed to clarify the difficulties, and he did not return for subsequent lectures.

Despite these difficulties Austin was much pleased with his class, since it was larger than he had expected (about thirty-two) and included many exceedingly capable young men 'who can understand anything,' that is, the most abstract argument. This group included John Stuart Mill, George Cornewall Lewis, John Roebuck, John Romilly, Edward Strutt, Charles Buller, C.P. Villiers, and Edwin Chadwick.[8] Of these all but Chadwick were to become members of Parliament, and many in the class were Benthamite radicals. Austin was 'much impressed and excited by the spectacle of this noble band of young men, and felt with a sort of awe the responsibility attaching to his office.' He saw himself as the medium through which more precise ideas on the foundations of law and morals would be transmitted to future legislators and other men of influence, but his ardour for his mission was mingled with intense anxiety for its success. After a month Harriet Grote reported that Austin's lectures confirmed the high expectations of those who knew him. There was also a pleasant social dimension to the course, for frequently after the twice-weekly Tuesday and Thursday evening lectures some of the students returned with Austin to his house around 8 o'clock. At one of these social evenings Sarah was gratified to be told by one of the students, 'It is really very agreeable to attend Mr. Austin's class – it is such a gentlemanly one!'; and she chose to ignore that this fact may have signalled a narrow range of students. She was also proud that Austin brought in £120 by student fees, and although this did not add to his income, since the university guaranteed a £300 salary for two years, it reduced the burden on the financially shaky university and held some promise for his future success. 'Even if the University were to fail,' and this was a real possibility in those early years, Austin felt he 'should by that time have established a reputation as a teacher of Law which would always enable him to get a class somewhere.'[9]

Austin's satisfaction with the lectures was not fully justified. As the first session drew to a close he was once more unable to meet the demands of the schedule. 'The class were extremely delighted with the course as far as it went,' wrote John Stuart Mill, but the proviso indicated one of the flaws. Austin had found it impossible to present all that he had planned in the prescribed time. At the end of June, pleading illness, he abruptly abandoned the course several lectures before its scheduled termination. It fell to Sarah to write to the university on his behalf to request that his students might be allowed to attend the last part of his next course without extra payment. This the university granted, and by such a clumsy arrangement one more problem was circumvented.[10]

There were other problems that could not be solved so readily. He had hoped to stimulate discussion, to 'wax in boldness and fluency.' He planned to get to know his students by name so that he could address them individually. He intended to ask his class 'to demand explanations and ply me with objections – turn me inside out … From this collision [there will be] advantages to both parties more advantageous than any written lecture.' He wished to extemporize; yet he was afraid of being tongue-tied. In the end he read to avoid the terror he experienced before an audience. There was something distinctive about his voice and delivery. Carlyle mentioned its 'clanging metallic' tone, his grand-daughter his 'musical rolling voice,' and Mill the 'slow delivery and splendid articulation,' yet it is evident that some were mainly struck by the first of these characteristics. Also, the lectures were marred by being repetitious; as Mill put it, 'different points are over explained … [and] are dwelt upon longer and repeated oftener, than is necessary to a complete understanding of them.'[11]

Austin's disappointing performance on the lecture platform contrasts markedly with his brilliance and flow in conversation. It was not only his daughter, Lucy, who judged him 'glorious in talk.' James Stephen said, 'In conversation I really know not a more interesting or eloquent man.'[12] The daughter of the economist Nassau Senior also recalled how astonishing and delightful it was to hear him talk: 'Every sentence that dropped from his lips as definite and bright as a newly coined sovereign.' Even the most famous talker of the time, Thomas Babington Macaulay, described his outpouring of words with awe: Austin 'talked with a nervous loquacity wh[ich] was quite extraordinary,' and he added, 'I, who generally get my share of the conversation, could hardly put in a word.' Yet Austin's impressive fluency deserted him when he mounted the lecture podium for the simple reason that the eloquent talker read from a text written in a style in which there was (as Stephen put it) 'an involution and a lack of vivacity which renders his writings a sealed book to almost everyone.' Only very occasionally can one find in his writing some of those pungent phrases that spiced his conversation. In writing he was so obsessed with precision that he tired himself and his reader with qualifications and repetitions. Senior alluded to the fact that a pen made Austin perfectly dull: 'If [he] would only write just as [he] talk[ed] it would be perfect,' he commented. Unfortunately in his lectures Austin talked as he wrote.[13]

Mill, his most sympathetic student, suggested remedies for some of the flaws of the lectures. He wrote a tactful analysis of them for Sarah, knowing that his appraisal (for which Sarah had asked) was destined for her husband's ears. The lectures were burdened by excessive details; 'They should be *very* much abridged.' Above all, Mill deplored Austin's failure to complete the presentation of the essential structure of jurisprudence; 'only a *complete course*' could do much to spread the reputation of the lecturer, he pointed out. Austin should not spend much time on improving that part of the course he had given, but should content himself instead 'with using the scissors abundantly' and then apply himself to the preparation of the subsequent lectures so that he would avoid 'that fatigue and harassing excitement which destroys his health.' Mill also urged the importance of an interesting introductory lecture which would explain what was meant by jurisprudence, why it was a science worth studying, how it differed from subjects covered by other law lectures, and how the study of law unaccompanied by the study of jurisprudence led to confusion. With considerable affection and tact, he was trying to steer Austin towards making jurisprudence more appealing to that larger audience which was vital for the survival of the professorship.[14]

Even the most engrossing lecturer would have had to contend with considerable obstacles in attracting a sizeable audience, for jurisprudence was a new and abstract subject without apparent relevance to practice. In those days, before theoretical classroom instruction had become a conventional part of legal training, barristers were trained only in chambers, and there was no inducement to spur attendance at classes. Yet jurisprudence did not have to be as forbidding as Austin made it. Mill had not asked for popularization, since he appreciated Austin's 'well grounded aversion to vague generalities,' but he tried to encourage his friend to be less abstract and less narrowly definitional. It was the method of presentation, not the subject-matter, that Mill was trying to amend.[15]

Hopes for the second session withered when Austin's class opened in November 1830 and there were no hearers. Austin's letter to the university reveals his anguish: 'I waited last night in my Lecture Room from 6¾ to 7 o'clock but no pupil appeared ... If I shall have no Class during the present Session, I shall be somewhat surprised as well as discouraged.' After postponing the course until January 1831, he lectured to eight students, telling Sarah that 'he would go through his course as well as if his class were ever so numerous, and at the end of it send in his resignation.' Austin's reputation as a dull lecturer had spread. A friend of Henry Cole's scathingly gave as an 'instance of John Austin's brilliant success, [his] having found two fellows to come to his lecture and stay till the end.'[16]

At the close of this second session, a new problem arose. The university's commitment to support the professorship terminated, and it was not feasible to continue the lectures merely for the fees of a handful of students. Austin's friends now came to the rescue. James Mill and Grote organized a subscription to raise £200 per year for three years and arranged with the university to continue the professorship from November 1831 to June 1834. In addition to James Mill and Grote, several persons, including Thomas Denman, William Erle, and John Romilly (all destined for judicial office), and John Stuart Mill, each offered to put up from £10 to £20 per year. John Mill broke the news in an affectionate letter to Sarah: 'You may lay down your anxiety, my dear Mütterlein, I hope never to resume it ... it is now certain or nearly certain that a Professorship of Jurisprudence will be endowed by subscription for three years. I do not know whether I ought to have told you this as long as there could be even the slightest doubt: but I do not think there can be the slightest, from the manner in which [Romilly] spoke of it, and besides I could not help telling you. However let us keep our joy to ourselves for the present.'[17]

The subscription permitted Austin to continue, and he offered the course of lectures for the third time during the 1831-2 session. He tried to promote his subject by publications: first he wrote a fifty-seven page *Outline of a Course of Lectures on Jurisprudence* (1831), which was an advertisement of sorts; and on Sarah's initiative, he agreed to publish the earliest and most general lectures, which became the *Province of Jurisprudence Determined* (1832).[18]

The number attending the third course is not known, and once again he did not begin until January. For the second time John Stuart Mill was one of the class. The experience of facing an ever dwindling class would have been discouraging to a more self-confident person. During the autumn of 1832 John Austin deliberated about the ensuing session and decided not to lecture again – only to change his mind in late November and begin lecturing in early December. Five students had signed up for his fourth session, and at least one more, Henry Cole, paid his £4.10.0 fee in December.[19] John Stuart Mill called this group 'a very small but really select class,' and there are indications that James Mill listened to lectures on about four occasions.[20] Cole's brief descriptions of the subjects of the lectures show that Austin followed John Stuart Mill's advice to ask the students to read his *Province of Jurisprudence Determined*, which made it unnecessary for him to read the lectures on the definition of jurisprudence and its relation to other sciences and to positive morality. This device greatly narrowed the subject on which he lectured, but it also improved the chance of completing the course before the summer. Although Austin missed as many as eight lectures (out of about forty-eight scheduled) because of illness and three more in March 1833 because of his mother's death, he did appear fairly regularly.[21] Cole, who had been so disappointed with Austin's first lecture in 1829, now shifted his judgment and noted 'an extremely pleasant and encouraging earnestness about Mr. Austin which speedily familiarizes you with him.' But on 2 July 1833 Cole heard the last lecture, indeed, the last one given by Austin at the university. Although the subscription would have paid for another year, Austin, faced with practically no students, decided to call a halt.[22]

Two more disappointments followed in short order. In 1833 Austin was appointed to the Criminal Law Commission by Henry Brougham, who had become Lord Chancellor. Mill as usual was encouraging: 'This is work for him of the kind which he most likes, and for which he is best fitted: it is also a provision for him: he is to have £500 a year while it lasts, and it will doubtless lead to other employment in the same line.' No details are known as to what precisely brought Austin into conflict with his colleagues, but he soon found that his ideas for fundamental reform ran contrary to the limited powers granted to the commission. The others on the commission were quite content to make what Austin regarded as patchwork recommendations, whereas he wished to survey the entire field of criminal law and draw up a draft criminal code: '*Then* let them appoint a Commission to pull it to pieces.' He returned from meetings of the commission 'disheartened and agitated' and found it repugnant to be paid public money for work from which the public would reap little advantage. Eventually he accepted the money, but not without misgivings. He gave up his place in 1836.[23]

At about the same time the Inner Temple established courses of lectures on Civil Law and Jurisprudence and English Law which were to be open to all members of the Inn. Austin was appointed, apparently at the suggestion of his friend Henry Bickersteth, as lecturer on Civil Law and Jurisprudence, and once more he prepared with great intensity. Again, in keeping with the earlier pattern, on the day the first lecture was to have been delivered, he sent a messenger cancelling his class. Also, as before, there was a rapid decline in attendance, and again he took it as a defeat. Sarah Austin, in sad recognition of the situation, wrote to Brougham that her husband was 'a man too scrupulous to take the public money for doing nothing and too sickly for constant, regulated labour, too conscious of his own capacities and incapacities to be easily adjusted to any work or to any workfellows. I know it all, my Lord, better than any body.'[24]

The repeated blows to Austin's self-esteem were more damaging than the other deprivations – lack of money, exile, and intellectual isolation – that were soon to follow from his failure. He was so scarred by disappointment and humiliation that henceforth he refused even to consider permanent residence in London, as it was the scene of too many memories that he could not recall 'without pain and a sort of aigreur.' As the lectures ended Sarah described how 'care, vexations, and disappointments have [soured] his blood and worn out his reserves.' The drawn out London defeat had a crushing effect; it was, according to Sarah, 'the real and irremediable calamity of his life – the blow from which he never recovered.' Even his appointment in 1834 as corresponding member of the Academy of Moral and Political Sciences of the Royal Institute of France failed to lift his spirits. The years between 1833 and mid-1836 were desperate ones.[25] Austin was deeply depressed and as often as not sick. Even when he was not physcially ill, melancholy and bitterness became, not, as formerly, a periodic mood, but a prevailing mode of feeling. What his daughter, who revered him, said later, was true at this time: 'Da is gloomy, I fear 'tis his normal state.' And others confirmed this. When Austin's fortune improved in 1836 with his Malta appointment, Carlyle, in reporting this change, added, 'Nevertheless one may doubt if it will do much for him; so aci[di]fied a man has he grown; and *produces nothing but acid.*'[26]

The symptoms of some malaise had always been there. The 'lethargy of the faculties' and the 'listlessness of indolence and ennui' which he noted in himself as a young man were possibly the early symptoms of his uncertain health. Austin may have inherited a lack of resilience from his mother, who was reputed to be melancholic. The diary he kept in the army was described by his granddaughter as 'grey, austere, and inelastic' in tone.[27] His 'sinking spirits' and 'damps of anguish' were no secret to Sarah as a young woman, for his letter of proposal had included an appeal to her to save him from low moods and lethargy. Immediately after the engagement he complained to her about a sense of 'oppression and stupidity,' and Sarah began apologizing for his manner right from the start. Writing to her brother in London, who had invited him to dinner, she explained: 'I hope you will find him [John] tolerably *agreeable* – for if he fails in any thing I *believe* it is in that ... I know he can be so if he tries.'[28]

Certainly, as Sarah noted, he had never been sanguine. Mill described the 'generally melancholy cast' of his character and his habitual bitter manner of expression. Well before he began teaching, he wrote to Sarah that he prayed that 'God, above all, strengthen us to bear up under those privations and disappointments with which it is but too probable we are destined to contend.' It seems he had forebodings of the terrible struggle and unmanageable stress that his ambitious career would create for him. Sarah's letters in the 1820s and early thirties are filled with a litany of references to Austin's indisposition and despondency and his need for recuperative trips to Cornwall, Hastings, Jersey, and Boulogne.

He suffered from indigestion, migraine, feverishness, skin disorder, and feelings of enervation and prostration. During one of his episodes he excused himself for his 'stupidity and gloom' and complained about his 'cursed stomach' and of being 'feverish and racked with headache.' He explained: 'In this state I am not fit company for anything human ... As is usual with me when labouring under this malady, I cannot endure society of any kind, being oppressed with a painful sense of my utter inutility to others, as well as of the burthen which weighs so heavily upon myself.' During severe episodes he retired not only from society but to his bed, and his loss of weight and energy was such that Sarah became thoroughly frightened.[29]

Friends naturally spoke mostly about his physical illness; for example, Grote lamented, 'It is truly unhappy that bodily circumstances should so cruelly cut up both his happiness and utility.' All sorts of physical regimens, diets, and water cures were tried. In 1835, when Austin would make no further effort to establish himself in London, he once more became ill. Homeopathy was fashionable at this time, and Frederick Hervey Quin, a physician who was already treating a friend of the Austins' also began treating John, 'with the most *marked* success,' according to Sarah. This optimism did not last long, and Carlyle, who thought homeopathy an absurd quackery, soon announced triumphantly, 'Austin has paid off Quin.' It was not the first nor the last search for treatment, for Austin's condition continued unstable in the extreme. As Sarah wrote a few months later, after they had moved to Hastings, 'There is no *progress* tho' there are variations.' The assumption as ever had been that a change of scene (especially absence from London) should have done him good.[30]

Some of those closest to Austin, especially Mill, who himself had experienced great stress, were more perceptive or more forthright about Austin's condition. Mill told Carlyle in 1833 that he 'always thought that anxiety was the chief cause of [Austin's] illnesses,' which he summarized as 'attacks of disabling though not dangerous ill health.' Sarah vacillated in her attitude to her husband's health, but she recognized the psychological dimensions. In 1828, when Austin could not bring himself to start at the university, she feared 'the terrible consequences to a hypochondriacal man of living without a fixed employment.' Austin himself recognized that stress was one of his enemies, for he wrote about expecting to continue working assiduously at Bonn 'unless I be crippled by a return of my old disease, or by the intrusion of some unexpected cause of anxiety.'[31]

The precise nature of his illness was a puzzle in his own day and it remains enigmatic. If a label had been given to his condition of extreme sensitivity and depressiveness it might well have been called 'neurasthenic' in the later part of the century. At the time the word 'psychosomatic' was obviously not used, but it is present by implication. The assumption that there was such a component is evident in the speculations of friends about the sort of sheltered employment that might suit him. Mill suggested that he might apply for the position of assistant examiner in the East India Company, where he himself was employed. It was the 'sort of employment which probably would not knock him up, like writing – and the improvement in his circumstances with leisure and freedom from anxiety, might give him a better chance than he ever had before of being well in London.' Charles Buller felt he should be given a pension or an appointment. Sarah also came to agree that he needed a protected niche – one of those 'harbours of refuge' which existed in the German states 'where such men can work for the world, in whose vortex they cannot live.'[32]

The obvious practical consequence of Austin's precarious career and uncertain health was a gnawing anxiety about the wherewithal for existence. During his entire life, and he lived to the age of sixty-nine, Austin was gainfully employed for only seven years – from 1829 to 1834, while he lectured and served on the Criminal Law Commission, and from October 1836 to July 1838, while he was a commissioner in Malta. (This calculation leaves aside the years he spent in the army and the brief period when he served as a conveyancer and an equity draftsman.) After these years of brief and intermittent employment Austin gave up any attempt to earn a livelihood. One can estimate that in the course of his life his total earned income was approximately £8000.[33] This sum gives an unrealistic picture of what the Austins had to live on even during his employed years, for half this sum was earned in the two well-paid years as commissioner in Malta, while his salary during the four years of the lectureship at the University of London was £300 per annum at first and then £200, when his friends' subscriptions supported the position. This was a meagre income with which to maintain a middle-class couple and child, and most other professors supplemented their fees by second occupations or by private means. Those who, like the Carlyles, lived on sums approximately of this magnitude also had a terrible struggle. In 1833, when he had in prospect £450 for the Inner Temple lectures and £500 a year from the Law Commission, Austin's income took a great leap, leading Mill to write optimistically, 'All his good fortune comes to him at the same time.' Both ventures, however, were short-lived. In fact, at one stage Austin was reluctant to take money from the Law Commission, and considerable persuasion was necessary before he would accept the £800 owed to him.[34] He was too proud to take unearned public money, but in his circumstances he had to be less fastidious about accepting money from parents and parents-in-law.

The marriage settlement, £100 from Sarah's father and £300 from John's, helped the Austins to scrape through the first years of married life, but with intense anxiety. All along Sarah's father was greatly concerned that his son Richard, who was responsible for sending Sarah her allowance, sent the money promptly, since she was 'housekeeping upon a frugal, *self-denying*' scale. A glimpse of the Austins' plight in the early twenties is given by John Neal, an American, who recalled meeting Sarah 'with tears in her eyes'; she told him that 'all her husband could earn, together with the allowance ... [was not] enough to make them comfortable. They had only one child [Lucy, born in 1821] ... but so straitened were they in their circumstances that they should look upon the advent of another as quite a serious calamity.' The allowance from Sarah's father continued until his death in 1826. It is not clear for how long Austin's father continued his support, although it is conceivable that he may have made it conditional on Austin's continuing at the bar. There is a letter to Sarah from Santorre Santa Rosa, the exiled Italian patriot who became her close friend, written in 1824 while Austin was still attempting practice. Santa Rosa expressed his distress at Sarah's news that Austin was not progressing in his career and was doing less well than in the previous year. He urged Sarah to speak frankly to Austin's father, and though he did not specify about what, it probably concerned money. What is certain is that John and Sarah were in such financial straits in the twenties that they borrowed money from their friend Nassau Senior, who had an office next to Austin's in Lincoln's Inn; and though they paid it back in instalments, they still owed him £75 in 1829. Senior graciously declined to be paid the remaining debt since he did not need the money and Austin's future was still uncertain.[35]

The Austins' financial worries were not ended when Sarah's father, who had been widowed in 1823, died on 23 June 1826 as a result of a carriage accident. Even though she was left £1700 under his will, if they used only the interest it yielded, their yearly income from these funds would have been significantly less than what it had been during her father's lifetime.[36] The period 1827-9 was still a time of 'the most rigid economy' for them, but after Austin finally began lecturing, Sarah wrote with increased hope to her sister about being able 'to fetch up our leeway, for the two last years were cruel ones, and put us sadly back in everything. We shall now get afloat again, and then, come what may, shall start clear.' Unfortunately a year later when there were no students for Austin's class, the old refrain – 'We cannot live on air' – recurs.[37]

John Austin was somewhat disdainful about money. In an early letter to Bentham he offered his allegiance and showed no enthusiasm for working at the bar. He was obliged, he explained, 'for many years to come, to give most of my time to Grimgribber.' His wife, he added, was in perfect agreement with his intention to devote himelf to the public good, and 'a very inconsiderable income (or what most women would think a very inconsiderable income) will satisfy her as much as myself.' Meanwhile, he had to conceal his feelings; he wrote, 'If my father imagined that I entertained any other views than those of getting money and power (but particularly the former) I am convinced he would not leave me a shilling at his death.'[38] Austin's aversion to legal practice combined with his reluctance to defy his father may have drawn out the decision to turn away from the conventional career for a barrister.

Jonathan Austin was a wealthy man, and Austin's expectations of an inheritance may also have influenced his decision to dedicate himself to jurisprudence with its foreseeably modest financial rewards. He certainly never held out glowing financial prospects to Sarah, to whom he confessed before marriage, 'It is also very probable that my profession may never bring me into one shilling.' His motives and thoughts about money are largely matters of conjecture, but after the failure of the professorship he seems to have been quite willing to follow his inclination to live very modestly and dedicate himself to legal philosophy and scholarship. His friends rather than he appear to have been concerned to find him employment. When the lectureship was on the brink of failure he told Sarah he would 'devote himself entirely to constructing a complete Corpus Juris – such an one as might live for ever and be a text-book for all future codifiers.' She loyally endorsed this: 'You may imagine that I could willingly make any and every sacrifice to so noble a project.'[39]

Austin's calculation that he might have just sufficient private income to eke out a frugal but scholarly existence in some inexpensive foreign country may explain his reluctance to follow up John Stuart Mill's suggestion that he apply for an appointment at the East India Company office. He also seems to have declined or ignored Mill's offer in 1837 to intercede on his behalf for a professorship:

> Would Mr. Austin like to be the Professor of Moral Philosophy at Glasgow? The chair is vacant, and it is worth £700 a year, but so long as old Mylne lives (he is 83 years of age) it will only be worth £300. It is in the gift of the Professors, and one of them, my friend Nichol, who is an admirer of Mr. Austin has written to ask if he would like it and to say that he could perhaps carry Mr. Austin's election to the chair with such testimonials as it would be easy to get.

In 1842 Mill was once more attempting to work out some plans for Austin, but by now he realized that Austin's co-operation was not likely to be forthcoming. 'How much I wish that any way could be found such as he would not reject,' he wrote to Sarah. Meanwhile Austin, with 'no distaste to a life of comparative poverty and obscurity,' was determined not to submit himself to the struggle for a place in life once more; he was content to live on the sidelines.[40]

JOHN AUSTIN'S INACTIVITY spurred Sarah on to heroic industry and self-discipline. She wrote to Carlyle that she felt numb when faced with the implication of Austin's false starts and poor health: 'When I think of it my heart seems to collapse and my head to be stupified. But *that* is not the part I have to act,' she explained, 'for if I sink, he falls.' As his spirits failed and paralyzed his effort, her energy and resourcefulness came to the forefront, and she became the dominant partner in an unusual marriage. As one of her brothers mused after John Austin's death: 'How unequally the power of working was bestowed!' Nearly all the practical management of their lives became her task; she was housekeeper, nurse, intermediary with the world, but, above all, she became the earning partner of the marriage. It was no empty boast when she said, 'I am the man of business in *our firm*.'[41]

Sarah had married Austin with a desire to be his helpmate and partner; circumstances were to put this resolve to a lifelong test. From the start she was searching for ways to supplement their income, and she was willing to turn her hand to any task that could be combined with caring for her young daughter. The languages she had learned for pleasure and as a possible resource in case of want now came to her aid. Driven by the need for money, she turned to her Italian, French, and German, and even her Latin proved useful. It was an uphill struggle to break into the poorly paid, difficult market for translations, and at first she was forced to take on all manner of tasks.

She tried her hand throughout the 1820s on a variety of anonymous translations, and those we know about indicate the range of work she was willing to consider. Her oldest brother, John Taylor, who was one of the outstanding mining engineers of the century, tried to help by offering her technical translating and compiling tasks. In 1823, when she was struggling with one of his publications, Santa Rosa, who knew how uncongenial she found this work, wished her 'some leisure and some rest' and an end to the tedious 'scientific rubbish,' but she continued struggling with it till at least the mid-twenties. By 1824 she was 'translating a quantity of stuff,' including an account from Italian of an expedition to Mexico to explore silver mining opportunities that her brother was supervising from London. In 1825 she bravely tried her hand at a technical dictionary, *A Vocabulary, English and Spanish*, for use by Englishmen working in Mexican mining ventures. Since Spanish was a language Sarah barely knew, it is not surprising to find that she borrowed a Spanish-English dictionary from Bentham and that she made some errors. Later she translated French letters for the *London Magazine* and found herself the recipient of charming and 'droll' letters from the author, M. Beyle (Stendhal), who addressed her as Mister Translator. Both Stendhal and she were to find it difficult to get their money from Southern, the editor, 'who paid nobody.' While continuing to translate various articles, in 1825, in collaboration with her cousin Edgar Taylor, she published a volume of early medieval lyric poetry from Germany and other parts of Europe; Sarah provided translations from middle high German and Provençal French, and Edgar wrote the historical and critical commentary. The difficulty of the endeavour was acknowledged in the *Edinburgh Review*, whose reviewer praised the facility and flow of Sarah's verses and their resemblance to the original. Her next known major translation was Voltaire's *History of Charles XII* (1827), the first three books of which she presented in a literal English translation on the Hamiltonian system with parallel passages in the original French – a method that aimed to facilitate the learning of languages. On her return from Bonn, she published a brief essay, 'Life of Carsten Niebuhr' (1829), which was republished in *Lives of Eminent Persons* for the Society for the Diffusion of Useful Knowledge.[42] She was gradually inching her way into the translating profession.

During the mid-twenties Sarah also translated for a group of gifted intellectual political refugees from Naples, Piedmont, and Lombardy, who now were congregated disconsolately in London. Sarah could converse in Italian with 'these martyrs to the cause of freedom' and offer them sympathy and help. She introduced them to editors and literary friends and sent two of them (Cucchi and Radice) to her family in Norwich to help them find employment. When Pecchio spoke of her as their protecting saint, 'as beautiful as any Raphael painted,' he was paying tribute to her charm but also to her unusual ability to translate their work from Italian directly into English, instead of following the usual clumsy practice of using French as an intermediary. Yet it was not easy to place their articles since many editors could not judge the work until it was rendered into English, and consequently the usual hazards of acceptance and payment were increased. In the case of the famous poet Ugo Foscolo (who did not think her a saint) such uncertainties were compounded by personal mistrust and misunderstanding. Sarah's relations with him were as cool as those with Santa Rosa were close. She was involved in 'an endeavour to give a perfectly English dress to his meaning,' she explained irritably, in response to his objections about her changes in his text. 'Mr. Foscolo is aware that there are terms of expression which without being grammatically wrong offend – one hardly knows how – against conventional habits of speaking and thinking.' In spite of such strains she helped him place his articles and translated and edited several lengthy ones for him, two of them for the *Edinburgh Review*, but, when he suggested a book, she explained that she was very busy and anyway could not undertake such work on a speculation. Many years later Sarah declared that Foscolo would have 'robbed' her of the small reward of her labour, had not the editor, who knew him well, sent her the money directly. Whatever underlay their mutual suspicion, the relationship was not helped by the sad fact that they were both in dire need of money.[43]

Sarah's pride did not stand in her way of taking on other poorly paid tasks: 'I have now, too, undertaken another trade, namely, giving lessons in Latin ... So Lucie [sic] and I trot down to Bentinck Street with our bag of books, and quite enjoy it. I do not fancy myself at all degraded by thus agreeably earning a guinea a week, and if anybody else does, he or she is quite welcome to avoid my society, as I inevitably should his or hers.' She also taught German to the younger brothers and sisters of John Stuart Mill and gave him lessons as well.[44] Her versatility and willingness to take on any work that came her way contrast painfully with John Austin's retreat in the face of setbacks.

During their stay in Bonn in 1827 and 1828 Sarah perfected her German, and by the mid-1830s she had transformed herself from 'a poor, unknown' young woman who did hack work from necessity into a literary woman who wrote review articles and had a growing reputation as a translator, especially of German. By 1830 she could write to John Murray that she had 'translated a good deal from that language ... The last translation I attempted were Specimens of the most distinguished prose writers of German.' The translations had been done to gratify the curiosity of a friend, John Sterling, who afterwards gave them to the editor of the *New Monthly Magazine*, where they appeared as five articles. Later she included them with explanatory notes in a volume entitled *Fragments from German Prose Writers* (1841). In 1832 her name became better known as the translator of a gossipy travel book that was to become the talk of the town – Pückler-Muskau's 'A German Prince,' as it was popularly known. Her 'felicitous rendering of each original phrase ... with accuracy and freedom' was again praised by an Edinburgh reviewer: readers persisted in believing that the book was not a translation but the work of an Englishman, 'merely because the language did not offer the slightest trace of transfusion from a foreign origin.'[45]

A list of Sarah Austin's major translations in the early and mid-1830s demonstrates her astonishing industry and adaptability. At this time she also began to contribute to a variety of quarterly journals and to the *Athenaeum*, and this remained a modest source of additional income throughout her life. She also embarked on what became a favourite alternative to straight translation – the creation of books by illustrating themes with extracts from various sources. It was fitting, in view of her family background, that one of her first such efforts was *Selections from the Old Testament* (1833), which presented extracts from the scriptures that were 'persuasive, consolatory, elevating.'[46] A very popular translation was Friedrich Wilhelm Carové's fairy tale *Story Without an End* (1833), about which a reviewer said that it 'would have a sale without end.' In the early thirties she also worked for the Society for the Diffusion of Useful Knowledge on a grammar and received John Stuart Mill's advice and corrections, but it is unclear if this ever saw the light of day. At this time she also translated two major French scholarly works by Sismondi, *The History of the Italian Republics* (1832) and *A History of the Fall of the Roman Empire* (1834), and part of an official French document, Cousin's *Report on the State of Public Instruction in Prussia* (1834), and she wrote articles on education as well. From mid-1835 to mid-1836, during their melancholy 'exile' in Boulogne, she made sure of work by contracting for Raumer's lengthy *England in 1835* (1836); and while she was 'drudging' at this, she was also completing a translation of Heinrich Hase's *The Public and Private Life of the Ancient Greeks* (1836) – for this, Sarah liked to point out, she had help from no fewer than two learned doctors – E.C. Hawtrey and F.A. Rosen.[47]

In the face of Austin's precarious career she steeled herself to the difficult life of a professional translator and reviewer, and every inch along that road was gained by hard, unremitting toil. Later she recalle this period and spoke of the discipline which she felt had 'been mercifully allotted to [her]self.' As Austin faltered, she became 'the busiest woman in the world,' and her daughter was left for days and weeks to her own devices as Sarah sat chained to her task. 'I must fag night and day' was her comment while under the invariable pressure to finish a long work at breakneck speed.[48]

One of Sarah's more adventurous efforts in the 1830s – an attempt to present something of Goethe's achievement and life to the English – was also one of her less successful ones in terms of sales, although it evoked the interest of Mill and Carlyle, who hoped it would stimulate greater interest in German literature. The core of *Characteristics of Goethe* consists of diverse recollections of the poet by some of his contemporaries; it was, as Sarah herself was the fist to admit, a compilation of materials that she had collected from various friends and sources and to which she attached notes and explanations. Unfortunately she rejected Henry Crabb Robinson's suggestion that she attempt a regular biography of Goethe, since she felt 'it would be absurd in [her] to attempt to write about Goethe otherwise than as a very humble reader of him.' Even so, her effort was the first (admittedly entirely inadequate) attempt to present something in English even in the direction of a Goethe biography, and it preceded Lewes' work by twenty-two years.[49] The idea of such a book (it was published a year after Goethe's death) was enterprising but the 'morsels' available to her were dull, and the lack of a connected narrative gave the three octavo volumes a desultory and timid air. Her extensive notes, however, displayed great enthusiasm for Goethe and German literature and a willingness to attempt literal translations of Goethe's poetry, 'those wonderful transfusions,' of which she gave some illustrative examples. 'You can *actually translate Goethe*,' Carlyle told her encouragingly, 'which (quietly, I reckon) is what hardly three people in England can,' but Falk, the principal commentator, as he bluntly put it, was 'a kind of *dud*' and certainly no Boswell.[50] The notices of Goethe were 'little more than so many funeral eulogies,' commented a reviewer irritated by the sycophantic tone adopted by Goethe's friends, yet he showered praise on Sarah's unusual grasp of the language, her ability to translate 'metaphysical reasonings, political declamation, and social dialogue – into correct, nervous, vernacular English,' and he hoped she would in future undertake the sorely needed translation of Goethe's works. He knew of 'no translator who [had] shown one-tenth part of the capability which she has evinced for undertaking so difficult a task.' The book stirred interest among enthusiasts for German culture – it was, according to Carlyle, 'a little flame' kindled for Goethe in England – and it helped to confirm Sarah's reputation as a translator, but her attempt to make Germany's 'noble and beautiful literature' better known in England did not get off to a promising start. The volumes failed to sell sufficiently to encourage her to continue with her plan to translate Goethe's correspondence with Zelter or with other schemes, such as translating Schiller or Tieck on Shakespeare. While in 1832 she had thought German literature was 'the rage presently,' after the poor sales of *Characteristics* she concluded sadly, 'The taste for German literature is growing but is still very limited. The mass of our reading public is impatient of anything that calls for a minute's reflection. Need I say they complain that Goethe is obscure.' Unfortunately the discouraging reception of the Goethe volumes turned her away from translating German literature, for which she had not only enthusiasm but talent.[51]

All Sarah Austin's effort during the early 1830s took place against the background of her husband's failure and collapse. She managed to establish what Francis Jeffrey called 'a fair measure of fame' just at the time when Austin's health and career prospects were most wretched and 'the source of as much grief and care, as much disappointment of hope and frustration of purpose as can well be imagined or borne.'[52] When Dionysius Lardner described his 'great confidence in the ability and zeal of Mrs. Austin' and told Sismondi she was 'our best living translator' (this time of French), he was, of course, the editor reassuring the author, but he was also reporting on her reputation as a major intermediary in making French and German literature and thought accessible to the English. That Heinrich Heine at this time, perhaps thinking of what she had done for Pückler-Muskau's work in England, was apparently hoping that she would translate him also points to her increasing renown. Sarah's wry comment that she was 'quite "the fashion" – but that will not enable us to live,' perfectly expressed her anxieties amidst this Pyrrhic success.[53]

Carlyle's double-edged comments about her rise from obscurity at this time illustrate her increasing reputation as well as the mixed reception that it received even from a friend who knew her thorny path. He himself was chained to an agonized labour and bid for fame with his three-volume work on the French Revolution, while anxiously counting how long his meagre means would suffice to maintain him and Jane Carlyle in London without regular income from employment. He noted Sarah's efforts with a mixture of admiration and denigration. She was, he felt, 'in a kind of trial-state; risen or rising to where she cannot hope to *stand*, where it will be well if she feel *no* giddiness.' She was in danger of becoming 'that unfortunatest thing in nature, a "London distinguished female,"' and so could be lashed by his tongue-in-cheek special language. She was 'a certain "celebrated Mrs. Austin" (called also the "celebrated Translatress of Puckler Muskau")' whose real worth lay in her qualities of character and ready helpfulness as a friend and not in her literary endeavours. Yet he noted her determined struggle with a side-glance at his own so talented but less financially driven wife. 'Envy no "celebrated woman," thou my little uncelebrated Darling! Envy not even the celebrated Madam Austin!' Evidently he was not entirely unimpressed by Sarah's efforts, and he granted that Sarah had weathered the trial by declaring she was a really good woman, only 'nearly ruined' or 'half ruined by celebrity (of a kind) ... the only woman I have seen not wholly ruined by it.'[54]

Sarah hardly needed Carlyle to be reminded of the double edge of her acclaim. Her literary projects were 'successful enough,' she said, but her satisfaction with the achievement was overshadowed by dependence on the earnings and by the fatigue of continuous translating and the constant anxiety about her husband. She valued success not because it brought her fame, she claimed, but as a means of earning money. In 1831 she told Carlyle that they were 'Teutonically poor,' and later she spoke of having 'fought poverty single handed.' To Brougham she said, 'My own fingers and my own head such as it is have sufficed to secure us against the want we must otherwise have felt.'[55]

How much did she actually earn? When she started working in the 1820s, she evidently felt she was in no position to bargain. Of the Voltaire translation, for example, she said, 'I got neither money nor renown for it ... they cheated me – of course,' but by the mid-thirties she could command better rates. Some information about the magnitude of her earnings can be gleaned from publishers' records. Murray paid her 100 guineas in 1836 for her two volumes of Raumer's *England in 1835*, though she was paid less than this for Pückler's travels. Longman paid her £60 for Sismondi's *History of the Italian Republics* and £145 for his *Fall of the Roman Empire*. The payments seem scant enough in relation to the magnitude of the work, but when one extrapolates from these sums and compares her earnings with Austin's annual salary of £200 and £300 at the university, it is evident that her contribution to the family income was not negligible. That her earnings were of consequence to their budget is confirmed by her various requests to publishers for prepayments of £7 here and £20 there. In the summer of 1835, for example, she wrote to Murray: 'I should be very glad of a little money just now to wind up all my English affairs, and if you think what I have *done* sufficient security for what I have *still to do*, and could conveniently let me have an instalment ... I should be obliged to you.'[56]

For the first decades of her married life Sarah, in pursuit of the pressing need for money, put aside thoughts of seeking fame or gratification. Later, she approvingly recalled another gifted woman (Madame Peyronnet) who, in the face of financial difficulties, had turned to translating: 'She had no taste for being conspicuous or famous – not the least – she wrote exactly as I did, *to earn money*.' Even some major translations of Sarah's do not carry her name and no complete bibliography can be established for her. When Lardner expressed regret in 1834 that no mention had been made of her as Sismondi's translator, she told him that she had thought it 'of no importance.'[57] Throughout the 1830s Sarah explained that she was content with 'the somewhat toilsome business' of translating, which she sometimes referred to as mere drudgery, because independent authorship was more speculative than she could afford to be and needed greater tranquility than was attainable in the face of John's unsteady course. As she told Jane Carlyle, 'My business is not to do as I like.' This choice to stick principally to translating elicited conflicting responses from her friends. Mill, in 1833, in the first flush of excitement over Austin's greatly improved financial prospects for the following year, wrote to Carlyle: 'Mrs. Austin is now overloaded with proposals for translating; her fame as translator has been, very deservedly, raised much higher by this "Falk" [*Characteristics of Goethe*].' Now that she was no longer dependent on the earnings from her work she could, he felt, branch out: 'She will now be at liberty to consult only her own judgment of what will do most good: she will persevere, I have no doubt, and be useful.' Carlyle, a great traditionalist in such matters, supported her inclination to subdue, at least for the time being, wider ambitions for the sake of being a loyal wife, 'living faithfully,' and conducting her 'brave life-fight' – that is, supporting Austin until his talents came into view. This mattered more in the long run, he declared, than whether 'the voice of the Reviewer be high or low, and millions of caps or none at all leap into the air at your name.' Carlyle's advice prevailed, and Sarah worked primarily for the money; but she was not always happy about her choice.[58]

Translation, which often involved abridgement, was a particularly onerous occupation. She had to show the initiative of an entrepreneur while remaining in a very dependent and vulnerable position, with a need to please many masters – bookseller, author, and public. Her correspondence with the Murrays shows her persistence in bringing projects to their attention; her cleverness in judging what might be a good speculation; her dexterity in dealing with a delicate relationship that was a mixture of business, friendship, and subservience: 'Lastly dear Mr. Murray I must ask the horrid question – what do you think you can give me for this job? You see I put it in the most thoroughly workmanlike manner. *Au reste*, I am quite sure you'll do as well for me as you can.' She was also astute in judging what books would succeed, and Murray must have regretted that he failed to follow her strong recommendation to publish Pückler. She was equally clear-sighted about Raumer, whom she praised for his 'vein of great good sense and a very luminous way of putting things – not the usual merit of Germans,' and about Carové, whose poetical, 'luxuriant fancy,' charm, and fairy-tale qualities she recognized. Yet when a suggestion of hers was turned down, she quickly rallied and presented another: she had all the worldly agility in dealing with circumstances and people that John Austin lacked, and she brought them all to bear on the task of acquiring work.[59]

Yet for every translation published there were at least two that foundered. An example of such a stillborn project was the proposal in 1834 that Sarah translate Bettina von Arnim's innovative and extravagant *Goethes Briefwechsel mit einem Kinde* (*Goethe's Correspondence with a Child*), the child being Bettina von Arnim. When Sarah pointed out that this 'epic poem' was too fanciful for English taste and that she would translate only excerpts from the three volumes, and when the London publisher offered only £100 for it, Bettina took umbrage and eventually claimed that she had translated much of the book herself, even though she knew no English and had resorted mainly to the treacherous help of a dictionary.[60] The strange concoction that resulted failed to sell in England, as Sarah had forecast, but meanwhile, as in similar cases, there was no recompense for the effort that went into aborted projects.

The strain of Sarah's life was not helped by the frenzied pace at which so many translations had to be completed to satisfy publishers who aimed to be first on the market. 'As matters are now, every body is in the dark as to his neighbour's designs; – three or four begin upon any promising book,' and booksellers wishing to secure themselves against loss had no other means 'than by hunting translator and printer to death. In this state of things, the quickest translator is the best.' The spirit of a race entered into her work: 'I am working my eyes out to get on,' she said when she began working on Raumer's massive *England in 1835* and Murray and Raumer were pressing for greater speed in order to achieve simultaneous publication in the two languages. The problem became more acute when the German edition appeared early and translated excerpts began to appear in the *Athenaeum* and Murray feared they would be forestalled. 'I cannot reproach myself with laziness,' she told him, and pointed out that 'the first Volume contains above 600 pages – no trifle!' In face of the pressures she reiterated, 'Want of industry and perseverance is not one of my faults, I may venture to say.' This time, however, she had to bend and agreed to accept a co-translator. She protested, 'I *do* doubt *anybody's* ability to write *anything* correctly in such a hurry and with so little revision,' and explained, 'It would not answer to me for any sum to throw away the little credit I have earned by taking great pains.' Nevertheless she agreed to a joint arrangement, 'provided it be stated in the *title page* the 1st and 2nd vols. translated by me and the 3d. by Mr. Lloyd. On no other terms, however, can I consent to it, and I must beg that to be *distinctly understood.*' She aimed to produce colloquial translations, but her standards, she felt, were under constant threat from the speed-at-all-costs approach.[61]

To immerse oneself in work: what other antidote was there to wearing anxiety about the future? The best wisdom was to fight off reflection till one's hopes revived. She would sink, she said, were it not for that '*daily labour* so falsely called the primal curse.' She applied to herself the counsel she had given her sister when she became a widow: 'Occupation is ever the best remedy.' When in the forties she began the massive task of translating Ranke's *History of the Reformation in Germany* (1845-7), having already translated his three-volume work *The Ecclesiastical and Political History of the Popes of Rome during the Sixteenth and Seventeenth Centuries* (1840), she said it would be 'an awful undertaking.' Yet, she explained, 'I have ... put my head into the yoke very willingly. I welcome the forced absorption in drudgery, as a potent reason against painful meditations. My nouns and adverbs keep me out of myself, and the honest pride of earning is also a resource against the worse pictures of poverty.' Mill recognized that she often clung to translations as a prop: 'I know how much better suited the business of translating must often be to the state of your occupations and spirits than the more continuous exertion of even a review article and it is very desirable that you should have something of the kind in hand.'[62]

WITHOUT SOME EMPLOYMENT FOR JOHN, the Austins could hardly support the expense of life in England, and the likelihood of having to take up residence abroad loomed ever nearer. Austin, who disliked London, may well have looked on this possibility as an escape from the scene of his humiliation. Sarah, however, for whom friends and family were a lifeline, dreaded the thought of this physical isolation superimposed on the inevitable loneliness of translating. To live abroad permanently threatened banishment from family and from much that made life endurable; it also severed Austin from even the possibility of employment; and it impeded her relations with publishers. She was so dismayed at the thought of leaving England that she usually spoke of residence abroad in dire tones of lament as an exile – an exile that was 'an aggregate of evils' which left one 'uprooted and cut afloat on the surface of the water.'[63]

The possible need to move to the Continent had loomed periodically during the previous several years. As early as 1831, when Austin had only six or so students and before the subscription from his friends extended the tenure of his professorship, Sarah said he would 'quit the University and England,' adding '[We] must go somewhere where our little means will support us. Plan we have none.' Two years later, as Austin's career still faltered, Carlyle reported that the Austins were talking of going to live in Berlin (Bonn was another possibility), as they were 'too poor for continuing in London.' A few months later, after receiving Sarah's mournful letter, Carlyle asked, 'What can one advise? A's is a hard case.' To Sarah, however, he sounded a less pessimistic note: 'We shall see; we shall hope, and to the last keep hoping.' By March 1834 Sarah looked back sadly on 'all the sanguine hopes we then had about that abortion the London University,' and soon she could say the same about the Criminal Law Commission and the Inner Temple lectures. The move abroad was not to be averted. In the spring of 1835, Carlyle, who had been spectator to the long ordeal, finally announced the long expected verdict: 'We are to lose Mrs. Austin: her husband is in perpetual ill-health and depression here; so determined to go to Boulogne in France, where he was once better, and leave all: employment, society, and what not.'[64]

Incongruously, as the farewell to London loomed closer, Sarah threw herself with increased fervour into the role of the literary hostess. Before she dissolved their household, she gave tea parties, receptions, and gatherings of literary and political luminaries in a final attempt perhaps to find encouragement or patrons for her husband or to deflect anxiety and reassure herself that they would not be forgotten in exile. Carlyle described this social whirl of the early months of 1835 with graphic distaste. The Austins' door 'was like a *winning-post* on a race-ground-for (aimless) carriages, and carriage-ladies.' At her house one could see 'floods of people; but people barren as the East wind.' His later, more charitable comment, 'We are sorry for her, very sorry for *him*,' was also more insightful. The final round of parties was the bravado of near-desperation; the mistress of the salon – and this is how Sarah has most frequently been recalled in the diaries and letters of the 1830s – was in anguish for fear of the future. She who had been accustomed *'to do all the hoping in her family'* was disconsolate at the prospect before them.[65]

As the first step in the intended migration to Boulogne, where they would 'once more attempt to cast anchor,' they moved at the end of April 1835 to Hastings, where Sarah came near to a complete breakdown. A month later, she returned to London briefly and 'dispersed [their] household Gods'; she was, she said, living like a strolling actress. 'I am now subject for the Vagrant act having neither house nor home,' she told Murray, and to Jane Carlyle she confessed at the end of July, while lodging with a brother preparatory to their final departure: 'I begin to long for even so much of a home as Boulogne holds out to me. I am quite shaken and shattered in pieces as to time, thoughts, chattels, etc. – *zerstückt.'* Her apprehension about the move was not unjustified: they would never permanently reside in London again.[66]

4

Escaping marriage

INNER AND OUTER TURMOIL pervaded Sarah's life in the early 1830s. She was approaching forty and was inclined to stock-taking. The strict notions of duty, restraint, and self-denial which her family had impressed on her were seemingly not to bring their reward in this life. Were her talent and spirit to be burnt out in the struggle to find a niche for Austin? Was it too late to escape a fate that was inexorably becoming clearer? Looking back on this time, Sarah said the middle period of her life was stormy; it was also tragically revealing.

She who had shuddered at the thought that her family name might be tarnished by a brother becoming a public singer, who was offended by the behaviour of her cousin Harriet Martineau, whose editorial pencil struck out anything *risqué* in translations, now let herself slide into an astonishing situation – an infatuation with a German prince. While appearing to be the very model of the supportive and devoted wife, she mentally took flight in an improbable and unsettling romance. Nor was this a mere momentary aberration. The attachment continued for some years, and its peak coincided with the last years of Austin's drawn-out failure in London – from about 1832 to 1834. That her passion was sustained by letters alone, and that the correspondence continued in spite of considerable risk of exposure, gives a melancholy insight into her unsatisfied yearnings and her bitter inner struggle to accommodate herself to circumstances.[1]

A clandestine affair might have been less dangerous than those tangible letters, which survived until recently in the manuscript department of the Berlin State Library. If a word had leaked out about her imprudence, the entire edifice of her life including her hard-won reputation as a learned translator would have been threatened. The fact that her postal 'lover' – for this strange affair did not go beyond an exchange of letters – was one of the most spectacular eccentrics of his age, a womanizer, a notorious publicity seeker, and, according to rumour, one of the least discreet of men, did not help her peace of mind. Yet she persisted. She persisted even though she was told he was 'universally regarded as a slippery person,' known as 'decidedly not a man to be trusted,' and feared as a gossip with 'no *delicatesse* about betraying to the world all he sees and hears.'

The more specific accusations against him that reached her ears were more disturbing still. There was the story, for example, that he had threatened to publish letters written to him by a married woman with whom he had had an affair in London and that he had extorted £2000 from her family. Sarah preferred to confront him with her knowledge of his reputation: 'I know you only from report ... I must be mad or stupid not to see the risks I run, nor could you, as a man of sense, be flattered by such blindfold, insane security.'[2] Confessing her anxiety did not, however, relieve it for long.

At times her nerves were near breaking point. Yet in spite of all her anguish, she continued to correspond, to declare her love, and to live in fear of the consequences:

> Therefore, Hermann, know fully and distinctly that my life is ... in your hands ... and that an indiscretion on your part – the vanity of shewing a letter – of quoting a fond sentence, might as effectively kill me, as if you poured down my throat the poison I should swallow ... Nevertheless I love you so dearly, and my nature is so frank and confiding that I shall invent no pretexts to back out of my dangerous position ... If you can trust yourself with the sacred deposit of the lives and happiness of three persons – each of no common value – then I will trust you. But in the name of God, Hermann – as you are a man and a gentleman – if you doubt your discretion, your self-command, your earnest sense of the solemnity of what I say to you – in the name of God – be frank and candid and save me, save us all from peril. – Imagine me on my knees before you and with streaming eyes.[3]

The esteemed translator, the respectable wife, the close friend of Mill, Carlyle, Sydney Smith, Francis Jeffrey, and Nassau Senior could at any moment have been exposed in her secret role as a love-struck devotee of a Byronesque princeling.

The prince's very name – Prince Hermann Pückler-Muskau (known as Prince Pickling Mustard to some London wits) – establishes the operetta-style background for this curious relationship. He was a minor German nobleman, the ruler of forty-five villages, a man with the most extravagant tastes and an unceasing need for money to indulge them. Handsome, eccentric, flamboyant, he had at various times served in the army, a dashing cavalry officer living in a whirl of daredevilry, dissipation, and debt. Women, horses, gambling, and displays of reckless courage occupied one part of his early life. A legend in his time, this extraordinary man's character was paradoxical, and he was no mere dilettante. In fact he was to prove himself a talented writer who worked diligently at his craft, and he had a wide range of other interests. Thus, though it would seem that he was entirely absorbed with countless romantic conquests, one of his most abiding passions was an obsession for designing and planting magnificent parks and gardens – his parkomanie, he called it – and he is still revered as one of Germany's distinguished landscape gardeners. His imaginative flair also inspired his literary productions; he was a superb romantic illusionist – in his life, his park designs, his books, and, of course, his letters.

In his unusual fashion he was also one version of the devoted husband. He had married for money in a frankly business transaction a divorced woman of forty-one – nine years his senior, and he spent the first years of their married life pouring out her wealth in creative fantasies that transformed sandy, prosaic Muskau into magical parkland with lakes, waterfalls, shady groves, and, naturally, a grotto with a hermit. Whole forests were planted to give reality to his grandiose designs. He lived with his wife, Lucie (Countess Lucie of Pappenheim, daughter of the Prussian chancellor, Prince Hardenberg), not always harmoniously and with little pretence as to conjugal interest, but on terms of a close and understanding partnership nonetheless. She was the all-forgiving partner, his 'second self' to whom he bared his soul and signed himself as 'Lou' (conceivably, wolf), while she was his 'Schnucke' (ambiguously, darling, sheep). The psychological and financial web that enmeshed them included a shared passion for the estates of Muskau, Groditz, and Branitz. As he aptly said of them both: 'Money with us is like water on a hot stone.' Since he was soon enough hounded by creditors, weighed down by encumbered estates, and in danger of complete financial ruin, Lucie and he reluctantly agreed on the device of a divorce so that he might be free to seek another heiress.

This search brought him to London in late 1826. It was his second visit to England, where he had already in 1815, before he condescended to marry Lucie, surveyed the fine gardens and the possibilities for acquiring a rich wife. Unfortunately for him, when he now reappeared in England his reputation as a fortune-hunter and talk of his dubious divorce preceded him, and while this was acceptable for men of his class on the Continent, in so blatant a form it was regarded as disreputable in England. Equally bewildering to the English was his insistence that his relationship with Lucie was that of son and 'mother' and that, as he put it, 'a sum of ten million and Venus herself' could not tempt him to jettison her in any future matrimonial arrangement: no matter what, she would continue to live on the estate. There were many raised eyebrows at such announcements, but since he was clever, charming, and bizarre, fashionable society was happy to be entertained by this outrageous foreigner who could play the roles of dandy, charlatan, and aristocrat with such panache. He and Sarah did not meet during this visit. While in London he claimed he came within a hair's breadth of marriage to a number of heiresses. Each of these escapades he dutifully reported in journal-letters to Lucie (who showed them to K.A. Varnhagen – a major literary figure in Berlin – even before he was back) until, finally, he returned to Muskau with a good command of English and new plans for Muskau but, obviously to his great relief, without a bride. His distaste for his own mission is a fascinating thread in his letters to Lucie. 'The truth is,' he moaned, 'the whole idea of marriage is unendurable to me: every woman appears repellent to me when I consider her in this light.'

It is ironic that England, which had proved such a poor hunting ground for heiresses, brought him fame after all and set him on a path to a dazzling literary career and the wherewithal to maintain Muskau. On his return to Germany he published his breezy letters, which were good-naturedly critical of the ostentation and shallowness of fashionable English society and mocked many well-known persons but also un-stintingly admired the beauty of the scenery, parks, great houses, and pictures. His book became a best-seller. Its chatty, intimate manner and irreverent portraits of some society notables and aristocrats were welcome on a Continent happy to see England deflated. The macabre German title, *Briefe eines Verstorbenen* (Letters from a dead man), and the thinly veiled anonymity of the outspoken aristocratic author added a certain piquancy and helped to make the letters an enormous success and a landmark in subjective travel literature. Pückler was compared to Heine, and his letters earned him the largest publisher's cheque of any author in Germany other than Goethe.[4]

Sarah was captivated by the book and its author right from the start. There was as much of Pückler as of his travels in a book that was a string of impressions, musings, and digressions. Even before she knew how to spell his name correctly, she wrote a breathless endorsement of the book to John Murray: it was not a matter of whether the letters should be published in England, 'Nine people out of ten would say that they *cannot escape* being translated.' The author's 'very acute remarks on English and Irish manners and character, and extremely picturesque descriptions of the respective countries, a vast number of personal anecdotes, conversations etc.' destined the book for popularity. Above all she was charmed by what she described as 'the peculiar and interesting mind of the author – the philanthropy, freedom from all prejudice, and the gentle and somewhat melancholy philosophizing mingled with a strong sense of the ludicrous and great power of describing it.' She also noted the 'high and gentlemanly tone of the letters,' their vicacity and spontaneity. Murray should understand that the author 'was a Prince – an eccentric man – a German – and a man who travelled to see men and things and not to make a book.' She was mistaken in believing that the letters were not written with an eye to publication, but her estimate of them and the man was insightful. When Murray dragged his heels, worried about the propriety of the anecdotes and whether the reform bill controversy would swamp interest in travel literature, Sarah swept his scruples aside: the reform bill debate was no obstacle: ''tis to be sure a stirring sort of subject but we are not so political nor likely to be, as that all the light-reading public are to starve for these twelve months to come while that is discussed.' She was not going to let this opportunity slip out of her hands: 'I adhere therefore to my resolution and shall begin forthwith to translate – certain of finding a publisher if you decline it, which for your sake and mine, I hope you will not.' Her only fear was that she might be forestalled by another translator. If Murray failed to act, she would offer the book elsewhere; and not long after Effingham Wilson contracted with her for the translation.[5]

Sarah captured a good deal of Pückler's spirit in her translation, which appeared in four octavo volumes. When the first two volumes appeared in 1832 (printed by her brother Richard Taylor) under the sedate and unwieldy title *Tour in England, Ireland, and France in the Years 1828 and 1829; with Remarks on the Manners and Customs of the Inhabitants ... by a German Prince*, she found herself associated with a book whose sales were fanned by a whirlwind of gossip. Her translation also received its share of attention. The letters had been 'so perfectly translated,' wrote an Edinburgh reviewer, 'that from beginning to the end there is not a turn of expression, by which an Englishman can be made aware that he is not reading a spirited original.' She could thus tell a Norwich publisher that, while she only desired to be left alone to do her humble work, she had to

put up with 'a quantity of puffing.' She also wrote triumphantly to
Pückler: 'Our book has had immense success in America. Romilly tells me
eight editions have appeared so far. Naturally the Yankees are delighted
with your account of England.'[6] As it happened, the triumph of the book
had a bitter-sweet taste, for it all took place against the background of
Austin's ordeal at the University of London.

Pückler was hardly the sort of person to maintain a formal relationship
with a translator who was so appreciative of his talent and character and
who was reputed to be attractive, and before long he was writing Sarah
letters in his much practised, intimate, and uninhibited manner. And
Sarah, who in the early thirties, after her stay in Bonn, saw her mission to
be that of extending knowledge of German literature to England, was
glad to establish ties with a German who had the endorsement of Goethe,
Heine, and Varnhagen and was in touch with so many major German
literary notables. They soon got to know each other better over a
confrontation about Sarah's determination to prune a text that had
already been carefully expurgated by Pückler and Lucie. In fact the
published German version was only a fraction of the original letters and
omitted most of the account of the fortune-hunting quest that had initially
led him to undertake the journey. The original letters, or what has
survived of them in the heavily edited nine-volume edition of his letters
put out by Varnhagen's niece, Ludmilla Assing, contain humorous
accounts of a fortune-hunter who felt hampered by his poor dancing, was
disheartened by his quest, and was always getting worsted in his efforts to
capture that rich and willing sacrifice to Muskau's glory. The letters also
contain interesting material that throws light on his unusual relationship
with his wife. Most of this had been renounced for the sake of propriety:
the German version was already a highly diluted one.

Sarah, even more squeamish than Lucie, now found additional
passages to cut. She left out, for example, Pückler's supposedly romantic
encounter with some beautiful girls in the Vale of Llangollen and his
flirtation with a 'fair African,' whose blue eyes and black hair enchanted
him and to whom he gave lessons in pistol marksmanship, but who
resisted his charm and called him 'a great rogue.' She also softened or
deleted many of his satirical references to contemporaries and what she
considered his indefensible gossip. As her sanitized version reached him,
he wrote good-naturedly, 'Really, Signora, your womanly fear to offend
one or the other insignificant person, and still more the consciousness of
your sex being known to the public, makes you such a little coward that
you are taking away almost every "sel" [spice] of my books. But a

translator ought to be of no sex at all.' She replied with spirit that her editing and judgment would save the book: 'Those passages which you are pleased to call the "sel" ... I take leave to call the dirt of your book.'[7] They were good sparring partners, and he appears to have relished the novel pleasure of corresponding with a woman as intelligent and nimble-witted as himself (and who, after all, had blue eyes and dark hair).

No matter how much she savoured the spontaneity and zest which made him such an appealing contrast to her husband, Sarah's public attitude to Pückler was naturally guarded and her praise circumspect, modulated to suit the occasion. In her preface to the book she endorsed him as a man of 'fertile imagination; of unfettered and intrepid understanding; and accustomed to consider every subject in a large, tolerant, and original manner.'[8] In writing to a Norwich publisher, she commended Pückler for his political insight, for at this time she shared his critical attitude to the materialism and snobbery of what she also called England's 'purse-proud society.' He was admittedly 'imprudent, flighty and far too careless of what he said either of himself or others. But ... toward *mankind* his heart is in the right place and his sympathies kindly and not limited by station.'

Yet she was careful to distance herself even from his congenial political attitudes, for she feared she might 'have to share in the bitter vengeance of the Aristocratical part of the Press against a man who has exposed their insolence, stupidity and illbreeding.' In soliciting for a good review of the book, 'desiring its good word if it might fairly be given,' she stressed, '*Nothing would annoy me more than to be named*,' and explained, 'You will *not* think that I espouse that Author's opinions because I have been the interpreter of them ... I fear his notions are too peculiar not to annoy routine people. I wish them to be regarded as I regard them, simply as the manifestations of an individual mind.'

His deplorably indiscreet tongue gave her most misgivings. She made sure that her name did not appear in the volumes, and she avoided the feminine gender in the preface, in which she was 'a mere translator,' in no way responsible for the contents of this 'slight but clever work.' To be too closely linked with the author might not only bring on her 'the fury of the fashionables' but also jeopardize her reputation as a translator of substantial literary works.[9] Above all, she was determined to disclaim any personal knowledge of the scandals and publicity that delighted Pückler. Without involving herself in a printed falsehood, she managed in the preface to create the impression of entire ignorance of him: 'All that I now know of the Author's personal history while in England (if information from such sources may be called knowledge,) is gained from the writings of his reviewers. Whether their representations be true or false I have not the slightest interest in discussing.'[10] It is true that she had not met him when he was in England, but this disinterestedness was affected, of course, a carefully contrived self-protective cover.

Apparently she succeeded in this strategy. While friends, such as John Sterling, assumed that she could 'not admire or respect' Pückler and wrote to her about 'Prince Prettyman to whose book you have shown so much more favour than you would have bestowed on the author,' Sarah privately showed considerable interest in the prince's life and even his appearance and reported to him that she had heard that he was 'a fine-looking fellow.' (She was apparently unaware that he periodically spent twelve agonizing hours dyeing his greying hair.) She also made herself useful to him in London and was available to make small purchases for him, to arrange for payment of his travelling debts, and to negotiate with publishers; and she diverted and flattered him by reporting some of the rumours that were circulating about him. She knew how to gossip, even on paper.[11]

From gossip about others, it was natural to turn to confidences about themselves. However, Pückler was bored by hearing of John Austin's troubles and dismissed that subject with the observation that 'if he were German things would be settled very soon here.' There were few other constraints. She was not reticent and questioned him about his reputation, and he was happy to explain with his disarming candour:

> You misunderstand me if you consider me as a fortune-hunter ... I am in no way 'dérangé,' but my big estates are 50 per cent. mortgaged (I inherited them so). I have still enough to live decently, but not enough to carry on my great and beautiful plans, and therefore I wish to marry a rich wife. C'est une affaire de convenance et très usité [sic] dans les grandes familles par tous les pays du monde. A woman with £100,000 would not bring in as much as I own myself, and my title and name would also come into the bargain on my side, and all that is very fair, I think.

As for his wife, Lucie, he was also quite willing to give his version of that relationship, and he conveniently made her older than she actually was. 'She calls herself my mother, and no mother could love her son more and better. She is ten or twelve years older than I am, and when we married she was a little in love with me, but I was not the slightest bit with her, and told her in plain terms and that I reserved every liberty on my behalf. This

passes your English comprehension, dearest Sarah, but we Germans are
"odd" people.'[12] With undaunted confidence, he explained some of the
unsavoury scandal that clung to him: 'Very often I invented in former
times horrid storys [sic] of myself only to have the pleasure to frighten
good silly people out of their senses.' He made it a rule, he told her, 'to
answer english impertinence allways [sic] by a dubble [sic] dose of the
same.'[13]

It was difficult to resist his high spirits. All his life he had an
extraordinary appeal to women, so much so that he was credited with
hypnotic powers. Sarah soon fell under his spell, and before too long her
doubts about him dissolved. He, in turn, sensed her heartache and that
she was hard-pressed and yearning for affection. His self-revealing letters
to other women and friends show why he was bound to be intrigued. Why
not try his hand at conjuring up some emotional pleasure for Sarah? The
role of fantasy and the power of the imagination to transform reality
fascinated him. As he wrote later, it was preferable to split wood than to
play the part of the cold seducer. A portion of illusion was essential to
create the magic of the sentimental attachment. What triumph could
there be without such sentiments? Sarah's case offered a novel experience: 'You know that out of curiosity and inclination I like to give way in a
mephistophelian manner to every mood,' he told Varnhagen; and on
another occasion he explained, 'In every situation, I promptly, and as it
were by instinct, discover the good side of things; and enjoy it, be it what it
may, with a freshness of feeling.' And Sarah was remarkably willing to
enter into the spirit of the game and was even willing to describe her
physical charms to him. Nor were his attractions unknown to her, for a
portrait of him graced volume three of the first edition. Pückler soon
enough tossed off featherweight wooing letters, and she had not
forgotten how to parry advances. 'Mon Prince, don't fall in love with me,'
she wrote to him, 'because il n'y a pas de quoi, secondly, because it would
be of no us – unless indeed you have a passion for writing love letters, no
matter to whom.'[14] She appeared to resist, but continued to write. 'The
only thing of which I suffer,' he wrote, 'is a longing for you, who won't give
me a sign of a similar longing, and who only translates books instead of
translating pleasures, as I do.'

Since most of these letters are not dated, we do not know precisely
when Sarah dropped the light-hearted, bantering tone, but there appear
to have been emotional, intimate letters, at least on her side, by 1832,
when she was writing, 'Hermann, Beloved, how did you have the heart to
write like that? I forget you? Thank God you do not know yet how

uninterruptedly my thoughts are with you – how tender, how passionate my longing is for you.' She told him later that she had just read a book of his based on a diary of a walking tour he had taken as a young man, which she 'would have given anything to have read with you – seated by your side, my hand in yours, my head on your shoulders so that when our hearts were moved by the same touching or burning words our eyes and lips might meet.' As his postal mistress, she waited anxiously for the letters and fretted when there was nothing from the 'Dear Original.' She had determined not to write again till she heard from him, 'but this sort of idea is unworthy of me and of all true affection and I disown it.'[15] She now no longer questioned his honour but told him how she gallantly attempted to defend him against scurrilous attacks: 'They call you, even to *me*, a liar, a swindler, an adventurer, a coward, they say you were compelled to quit England on account of the commission of an offence "inter Christianos non nominendum" (the black-hearted wretches, the priests must have invented that), in short my dear, je ne suis pas sur les roses, deinet-wegen.'[16]

The tone of the correspondence would have scandalized her friends. Yet after a decade of John's gloom, timidity, and precision, it is not surprising that Sarah eagerly awaited declarations of sentiment from an unhampered spirit who understood that the 'lovely woman, the dear unknown' was in need of sensual nourishment.

> Last night I had a dream of you, dear Sarah – a rapturous dream – Oh, it was life itself! I dare not say more; don't be angry, but indeed I believe I was your husband and you were my wife; fantastic charming vision. I pressed a lovely form in delirious madness to my heart and thought to feel her burning kisses on my thirsty lips. It was but a dream but had all the true sensations of reality. Oh Heavens! if I could by enchantment give you an equal one ... What power there is in nature. It not only enables you to love an unknown being; you can even possess it and sink into a sea of bliss with it, breast pressed to breast ... I must have the privilege of thinking aloud with you or no more write at all.[17]

The generous-hearted romantic hero fades a little into the literary hack when one discovers that he owned a sort of copying device and kept outlines of his old love letters, so that he could reuse them, and it is only because of this that we have even some record of their exchange.

Sarah was not just play-acting, nor was it just youthful flirtatiousness reasserting itself. There is pathos in her attempting to be 'la petite femme par distance' and reaching for this adventurer who has been called 'the last modern knight.' At the time of their courtship John warned her: 'You will, for your own sake, remember that no hypocrisy, however refined and vigilant, could eventually conceal the want either of truth or of mental purity from the earnest gaze of a lover.'[18] In the early thirties, however, he was gazing only inward, and his despondency blinded him to Sarah's plight. The days were gone when he could write, 'If I can make you happy, my Beloved, trust me I will.'[19] Four years after her marriage she already felt irrelevant in the face of her husband's all-consuming anxiety about his career. 'I have thought all society even his wife as indifferent, almost burthensome to him,' she had told a friend, and this withdrawal became more severe during the following years.[20] In an era when the psychology of depression was even more mysterious than it is today, it was understandable that she interpreted her husband's state as a rejection of herself.

Only rarely did Sarah lower her defences and hint at some of the realities that may have intensified her feeling of being unloved, and, given her sense of propriety, it is not surprising that she inclined to hint of her distress to foreigners – to Santa Rosa, Pückler, and later in life to Guizot and Barthélemy Saint-Hilaire. After her husband's death she wrote to Guizot, who had become a confidant, that he had not always been 'a very tender husband to me, nor easy to please.' Ill health, disappointment, and anxiety, she explained, had made all things distasteful to him. During most of their married life John did little to strive to improve their unstable financial situation, and he may well have failed her sexually as well. In deep distress, Sarah wrote to Pückler: 'I have all your tastes, animal, social, intellectual – above all, the urge for living and being loved, au suprême degré; and in that which is the life of life and the sense of my whole being. Oh! how have I been bitterly disappointed. No more of that, but you would not disappoint me.' Meanwhile she had to put up with her barren existence. Later she told Guizot, 'There have been days when young and full of pretensions to happiness I have felt as if I had more tha[n] I could bear.'[21]

Sarah's anguish over her fate was at its height in 1834-5, when even her spirits and courage, a matter of great pride to her, began to falter. Her husband's career in London was stillborn, his spirits were ever more uncertain, and a life of exile appeared to be one of the few certainties. Carlyle, curious about the state of things with Austin, called on him for a long talk and concluded that Sarah's gloom about their situation was justified. Austin was, he reported, 'evidently very unhealthy, little likely to be healthy, a painful, faithful, pitiable man.' Sarah, in a state of constant harassment, continued her nursing and buried herself in translation, but daydreams of German castles, parks, gardens, and special flower beds planted in her honour floated into her mind. It was a relief to confide in someone, even if only by letter: 'I am half killed,' she wrote to Pückler, 'with expenses, anxiety, sorrow and physical fatigue. Courage! I shall go through with it and remain what the Lord Advocate [Francis Jeffrey] calls me, "the Heroine of Domestic Life"; I must.' In spite of this oft-reiterated resolution, the strain began to tell. She had written to Carlyle that she was not well, though she did not reveal the depth of her despair to him. 'Your own health too, it seems, is bad,' he replied; 'You have to complain of dispiritment, now when you still need all your strength,' and he proceeded to exhort her with a rhetorical passage from Schiller: 'Rise, noble Talbott; this is not a time to faint and sink: force faltering Nature by your strength of soul.' More realistically, he added, 'Alas, it is so much easier said than done.'[22]

Pückler's letters created visions of adventure and pleasure for Sarah, but did she realize that she was trying to grasp a mirage, that Pückler was a conjurer, a jester, governed by impulse and whim and happy to ignore realities? As Heine noted, 'The adult child called Prince Pückler liked to play his harmless games in the sunshine.' But for Sarah these games were hardly childlike and the sunshine was bound to be fleeting. Even the comfort of a postal romance was threatened in the summer of 1834 when Pückler left Muskau for a six-month journey through Europe before embarking on a long adventure-seeking trek to Africa, Egypt, and Asia Minor. Meanwhile he continued to tempt and tease her. When Sarah was considering places where she and her husband might live that were less costly than England, he suggested that they should stay at Muskau Castle. Such a proposal may have appeared too shameless to contemplate for long; but that such a constellation was just conceivable even in her circle must have been painfully evident to her, since she knew about the John Taylor-Harriet Taylor-John Stuart Mill embroilment. Sarah witnessed this development with fascination, and when Carlyle returned from Scotland she poured out the latest news about that extraordinary relationship. Harriet Taylor, in spite of a husband and children, was managing to sustain a romantic attachment with Mill without deserting her family; 'the fascinating half angelical half demoniacal Mrs. Taylor,' as Carlyle described her, had settled into a triangular domesticity without sacrificing either husband or adoret.[23]

The irregularities of her brother Richard's life may also have led Sarah to ponder unorthodox constellations that could exist even within her own virtue-conscious family. The details of Richard Taylor's private life are obliterated by discreet family editing, and it is unclear when Sarah came to know that Richard, who apparently remained unmarried, had children. By 1834, it would appear that a daughter, called Sarah, was sent greetings by her aunt and namesake, who was daily becoming more familiar with marital ambiguities.[24]

In spite of such irregularities in the lives of people around her, Sarah rejected the invitation to Muskau. She continued to be distracted and torn, and she clung to the emotional release provided by the Pückler fantasy while recognizing its implausibility. In thanking Pückler for the garden he had planted in her honour – 'your flowers, in short for your love' – she acknowledged that the path he had laid for her was one 'where I shall never tread.'[25]

She was also aware that a mere postal romance would not continue to sustain his interest. 'I can hardly believe that your romance will last,' she wrote to him. 'Were you a young enthusiastic novice, I could, but alas! Dear One, you have taken the habit of enjoying the present and your pauvre petite femme par distance vanishes into the air while you grasp something more substantial.' He now challenged her to meet him. He was going to begin his travels by going to Paris, and he would make a small detour to visit her in London. As always he was not lacking in candour: 'If I please you then I shall be true to you as gold, because I am longing so much for a person who loves me and pleases me at the same time spiritually and sensually. Maybe that is possible with us, maybe not, in any case we shall be the best of friends for ever. I want to surprise you and at the same time test you – so beware! A thousand kisses for your sweet little one and a long tender kiss for you.'[26]

When it seemed that he might just arrive on her doorstep, Sarah finally abandoned the entrancing postal minuet and reaffirmed her resolution to lash herself to duty. In deep despondency she wrote to him: 'Do not think me either fickle or hypocritical and prudish if I tell you to lower your expectations of what I *may* and *can* be to you. Were I free I still think I could be everything to you ... let us not deceive ourselves – there is an object between us.' She concluded, 'I may be worn out; but I shall have done my duty.' Her husband's health was wretched and left little room for hope, but, as she wrote to a friend, 'I do bear it and with God's help I hope I shall continue to do so.'[27]

One anchor to domestic reality during these years was Lucy Austin, aged thirteen in 1834. Lucy, a superbly intelligent and independent child, was a great satisfaction and comfort: 'My child is well and that is my main prop,' Sarah told Francis Lieber. Pückler, sensitive to maternal feelings, had never overlooked Lucy and often included her in his letters, and Lucy, who shared with him a deep affection for animals, wrote, we are told, some charming letters to him. Some years later, Sarah told Guizot that she had a superstitious belief that she had 'born the malice of fate' for Lucy. 'If so,' she added, 'I am content.'[28]

Pückler embarked for Africa in January 1835. The publisher John Murray, seeking the autograph of an author who had eluded him, asked Sarah if she had any of Pückler's letters that she could let him have. With perfect veracity and *sang froid* she could tell him, 'I never saw him so that our correspondence is necesarily a very odd one'; furthermore, his letters were 'either too good[?] or too absurd to give away,' but she could offer him a cover or a letter of business.[29] Meanwhile she was writing Pückler loving and melancholy goodbye notes: 'Strange, and hard as strange, that one who could understand and love you so much should be for ever parted from you ... My mind returns constantly to the dream of seeing you, but with ever less hope. I embrace you, Beloved, and kiss your eyes, and – Oh – your lips! Keep well.'

After Pückler's departure Sarah was in the most despairing period of her life. There was little enough to support her spirits: John was depressed to the point of physical collapse; her fantasy was over; the dreaded move abroad was imminent. 'I am oppressed and dejected beyond description,' she wrote to Brougham. 'My courage which has stood him and me in good stead is breaking down.' Lucy remained, but, as Sarah explained, 'I cannot consent to lay any part of my burthen on my young and light hearted child. Let her go free, as long as she can, poor thing.'[30]

Sarah's unhappiness was intensified in the spring of 1835 by the confusion and restlessness brought about by the dissolution of her household. In Hastings, where they had moved temporarily as the first step in their migration to Boulogne, Sarah, isolated and left to brood in solitude over the problematic future, appears to have come close to a nervous breakdown. Her thoughts spun around on the theme 'What is to come of this?' What were their prospects if John did not rally? To a friend she wrote in deep melancholy: 'I never sit down to write a letter, or to sew, or to think, without rivers of tears which *will* come ... Oh, my dear I feel as if I could clasp my hands over my eyes and die. But *that* I must not and yet I am frightened at myself for it seems to me as if I could never hold it out. Pray for me that I may.' She was quite broken in spirit.[31]

Her fear that fortune, friends, and hope were on the ebb is corroborated by an account written by Carlyle at this time. The Austins had gone to Hastings, he wrote: 'No mortal seems to remember that they ever existed here.' He chose to draw a moral lesson on literary and social vanity from this:

> Mrs. Austin seems to be here again; half in secret; looking after the letting of her house. We are to go up and drink tea with her; and she promises Jane a chair; I and herself are to sit on stools or as tailors do, for the whole establishment is dismantled. It is truly sad to see how soon the place of the most popular public favourites is filled up: Mrs. A. had carriages by the score at her house daily, and you could not see her, or hear yourself speak to her for the cackle of admiring lady-visitors, and already it seems to be forgotten that she ever existed: nobody can give the smallest news of her; appears to think any speech on the subject a superfluity.[32]

Sarah's effort to regain some serenity is reflected in letters from Boulogne, where she and John now spent nine months in limbo – from August 1835 to the summer of 1836 – till they heard of his appointment to the Commission of Inquiry into Maltese affairs. During this and other forlorn periods Sarah found her religious faith a source of comfort. She was not, by her own account, a zealous Unitarian or upholder of any 'very defined dogmatic faith.' She kept, however, 'a foundless trust in the Source of all good – such as His Son reveals Him to us,' and this, as she told Harriet Grote, gave her 'a sort of reliance that encourages me in a thorny and weary path.' And she added, 'How natural it is to take refuge *somewhere* from the world![33] The extent to which she retained her religious sentiments is revealed in the comment of her friend James Stephen, who wrote that he regarded her as 'among those who belong to the "religious world" in the right and catholic sense of the expression.' That during this period especially her religious feelings came to her aid is evident in a letter to Heine, whom she had first met in Boulogne in 1833. In thanking him for a gift of his verses, she asserted that he was in spirit, and in spite of appearance to the contrary, fundamentally a good Christian. Then in an elliptical fashion she referred to 'a wound,' attempts to conquer emotions, a sense of guilt, and the consolation she sought in religious faith: 'Ah we are all worth so little! When I see dear Mr. Heine, how easy it is to inflict a wound, how difficult it is to heal it, what wisdom, what patience one must employ; what distaste one must endure; how many emotions of one's lower nature one must suppress, I believe truly in the divinity of him who could pardon all, who wished to appease all, to purify all – who had only tears for the evils that he could not reform.' There is also a hint that Pückler was still on her mind, for she told Heine that she was filling the solitude of the winter in a deserted summer spa by working on the translation of Raumer – 'an innocent enough occupation' and a great blessing for her. The letter abounds in tantalizing ambiguities. Yet Heine is not likely to have been in her confidence, for a few months earlier, while complaining bitterly to a friend about 'the prospect of passing a winter a hundred miles from any creature with whom I can exchange a thought or feeling,' she mentioned that Heine was in Boulogne and perhaps would stay longer: 'But you know me enough to know how little his manner of thinking and mine agree, or how little *épanchement* there can be in conversation with such a man.'[34]

Pückler was out of reach, but he was not entirely out of mind. Sarah's correspondence with him continued in a desultory fashion till the early 1840s. He did not return from his travels until 1837, and by the time they met for the first time in Berlin in 1842 her passion had cooled; unfortunately there is no record of what they said or thought. There is also no evidence to suggest that John Austin became aware of her feelings for Pückler. Sarah was so protective of her husband that she is unlikely to have revealed this. If others knew, they were discreet – as was Pückler himself, for he did not betray her. Though Sarah must have had an uneasy moment when John Wilson Croker in his review of Raumer's *England in 1835* asked why she had suppressed Raumer's denunciation of Pückler's impertinent gossip. Pückler kept her letters and his drafts, but neither he nor his literary executrix included Sarah's letters in the volumes of published correspondence. As Goethe had written in a laudatory review of Pückler's book, which Sarah quoted in her preface, it was natural enough that Pückler drew women to him: 'He attracts and is attracted; but his experience of the world enables him to terminate any little *affaires du cœur* without violence or indecorum.' And even John Sterling grudgingly acknowledged, he was 'as things go in Germany, a good deal of a gentleman' after all.[35]

The intense emotion of the Pückler episode faded, but of course her memory of it was never obliterated. In an account describing the cholera epidemic in Malta, she wrote of how a good Maltese woman, who all her life had been devoted to her family, had, in the face of overpowering fear, lost all sense of duty and failed to care even for her daughter; and Sarah observed, seemingly in an autobiographical reminiscence, 'How frail and precarious a tenure we hold our best qualities, unsustained by courage.'[36] The possibility that Pückler might publish her letters or give her away unwittingly seems to have given her twinges of apprehensiveness the rest of her life. 'We all do foolish and wrong things,' she told Guizot while commenting on an indiscreet book, 'at least I *do*, but I hope I am not a bad woman in the main, and why should my faults and follies be printed?' Her apprehensiveness may also have strengthened her later strictures about any disclosures of private life. The veil that she wanted drawn over her own indiscretions ought, she felt, to be extended to others; 'A woman's heart is best revealed in her life; and if she writes, in the tendency of her works,' she told Guizot. The Pückler episode was also reflected in a resigned comment on what life still held out. 'Thus and no otherwise should we speak of life – what [pitfalls] to avoid,' Sarah wrote. 'Is that all? Alas, yes. What to gain, to have, that we will leave to the young to dream of.'[37]

As the memory of her transgression faded with the years, she looked back on her struggle in a different context. She now tended to see her self-denial and adherence to duty as part of that disciplined English tradition: 'We are the only women in the world who are drilled from our cradles into government of our feelings. The French ... the Germans ... both have ways of equivocating with duty. If we *sin*, we do so with our eyes open and we don't call our sins by sentimental names.'[38] In old age she took a non-nonsense attitude to one of the most famous of all sentimental attachments, that of the young Goethe for Charlotte Buff, as transmuted in the *Sorrows of Young Werther*. Charlotte was quite willing to engage in a flirtation with Goethe, but in the end she married the man to whom she had been betrothed. Sarah felt that Lotte had acted wisely, for she probably recognized that Goethe (like Pückler perhaps) was not about to marry. Sarah was also understanding of Lotte's response: 'the adorations of Goethe were too flattering, and too charming to give up.' But her sympathy for Lotte ceased here: 'Lotte should have taken Goethe or left him. That is the English and *good* sense of the thing.' To prolong the flirtation while doing neither of these things – that was one of Goeth's 'absurd Verhältnisse [relationships].' Sarah now prided herself that she had, after all, acted with English good sense.[39]

5

Colonial service: reform and retribution

JOHN AUSTIN'S APPOINTMENT IN 1836 as the leading member of a Commission to inquire into the affairs of Malta gave him and Sarah a new lease on life. Austin had resigned from the Criminal Law Commission, and Sarah, eager for some new public employment for him, pressed his claims on those, such as Lord Lansdowne and Lord Brougham, who were in a position to help: 'I cannot but feel intense mortification at the thought that so much thought and learning and sincere devotedness to a noble science should be fruitless and should die with him.' In a mood of discouragement they had retreated to Boulogne in August 1835 to escape the expense and defeats of London, but it offered little solace, for the sense of humiliation went with them. Sarah felt isolated, and even Lucy, now fourteen, echoed her mother's judgment when she described the 'desperately humdrum life we lead here, perfectly wretched.'[1]

The Malta appointment provided public recognition and a dispensation from Boulogne, where the Austins had been for almost a year. Suddenly a brighter vista opened: from an obscure, impecunious, anxiety-ridden exile, they were launched into a position of prestige and influence. Sarah looked forward to Austin's using his great knowledge to enhance the public good. He was, as Carlyle put it, 'to be the Minos and Lycurgus of Malta.' It was also the first time his services would be rewarded by a munificent salary (£1500 a year plus £3 per day expenses).[2]

They were to sail to Malta from Marseilles. With the other commissioner, George Cornewall Lewis, who had been one of Austin's students at the University of London, but without Lucy, who was left in school in England in order to avoid the hot climate, they made their way through France in late September and October 1836. They travelled from Boulogne to Marseilles by way of Paris, Dijon, Chalons, Lyons, and Avignon, with diversions to Nîmes and to the Pont du Gard. At Marseilles they stayed with Sarah's brother Philip, now a very successful manufacturer of marine equipment. Since it rained continuously after they left Paris, they may have been glad to board the Royal Navy frigate which was to carry them to Malta, but the journey proved wearisome, especially as it consisted of 'ten days of tacking, watching, longing for winds that would not blow.' Finally, just outside the harbour at Valletta, they were rescued by a stream-frigate which came to tow them in. Sarah may not have been aware of the irony in her description: 'I shall never forget the effect which her [the steam-frigate's] rapid undeviating course had upon me ... It was like the course of a man who asks no help but of his own judgment and his own inflexible will, compared with that of a weak and dependent woman shaping her way by every changing mood.' Their entry into the harbour provided the sort of triumphal acclaim that she seemed always to have envisaged for Austin.

The magnificent harbour provided a perfect setting for a dramatic entry. It was filled with rowing boats; every wall, bastion, and balcony overlooking the scene was crammed with cheering crowds; and above the din the guns of anchored ships fired a welcoming salute. As so often, Austin left no record of his thoughts; perhaps he recalled his discontent in the army when he was stationed in Malta. Sarah was overcome by emotion as the cheers 'rang across the waves and re-echoed from side to side with an effect that to me, who expected nothing, was quite over-powering.' The passengers were placed in quarantine, where they remained for six days, because there was cholera in the Mediterranean and it was assumed to be contagious. When released (on 26 October 1836), they were again greeted by enthusiastic crowds as their carriage brought them through the outworks, into the city of Valletta. The scene, which is preserved in two lithographs, was festive; there was an enormous concourse of people and many bands, and the atmosphere was heightened at night when the town was illuminated.[3]

Although their welcome was exhilarating, it was also sobering. Lewis recognized that the enthusiasm reflected high and perhaps unrealistic expectations from the commission: 'They almost seem to think that we shall call down manna from heaven.' Sarah heard the cheering of the crowds as 'the voice of the suffering calling for help and justice,' and she recalled that her husband had taken on a great responsibility. Thus when the ship's officers congratulated her on the flattering reception, she said nothing and turned away to hide her tears, perhaps worried about how Austin would acquit himself.[4]

The Austins now began a novel style of life. They had a large, finely situated house at Sliema, and as many as five of their servants were men, a fact which, Sarah recognized, was a reflection of Malta's poverty and unemployment. According to protocol, Austin was third-ranking man at Malta, preceded only by the governor and the archbishop; and as the governor had no wife, Sarah took precedence, as she noted, of every woman in the island, which was a considerable change from having been 'la belle anglaise' to the fishermen at Boulogne. There were many occasions to enjoy her new status. Within days of their arrival there was a United Services ball, and many other festivities followed, among them a governor's ball, a ball to celebrate the queen's birthday, and a ball and supper hosted by Sarah and Admiral Sir Robert Stopford. She was experiencing colonial social life in its heyday.

Sarah savoured Malta and thrived there. She rode nearly every day, and having loved the sea in its varied moods since childhood, she especially enjoyed the bathing, which in summer was the only relief from the oppressive heat. ('You have not the faintest idea what *sun* means,' she wrote.) Moreover, Sarah was fascinated by the unfamiliar features of Malta – 'this little half-Arab nation' – with its strange mixtures of languages and cultures. She was stimulated by the exotic flavour of the beige stone buildings and the active street life and charmed by the frequent slightly discordant ringing of bells from the many churches and convents; she loved the intimacy of Valletta, a tiny metropolis where hilly, stepped streets led on three sides to harbours and the sea. With her usual energy Sarah threw herself into her new role. It was said that she was responsible for the commissioners' recommendation to increase expenditure for elementary education, and she arranged for the establishment of ten new village schools. She 'consider[ed] herself an equal member of the Commission,' and, as she put it, she regarded her time 'the property of the public.' Sarah recognized that Malta was a mine of valuable and unrecognized works of art and craftsmanship, and she arranged for the sale of gloves and lace in Valletta and in England. Much later her friend Barthélemy Saint-Hilaire speculated whether she might have been happier or at least more useful as the wife of a diplomat, and her life in Malta supported his insight.[5]

One is bound to wonder why Austin was given the appointment. He was an inexperienced barrister whose reputation for erudition and brilliance was confined to a few of those who had read his book or heard his lectures. Among public officials he may have been known for his connection with the Criminal Law Commission, but Austin had served on the commission so briefly before resigning that this probably did not affect judgments about him. In political circles, if known at all, he was associated with Benthamism, and this was not likely to enhance his reputation for sound judgment. Lord Melbourne, for example, on this score dismissed him as a fool, and Sydney Smith satirized him for being a philosopher and a spokesman for 'transcendental Benthamism.' Since he was little known and vaguely suspect, only a well-placed supporter could have influenced the decision on Austin's behalf, and no one was better placed to do this than Sir James Stephen, who was permanent under-secretary at the Colonial Office and one of Austin's few close friends. Conceivably Lansdowne also helped, since he was favourably disposed to the Austins, and Sarah never ceased promoting her husband in her correspondence with him. It was also opportune for Austin that a group of Maltese lawyers had just completed a draft criminal code, and their proposal was to be on the agenda for the commission and was very much in tune with Austin's interest in Continental codes and codification. Austin was appointed even though it was known that he performed poorly under the stress generated by a tight schedule. Lewis, although not eager to leave England, agreed to serve with his former teacher to help allay fears on this score.[6]

The decision in June 1836 to establish a commission of inquiry was made in response to discontents in Malta. Petitions for redress of grievances were submitted to the government in Malta at various times during the early 1830s, a committee was formed in Malta to press complaints, and an agent, George Mitrovich, was sent by the committee to present its case to the British public and Parliament. The complaints were above all directed against the lack of representation of the Maltese in the councils of government and against censorship. As a crown colony, Malta was ruled by a governor, a crown appointee, whose decisions were made in consultation with a council (established only a year before) on which Maltese subjects had only a minor role. Discontented with this arrangement, a group of Maltese complained that the British broke a promise, made in 1798 when Malta came under British rule, to restore an ancient popular assembly. They also agitated against the high level of taxation, excessively high pensions paid out of Maltese revenue, restrictions on trade, restrictions on the press, the predominance of Britons in important offices, and the failure of those who held office to perform their duties.[7]

The commissioners were given a very extensive agenda, despite their instructions that they recommend no change that would undermine Malta's role as a fortress. They were asked to consider nothing less than 'the introduction of a permanent and salutary system of polity,' and this required an examination of all the laws, regulations, usages, and every matter connected wih the civil government, judicature, civil and ecclesiastical establishments, revenue, and trade. Under this rubric the inquiry was to include such matters as a criminal code, a popular representative assembly, liberty of the press, education, charities, poor relief, and emigration. In fact, nearly every public institution was to be scrutinized. The order in which these topics were taken up was left to Austin and Lewis. For Austin, this was to be a first experience of practical politics, with its conflicts of opinions and factions, its tension and acrimony. It proved to be a formidable challenge to his skill and his temperament.

Despite the all-embracing agenda and severe poverty and resentment in Malta, Austin and Lewis, after their initial assessment, concluded that fundamental change was unnecessary. Although they made occasional vague allusions to Maltese rebelliousness and comparisons with the problems of Ireland, the commissioners were able to reassure the authorities in London that the Maltese were loyal to British rule. They explained that the General Committee of Maltese, which submitted the petitions, was dominated by 'able and respectable advocates and merchants,' a group that, according to the commissioners, was 'rational in its views, and temperate in its conduct.' Although a minority on the committee might be 'unreasonable, impatient, and violent,' the committee did not threaten general tranquillity. While the bulk of the upper and middle classes (as Austin and Lewis described them) were dissatisfied, the commissioners were confident that their grievances could be remedied without making extensive changes.[8] This was convenient, in view of the commissioners' obligation to recommend only changes which would be compatible with continued use of the military and naval stations in Malta.

Austin and Lewis began their work soon after being released from quarantine, and as a first step they interviewed the leaders of the General Committee of Maltese. That Lewis spoke Italian must have been a great help. They also attended sittings of the courts and consulted the judges, and they distributed a questionnaire, which in fact was a census, on the size of the population, its distribution by occupation, wages, mendicancy, crime, emigration, use of agricultural land, manufactures, and education.[9]

AUSTIN AND LEWIS could hardly have got off to a more disputatious start. They immediately became embroiled in a controversy with Sir John Stoddart, the chief justice, who was a former leader writer for *The Times* and a man with independent views and an abrasive personality. The controversy initiated a pattern of conflict with the English establishment in Malta that continued throughout their twenty-month stay. Ultimately the commissioners were successful in their battle with Stoddart, but their victory proved to be costly for the final outcome of their mission and for Austin personally.

The controversy, which began soon after Austin and Lewis were released from quarantine, was provoked by Stoddart's speech at the opening session of his court on 5 November. He often gave speeches from the bench on matters not connected with the cases before him, and this one was directed against a report on a criminal code which had been issued only a few months earlier by a committee of Maltese lawyers. Among other things the report cast doubt on the usefulness of trial by jury, an institution highly valued by Stoddart, in fact introduced to Malta by him in 1829. Knowing that the report, including its discussion of trial by jury, would be among the subjects taken up by Austin and Lewis, Stoddart requested the commissioners to attend his court to hear his speech.[10]

For Stoddart, as for many in England, trial by jury was nearly a sacred institution closely connected with the protection of individual rights and liberty of the press. Since he wished to see these things take root in Malta, the proposed new criminal code was unacceptable. In his speech he explained the rationale for jury trial in English legal practice and its close connection with a free press. He objected to the argument that the English jury system was not practicable in Malta because there were not enough competent jurors and to the treatment of jury trial by the Maltese lawyers 'with slight and indifference.' He pointed to the intimation from the Colonial Office that liberty of the press would be established quite soon and emphasized that, as in England, this made jury trial a necessity.

The commissioners were shocked by the chief justice's speech, and they informed the colonial secretary (Charles Grant, created Lord Glenelg in 1835) about Stoddart's conduct. They regarded his speaking on matters not related to cases before the court as inappropriate, and they asked the colonial secretary to restrain him so that in the future he would confine himself to his judicial functions. Austin, of couse, was still sufficiently a Benthamite to be sceptical about juries and favourable to codification. Thus the commissioners objected to the 'most hostile spirit and ... very invidious style' in which Stoddart criticized the proposal for a code and found his speech 'in itself indecorous.' They also complained that he had aggravated their difficulties by indicating that liberty of the press would be established soon when he must have known that since this was a matter for the commissioners to take up, the timing and extent of the change was still uncertain. In a subsequent dispatch Austin and Lewis described the many collisions between Stoddart and the chief secretary and observed that 'the petty and unseemly hostilities' lowered the dignity and weakened the authority of the government. They also pointed to Stoddart's connections with the popular party in Malta and with William Ewart, the radical member of Parliament who promoted the interests of the radical movement in Malta. Privately, Lewis described Stoddart – Austin undoubtedly would have agreed – as a hot-headed man and as one of the greatest demagogues in Malta.[11]

Lord Glenelg, speaking for the Colonial Office, shared the commissioners' view that Stoddart's discussion of liberty of the press was dangerous and ill-timed. Although this episode interrupted the commissioners' investigations he welcomed their observations; in their 'impartiality and wisdom I can place unhesitating reliance.' He endorsed their recommendation that the chief justice's functions should be carefully circumscribed, and he asked the governor, Sir Henry Bouverie, to assure the commissioners that their assistance was valuable and received with gratitude. This was only the first of many occasions when Austin and Lewis, although beleagured in Malta, would receive strong support from the Colonial Office.

The enmity between the commissioners and Stoddart arose partly from personal differences, but above all from disagreements about legal matters. Stoddart, in addition to wanting to introduce English law and procedure into Malta, especially trial by jury, also wanted libel laws in Malta to be copied from the English model, and he was sceptical about codification. Austin and Lewis were much less confident about importing English law into Malta. Austin was not enamoured of English law and practice, as his *Province of Jurisprudence* made clear; and Lewis thought French drafting superior to the English. They argued that there were many problems in adapting English law to Maltese circumstances; most notably, it would be unintelligible to the Maltese, including lawyers. Their low esteem of the chief justice was transparent even in their formal report: 'No English lawyer of distinguished talents and acquirements could be tempted to accept the office [held by Stoddart].' Stoddart summed up his own view of the disagreements by contrasting the commissioners' 'system of re-Italianising the Law of Malta' with his own attempt 'to breathe a little English spirit of freedom' into it.[12]

As early as January 1837, after only two months in Malta, Austin and

Lewis decided that Stoddart had to go. At that time they told Glenelg that it would be impolitic to remove him immediately, but it was clear that they thought the time would come. Meanwhile they informed Stoddart that they would report to the Colonial Office about how 'the most effectual security could be taken against future collisions between the administrative and judicial authorities in these islands.' Although Stoddart wrote a long defence of his conduct, it did not help him. If he had any doubts about where he stood, they would have been dispelled by Glenelg's dispatch of 29 March, which strongly endorsed the commissioners' views and authorized the governor to show the dispatch to the chief justice.[13]

When the commissioners filed their report on the state of the courts they recommended that the Supreme Council, which was the appellate court over which Stoddart presided, be merged with the Court of Appeal and that the office of chief justice, held by Stoddart, be abolished. They backed the recommendation with varied reasons: the existence of two appellate courts made for unnecessary complexity; the two courts were practically identical; of the two courts, Stoddart's was inferior in quality; Maltese judges could do the necessary work; and in addition to being a 'needless office,' the chief justice's pay was 'invidiously excessive.' A letter to Glenelg was even more outspoken: Stoddart received an 'exorbitant salary ... for doing nothing or worse than nothing,' and 'whilst as a Judge he is inefficient, his legislative powers as Member of the Council are nearly an insuperable obstacle to useful law-reforms.'[14] Lord Glenelg endorsed the recommendation and abolished Stoddart's office from 1 January 1839.

The elimination of Stoddart's job was not merely the consequence of personal animosity and differences in opinion, for it was Colonial Office policy to eliminate sinecures and rationalize the civil establishment. The commissioners were entirely in agreement with this policy, and they aimed 'to reduce the public revenue taken from this small and poor community to the lowest amount consistent with the public service,' and therefore 'to abolish every office appearing to be needless, and to diminish every salary appearing to be exorbitant.' The rationale for this policy varied. First of all, there was the drain on the meagre resources of the island, from which the civil establishment was paid. The entire revenue was approximately £95,000, and this came from a community so poor as to be comparable, as the commissioners put it, to a second- or third-rate London parish. Furthermore, it was 'necessary to the moral improvement of the people' to abolish sinecures, for they created wrong expectations and fostered habits of indolence, improvidence, and mendicancy. This reasoning reflected the experience of Lewis as a poor law commissioner and Austin's sympathy with the New Poor Law. Finally, their wish to abolish sinecures, about which they were unrelenting, also reflected a firm belief in Benthamite rationality. The governor, having observed the commissioners' determination to eliminate waste and reduce expenses, acknowledged that their advice was 'entirely unbiased by any considerations but those of zeal for the public service.'[15]

The severe policy was applied to other notable offices. Among them, the attorney-general's office was abolished, and its occupant, Robert Langslow, found himself without his job. The commissioners did not mince words: the office was unnecesary; since 1832 Langslow had prepared only twenty-one documents; although he had been away from Malta during the eight months previous to the date of the commissioners' recommendation, 'the law business of the government has not sensibly suffered in consequence of his absence'; Langslow could not perform certain functions of his office because his poor Italian was insufficient for forensic purposes; and his pay was excessive. The establishment of new offices (crown advocate, with an English assistant) was recommended.[16]

The abolition of the 'almost sinecure office' of treasurer was also recommended, and its few functions were to be assumed by the chief secretary. This proposal greatly complicated the commissioners' relationships with leading figures in Malta. There were rumours that Sir Frederick Hankey intended to resign as chief secretary, and the commissioners urged Glenelg to facilitate this outcome so that the present treasurer could replace him, thus performing the functions of both offices but without an increase in salary. Hankey, an able and industrious man, but extremely military in his bearing, was disliked by all classes of Maltese. The commissioners also criticized him for having 'scarcely a tincture of political or economical science; and, as it appears to us, he is nearly devoid of practical good sense and discretion in the administration of public affairs and in his dealing with men.' While Hankey was in London, Austin and Lewis, with a zeal for improvement but not much finesse, told the colonial secretary that they were willing that Hankey be informed that his resumption of office would be 'highly inexpedient.' Having made an enemy out of Hankey, Austin and Lewis also must have lost the support of Nugent, the treasurer, for although they recommended him as Hankey's replacement, another appointment was made. Consequently, Nugent not only failed to receive the appointment recommended by the commissioners, but he was also left without his old office, likewise on their recommendation. This episode complicated the commissioners' relations with the governor, for his intervention against the commissioners' proposals was made possible by his opening by mistake a letter not addressed to him in which the commissioners' recommendations were discussed.[17]

It was not only the chief justice, the attorney-general, and the treasurer who found themselves stripped of their offices. The commissioners' passion for economy was directed to many lesser offices as well. Among others, the following were abolished: collector of land revenue, auditor-general, lieutenant-general of the Island of Gozo, and superintendent of the post office. In addition, the commissioners recommended the abolition or consolidation of the following departments or offices: grain, marine police, government works, magistrate of markets for Malta, magistrate of markets for Gozo, collector of land revenue in Gozo, and collector of judicial receipts. There were also recommendations for the radical reorganization of departments responsible for tariffs, charitable institutions, and schools. Most of these recommendations were implemented by the Colonial Office while Austin was in Malta.[18]

Such drastic changes were bound to be disturbing, but more were to follow. Austin and Lewis urged the home government to be sparing in the grants of pensions, since one-eighth of the revenue was already used for this purpose. They also urged termination of the practice by which a great many government servants were able to enjoy use of crown property for their private dwellings without payment or at rents that were well below market values. In addition, the commissioners strongly recommended that in making appointments, including those for superior offices, 'natives of the island ought generally to be preferred to Englishmen.' This would reduce discontent and make the government more popular; it would encourage the cultivation of the qualities required for public office; it would put an end to the degradation that came from exclusion; and the salaries required by Maltese would be less than what was paid to Englishmen. Opposition to the commissioners among the English community in Malta was inevitable.[19]

The opposition was most direct and most hostile in *The Harlequin*, one of the newspapers that were allowed to begin publication in 1838, subject to censorship, in anticipation of the expected establishment of a free press. Here the commissioners' reports were ridiculed as ten-penny sheets. Austin and Lewis were called anti-British and their reports a blow against anglicism, and they were accused of having 'libelled British education, the British name, the British character.' More specifically, they were guilty of causing Englishmen 'to be turned out of their situations

with less ceremony than a man would turn a dog out of a kennel –
pretending that those situations were abolished – though in fact they only
changed the names of them, in order to give them to Maltese.' The
commissioners were also accused of promoting the fortunes of Maltese
favourites and, worse, of encouraging Maltese radicalism. Such conduct
was regarded as an extension of the commissioners' own radicalism,
which was said to have originated in 'the sublime regions of Malthus,
Bentham, and the host of ultra-radical economists, in ... cold, dreary
regions of heartless policy, and *fanatic* utilitarianism.' In such regions *The
Harlequin* located not only Austin and Lewis but also the 'lady commissioner.' Their philosophic outlook was regarded as the source of 'the crude,
absurd, and destructive innovations got up by these two-penny-half-
penny Commissioners.' A similar theme underlay the paper's description
of the ridicule heaped on the commissioners and especially Sarah at a
carnival where she was depicted as on horseback: with 'a piece of string
she drew after her an enormous jack ass, alias donkey; which same donkey
was loaded with an immense book inscribed with "*political* economy."'[20]

The commissioners' relations with the English community were made
worse by their unofficial attitudes. Privately they expressed their disdain
for the English in Malta, and some of this was discerned by their
compatriots. Sarah complained about the lack of intelligent society and
the want of breeding, and Lewis thought 'the scum of England is poured
into the colonies' and regarded his fellow-countrymen as 'the offal of
every calling.' He was intensely bored by them: 'one meets the same
people again and again; and it is merely the same pack re-shuffled.' A
'kleinstädtischer Geist' prevailed, and he shuddered at the thought of
living there permanently. What is more, he and the Austins were severely
critical of English treatment of the Maltese. Lewis thought the 'brutal
treatment by the English in society' was one of the great evils in Malta, and
Sarah suspected that much of the discontent arose from English insolence
and prejudice. When the Austins and Lewis established close relationships with Maltese merchants and professionals, especially those in the
moderate wing of the reform movement, they were accused of 'having
skulked off among the Maltese.' Sarah ostentatiously befriended the
Maltese – like Lewis, she spoke Italian – and she tried to overcome the
conventional barriers between the two communities, but she knew her
conduct would provoke criticism and during her first fortnight in Malta
asked, 'How will the English ladies bear this – so strong a censure, though
a tacit one, on their conduct?' And later she wrote to Mill, 'If I escape
poisoning you may rejoice. I think I have ... reason to have a taster ... I am

sorry to be an object of hostility to any body, but civility to the Maltese is an inexpiable offence in the eyes of the English ladies.'[21]

The commissioners clearly unsettled the Malta establishment: careers were cut short; emoluments were taken away; and expectations were disappointed. Even those not immediately affected were chilled by the new atmosphere of austerity. The governor, who was spared despite their severe scrutiny, complained about the commissioners' 'sincere but, as I think, mistaken and overstrained zeal for economy.' Although there is little evidence of acrimonious personal relations, the commissioners experienced the discomforts inflicted on those who rock the boat. Some of this was revealed by Sarah, who, however, also affirmed their resilience. 'Your Lordship [she wrote to Lansdowne] doesn't know what it is to be a reformer. When you meet the man whose sinecure you have abolished every day, when you have to encounter every disappointed claimant and every detected jobber in every ride and walk, you will pity us. But we are harder than the nether millstone.'[22]

THE MATTER OF LIBERTY OF THE PRESS should not have been a stumbling block for John Austin. His instructions directed him to look for ways of abolishing censorship; indeed, earlier in 1836 the government in London had announced its intention of ultimately establishing a free press. Apart from the clergy, all parties in Malta favoured abolition of censorship, including both the moderate and extreme factions of the Maltese organization agitating for reforms. Even Sir John Stoddart, the commissioners' antagonist on other issues, shared this wish. Since the opposition to it was insignificant, liberty of the press should have been established speedily and without difficulties.

Confident that they enjoyed considerable support both at home and in Malta, and aware of the importance attached to this issue by the Maltese, the commissioners took up the matter as one of their first tasks. They were occupied during much of November 1836 taking evidence from interested parties, and by the following March they submitted to London a report and drafts of proposed laws providing for extensive freedom of printing and publishing.

Since the commissioners assumed Colonial Office support, their elaborate arguments for liberty of the press were in all likelihood to arm Lord Glenelg should he face opposition within the government or in Parliament. The only newspaper on the island, which was produced by the government (the *Malta Government Gazette*), excluded all discussion of politics or any other controversial matters. The removal of most restrictions would, first of all, the commissioners felt, open the door to long-term improvement:

> Any considerable improvement in the physical and moral conditions of the mass of the population must proceed from an antecedent improvement in their opinions, sentiments, and habits; and we are convinced that this improvement will be utterly impossible, till such of the natives of the Island as are unconnected with the Government, but are superior to the prejudices of their countrymen, and are anxious to enlighten them, be permitted to publish their thoughts without submitting them to a government censor.

Furthermore, the absence of political discussion exposed the government to misrepresentation and to the odium created by a presumption that its acts could not endure scrutiny. Apart from its effects on politics, censorship prevented the diffusion of information of any kind, and thus it perpetuated 'much pernicious ignorance and many mischievous prejudices.' This was illustrated during the cholera epidemic which broke out some months after the commissioners' arrival. Many people believed that the government had conspired with physicians to spread the disease in order to reduce the population, a report that was 'readily swallowed by the malignant credulity of the multitude.' Such false notions, the commissioners explained, could have been prevented by a free press. They were astonished, however, to discover that books and newspapers could be freely imported into Malta without censorship, and since there was no effective libel law, there was no sanction against those who introduced genuinely dangerous publications. Consequently, the government was denied the protection that censorship supposedly provided. The system was 'odious and inefficient; combining, to a great extent, the evils of a rigorous censorship with those of an unbridled press.'[23]

A free press for Malta was a matter of strong conviction for Austin and Lewis. Its importance, they wrote to the colonial secretary, 'will excuse the perseverance (approaching perhaps, to pertinacity)' with which they pressed the matter, and Lord Glenelg noted their 'earnestness' with appreciation. This did not mean they were dogmatic or inflexible, however: 'We are far from regarding the plan with the blind partiality of authors' they explained. Nor were they ideologically rigid, as was evident in their willingness to appease some of the fears about the consequences of a free press. They were aware of concerns that a free press might lead to dangerous attacks on the government or the undermining of military security, but since there had been no difficulty with the imported press, they did not recommend restrictions in order to assuage such fears. On the other hand, they recommended restrictions on the press to prevent attacks on friendly foreign governments, insult or ridicule of (but not argument against) religion, and attacks on private character. Thus while strongly endorsing an extensive liberty of the press, they were careful to avoid provoking opposition to their proposals and did not risk losing a substantially free press by recommending absolute liberty. They also were willing to modify their recommendations: 'Any grant of a free press, not shackled with restraints which would render it illusory, will be gladly received by us, and gratefully hailed by the people of Malta.'[24]

Despite their caution and strong support from the head of the Colonial Office, the commissioners encountered difficulties. London was very slow in responding to their report, only partly because the king's illness delayed all deliberations. Lord Glenelg decided that greater restraints on the press than those the commissioners recommended would be necessary, but he did not say why. Austin and Lewis initially thought he was vacillating and that there was apathy in the Colonial Office; and later they correctly suspected that foreign policy considerations were being pressed, and that London was responding to representations from governments in Italy, including the Austrian, which feared criticism by exiles using a free press in Malta. They volunteered amendments in their proposed libel law in order to overcome these objections. Glenelg, strongly favourable, as ever, to liberty of the press, assured the commissioners that when they met he would satisfy them that the postponement was necessary. Finally, in November 1837, after eight months of deliberation, Glenelg announced the government's assent to the principle and outline of the plan recommended by the commissioners. However, he was leaving the revision of details to the governor and the council in Malta.[25]

Sir John Stoddart was on the council, so when the commissioners learned of London's approval of their recommendation, they experienced apprehension instead of delight. They immediately warned Glenelg, and this led to new and extended delays. To allow the council the power of modifying the commissioners' drafts of the new law in effect gave the power to Stoddart, for he was the only member of the council with technical knowledge of law, and he could easily sway the other members. The commissioners also explained that they had already rejected a draft of a libel law prepared by Stoddart, and that he would prevent any measure not produced by himself from passing through the council. Furthermore, his prejudice and 'his thirst for power' were so strong that he would oppose the commissioners' draft because it provided for trials without juries in libel cases. Juries, they warned, would pay no regard to restrictions on the liberty of publication, so that those charged with libel, if tried before juries, would almost certainly be exonerated. Thus Glenelg was asked to alter his instructions so that the council could be bypassed.[26] He was urged to rule that in the event of resistance in the council, the press law would be promulgated by the governor.

Glenelg was persuaded that Stoddart's foreseeable opposition to Austin's press law ought to be prevented. There was discussion within the Colonial Office as to whether the new law could be promulgated by the governor without approval by the council (as the commissioners suggested), but Stephen, the permanent under-secretary, argued that such a course was legally dubious.[27] Glenelg decided that 'the difficulties apprehended by the Comm[issione]rs may probably be overcome without ... resorting to the extreme remedy which they have suggested.' The council was to take part in the passing of the law, but the governor was instructed to subject it to informal pressure. The members of the council, especially Stoddart, were to be told that it was the government's wish that 'no alteration should be made in any of its essential provisions after it has been revised by the Comm[issione]rs and approved by yourself.' If such alterations were made, the council should understand, the governor would withhold his sanction of the law.[28]

The commissioners had no choice but to accept Lord Glenelg's decision, but such was the strength of Austin's wish to see his press law passed that he lingered in Malta despite Colonial Office instructions to return home. The inquiry had already lasted longer than expected. As early as August 1837 Glenelg gently encouraged the commissioners to bring their work to a close, and early in 1838 this pressure intensified. This, however, did not alter Austin's determination to remain in Malta to prevent Stoddart from undermining his law. Even after receiving Glenelg's letter of 1 March calling for the close of the commission 'with the least possible delay,' the commissioners proposed that Austin ignore these instructions. Lewis was to return for consultations with Glenelg, evidently to urge that Austin be allowed to 'prolong his stay in Malta until ... the law on the liberty of the press [and other laws] could be completed and passed through the Council.'[29] Lord Glenelg, although generally supportive of Austin, was dismayed. He had already been warned by the governor that Austin ought not to be allowed to remain in Malta after Lewis departed, and he sent another letter to Austin firmly calling for his return, which the governor was to deliver in the event that Lewis departed before Austin.[30] This letter was delivered when Lewis embarked for England on 27 April.

However, Austin lingered for almost another two months, finally leaving on 17 June.

During this period Austin suffered another breakdown. Bouverie had mentioned it as early as February 1838; and by April it was sufficiently disabling for Bouverie again to warn Lord Glenelg of 'the inexpediency of Mr. Austin being left here alone.' The governor also pointed out that little progress was being made on the small revisions in the press law which Austin had undertaken and that, 'owing to the uncertain state of his health, no definite time can be fixed for the termination of any work he may undertake.' Stephen was pained to receive a private communication about the same matter, and on his return Lewis was consulted about Austin's condition.[31]

Austin's departure was delayed until June apparently because of his 'continued indisposition,' which prevented him from completing his revisions of the press law.[32] Consequently he took this work with him to finish in London. One can speculate about the cause of Austin's breakdown: once again he had not completed what he had undertaken, and since he was being called home, there would be no opportunity to work on other items on his agenda. Moreover, the press law, which was substantially drafted and was an important achievement, was threatened by Stoddart, who remained in Malta, dominating the council which would review Austin's work.

When he settled in London in July 1838 Austin resumed making small revisions in the draft press law. But whereas the delays during most of 1837 arose from hesitation in Whitehall, now the slow pace of work could be traced to Austin, and one may suspect that it was deliberate. He had no confidence that Glenelg's way of overcoming Stoddart's opposition would work. Lord Glenelg assumed that Stoddart would bend to pressure from London; but Austin knew Stoddart as a stubborn man with a fanatical attachment to his favoured ideas about juries and English law as a model for the Maltese. Consequently, Austin, knowing that Stoddart's days in Malta were numbered because his office was about to be abolished, counselled delay so that the press law would be presented to a council of government in Malta that would not include Stoddart. Austin was in a good position to hold things up, as the Colonial Office was waiting for his revisions. Moreover, he recommended that he be allowed to work on other matters before turning to the press law. This, he explained, 'might perhaps be most advantageous, even with respect to the speedy passing of the Ordinance [on the press]; for I believe that so long as Sir John Stoddart sits in the Council of Government, it would not be possible to get the Ordinance through the Council without great difficulty and delay.'[33] Evidently Lord Glenelg was persuaded, for despite Bouverie's warning that delay would create difficulties in Malta, he yielded to Austin's request but also expressed the hope that there would be no material interruption of the final preparation of the press law. Sir George Grey, the parliamentary under-secretary, disagreed but disingenuously alluded to 'reasons of wh[ich] I am not aware for postponing the completion of the Ordinance on the Press to the other matters.' Grey, more sensitive to the climate of opinion in Westminster than to that in Malta, noted that more delay 'will hereafter be a matter of reproach.'[34]

At this stage a new difficulty arose as a result of the various delays, for they set the stage for a brief but intense combat between Austin and the law officers of the crown. In December Sir John Campbell and Sir Robert Rolfe, the attorney-general and the solicitor-general, whose approval of the new law was required, listed seventeen objections to Austin's work, all but one of them technical. They found Austin's language (the proposed law was Austin's work, not Lewis') imprecise, vague, obscure; they complained about 'unnecessary detail of enumeration as well as a great deal of useless subdivision'; they were disturbed by the use of a word (semi-public) 'not hitherto known to the Law, nor ... to be found in any English author'; they pointed to expressions which were 'extremely vague, and calculated to give opportunity for great oppression' and to a distinction which was 'very difficult to comprehend'; and they could not recommend the law for adoption.[35] These were the kinds of criticism that Austin himself had directed against much of English law, and the law officers' critique must have been particularly damaging to one who prided himself on his precision and clarity.

Austin defended his work vigorously and promptly. Only four days after receiving the detailed criticisms from the crown lawyers he and Lewis returned a forty-one-page reply in which the proposed law was given a spirited defence. Austin pointed out that if the law officers had examined his supplementary notes, which were to be published as explanations of the new law, they would have seen that their objections had been anticipated. It ended unapologetically: the commissioners recognized the considerable authority of the law officers, but they, after all, knew much more about Maltese circumstances. The commissioners made one grudging concession, and the draft was changed in very small ways as a result. In contrast to his limp conduct in many other situations, Austin fought hard.[36]

The colonial secretary faced a dilemma. On one side, the law officers, who were his colleagues in the government, opposed the draft law; on the other, the commissioners 'strenuously objected to every plan ... which involved any material departure from their original project.' As Stephen explained, 'It was impossible to effect any agreement or compromise between the opinions of the Commissioners and the Crown Lawyers. They held each other to be very grossly mistaken.' Glenelg decided for Austin and Lewis. He may have been moved by Bouverie's warning that further delay would cause difficulties in Malta, an argument repeated by Austin and Lewis. Glenelg privately sent the law officers' correspondence and the commissioners' reply to the governor in Malta with the suggestion that he consider whether modifications to Austin's draft were required, but he also instructed Bouverie to submit Austin's draft law to the council (now without Stoddart as a member) for modifications required by special circumstances in Malta, but 'with a view to the enactment' of it. Glenelg accomplished 'this half suppression of the objections of the Crown Lawyers' (as Stephen characterized it), and thus provided Austin with victory. The draft was altered in Malta in only one detail, and it was enacted in March 1839.[37]

Austin's views had thus prevailed over both the chief justice in Malta and the law officers in Whitehall. This must have been immensely satisfying to him, but his sense of victory was short-lived, for during the next few months his work on Malta was scrutinized in Parliament. One of the instigators of this development was his antagonist, now out of his office as chief justice, and back from Malta, Sir John Stoddart. 'I doubt not the Commissioners will deal me some ugly blows in their report,' Stoddart told Lord Brougham, 'but I am quite prepared to return them with *compound* interest.'

Stoddart encouraged Brougham to take up his cause. He explained that the commissioners lacked practical knowledge and enthusiasm for English law, that their press law would give excessive authority to the government, and that their court reforms would submit English defendants to Catholic judges; and he did not neglect to solicit Brougham's help in gaining a pension at full salary, should he fail to obtain another judicial appointment.[38] Brougham rose to Stoddart's bait. He was eager to attack his former colleagues in the Whig ministry, and he did so on many issues. He took Stoddart's suggestions and expanded on them in Parliament with criticisms that were little less than savage.

Brougham acknowledged that Austin was useful, acute, and learned, but he was not a lawyer in constant and daily practice of his profession; this was unobjectionable when Austin served on the Criminal Law

Commission (to which Brougham as lord chancellor had appointed him), for the others on the commission were practising lawyers. However, his appointment to the Malta commission was an error of judgment, as Lewis had only six years' experience and Austin none at all. Whatever his talents, because of his inexperience, Austin was 'utterly unfitted' to serve unless his colleagues had abundant experience. The bad law now before Parliament was 'one more of the consequences of sending out speculative men to report on practical matters.'

The press law, Brougham argued, was bad on political grounds. The punishments were far too severe: 'So far from that ordinance [drafted by Austin] being favourable to the liberty of the press, he contended that it was calculated to extirpate the liberty of the press in Malta.' The previous censorship was ten times more harmless than Austin's ordinance, which 'was worthy of the time of Charles 1st ... of the Tudors themselves.' In agreement with Stoddart, Brougham thought libel law in Malta ought to have followed the English model and that juries ought to have been used. If the chief justice had been on the council in Malta, Austin's libel law would not have been approved. Thus Stoddart found in Brougham an instrument for his revenge.

Brougham also claimed that Austin's libel law was inadequate when judged by technical legal criteria, and this aspect especially called forth his venom. The supplementary notes which explained the law, regarded by Austin as so important, were confusing, a 'curious assemblage of blunders' and without authority. The language was vague, and the ordinance was a 'most incredible document' and 'full of the grossest, the most monstrous, the most incredible absurdities.' He even taunted the commissioners with never having held a brief. It never would have become law, Brougham said, if the crown lawyers had been consulted. It is evident that they had been consulted by him.

Austin also had to endure Brougham's heavy sarcasm. The former chancellor spoke of 'these most astute and learned commissioners, these most learned Thebans,' and 'these sage legislators.' Furthermore, if Austin read *The Times*, he would have learned that Brougham's comments frequently elicited laughter. Austin, with Lord Glenelg's support, had been victorious over the crown lawyers and over Chief Justice Stoddart. His victories were not reversed, but he was being made to suffer for them.[39]

Others besides Brougham criticized the commissioners' work. The Duke of Wellington was worried about the effect of a free press on the usefulness of Malta as a military garrison, and he feared it might lead to insurrection in Italy. In view of the widespread illiteracy in Malta, he thought a free press hardly necessary. The Earl of Ripon was generally critical of the commission; however, he was defending his record as secretary of state for colonies, and this vitiated his arguments, as did his acknowledgment that one of his family connections, whom he had appointed as collector of land revenue, was now destitute because the commissioners had abolished his office.[40]

Glenelg defended the commissioners on behalf of the government, but no defence could have undone the personal damage from Brougham's severe and humiliating attack. Although Austin discerned the work of disappointed sinecurists, saying, 'The reckless selfishness of these two men [Stoddart and the former attorney general, Langslow], and of their patron Lord Brougham, fills me with indignation,' Brougham's barbed words penetrated this defence. Sarah, bewildered, said that Brougham's ferocity was beyond her capacity to describe. Austin was so ill he could not leave his bed.[41]

THE ATTACK IN PARLIAMENT was not the end of Austin's ordeal. He also had to pay a price for what he had not done. The commissioners were supposed to have looked into the Maltese demand for an elected popular assembly, but although they considered the question, they never submitted a report on it. By postponing the matter, they were resisting strong pressures from both the radical Maltese led by Mitrovich and Sceberras and the moderates with whom Austin and Lewis sought to establish rapport. Strong intimations from the government had encouraged the Maltese to expect some kind of elected legislative assembly, and consequently the commissioners were urged by the Maltese to make this the first question they took up; such were the expectations that many thought the commissioners 'came out with a Maltese Magna Charta in [their] pockets.'

The reason for postponing their report on a popular assembly, according to Austin, was to allow them to become acquainted with Malta, which they would do while resolving less difficult issues like the tariff and the civil administration. They also wished to observe how political judgments were formed, and thus they looked forward to the end of censorship before making recommendations about the assembly. Austin also described 'embarrassing difficulties' that arose from their recognition that they could not satisfy Maltese expectations and at the same time meet their obligation to recommend nothing that would diminish the military and imperial significance of Malta. They were especially worried that even the moderate faction in Malta would be disappointed by the very modest change in existing arrangements that they were likely to recommend. At one stage Austin was even considering a reduction in the already small authority enjoyed by the existing council. Their worry was unnecessary, however, for during the delay the moderate and radical factions quarrelled about their goals, and most of the disappointment and even anger was felt by members of the more extreme faction.[42]

Another matter neglected by the commissioners was the state of the law. They reported on the courts, but civil and criminal law, including procedure, were yet to be examined. Not long before their arrival a committee of Maltese judges and lawyers had completed a penal code and a code of procedure for the criminal law, but since the commissioners were not satisfied with these codes, action on them was postponed. Thus Austin had these codes to scrutinize as well as civil law to consider, but he failed to take up these matters, perhaps because Colonial Office instructions discouraged codification, and also because he recognized the complexity of the issues and the need for intimate knowledge of Maltese circumstances. In the end Austin accepted the Colonial Office's proposal for the revision and adoption of the code drafted by the committee of Maltese judges and lawyers.[43]

When the commission of inquiry was formed, the Colonial Office expected it to be occupied in Malta for six months. Austin spent about twenty months in Malta and still did not complete his task. A year after the attack in Parliament he felt defensive about the situation and answered the charge of negligence to which he was open by sending an explanation of the delay to the Colonial Office. In addition to the difficulties connected with the Maltese wish for an elected assembly, Austin explained that his health was so bad that he would have to go to Carlsbad for the waters during the summer and part of the autumn.

> In so far as the delay is attributable to myself ... [he wrote to his friend James Stephen], I have rather to express regret than to offer an apology. The subject is so extensive, and its numerous parts are so interlaced, that it was impossible for me to finish the Report without a very vigorous and sustained effort. But since an unusually severe attack of my chronic malady, under which I suffered last September, I have not been competent to any effort of the kind; my spirits, memory and powers of attention having so miserably failed me, that I have seldom been equal to the almost passive employments of reading and conversation.

Austin explained that in the circumstances he could not complete the report before the end of the year.[44]

The prospect of the commission's work being dragged out yet further was unacceptable to the Colonial Office, which was no longer led by Glenelg. Lord John Russell had been colonial secretary since September 1839 in succession to Glenelg and Normanby (who served from February to September 1839), both of whom had been supportive of Austin. Russell was impatient to bring the commission to a close, for he was nervous about the government's small majority in the House of Commons. Among the things not completed was a general report on the entire work of the commission, and although to Austin that would have been a mere recapitulation of the several particular reports, to Russell such a general report would have represented the completion of the Malta inquiry and made the ministry less vulnerable to Parliamentary criticism. Austin pleaded that the commissioners had completed most of their task and had failed to report on only three matters – the assembly, the law, and the practicability of a tax reduction. Whereas for Austin this represented a considerable achievement, to Lord Russell the neglected subjects were 'considerable deficiencies.' An under-secretary, Vernon Smith, recommended that they might 'decline giving the Comm[issione]rs any further trouble,' and even Stephen acknowledged that if the remaining reports never appeared there would be little cause for regret. Russell noted that the commissioners 'are not likely to report further to any good purpose. A report in 1842 of what was advisable in 1838 will lead to no good end.' Clearly Austin worked at too slow a pace for the Colonial Office. In June 1840 Austin and Lewis were told that they could at their discretion submit additional reports but that their commission was terminated.[45]

The débâcle had no single origin. In small part it can be traced to Austin's lack of affiliation at this time with a single doctrinal view. Having complained (in the *Province of Jurisprudence*) about 'unmeaning abstractions' and 'senseless fictions,' Austin was not about to use language or argument that identified him with any of the factions or parties in Malta or in London. Thus, although suspicious of colonial governments, Austin protected imperial interests; and he was severely criticized by both those wanting liberty of the press and those opposed to it. As a result, Austin, while demonstrating the independence of his views, also lost the support of most organized opinion. His independence also meant that he judged every question on its merits without preconceived ideas, and this contributed to the slow pace of his work. The successful official investigators among his contemporaries, such as Chadwick and Senior, had systematic, theoretical understandings of the subjects they investigated, which facilitated the organization of their inquiries and directed them speedily to their conclusions and recommendations. Austin was without this advantage.

If Austin went to Malta with any preconceived notion, it was a belief that in colonial governments there were many sinecure offices that ought to be abolished. He and Lewis recommended abolition of offices with a certain relish. It is doubtful that the savings from this were very great, but the cost to the entire inquiry was considerable, for the commissioners stepped on many toes. Stoddart's wish for revenge led him to encourage the radicals in Malta, and without his efforts Brougham might not have led the damaging attack in Parliament. Of course, Austin's illness contributed to the slow pace of work, especially after his return to London, but his symptoms might not have been so severe if he had experienced less anguish about being at the centre of controversy. Finally, Austin was unlucky, for after enjoying the support of Glenelg and Normanby, he faced in Russell an impatient and unsympathetic colonial secretary. Yet even this misfortune would have been avoided if the work had not been dragged out so long.

The Malta experience was a personal débâcle for Austin, despite his and Lewis' considerable achievements. Most of their recommendations were adopted: liberty of the press; reform of all administrative departments, some of which were entirely remodelled; reform of the tariff office, and custom duties, and abolition of the grain system; reform of the government charities; improvements in the university and the lyceum, and the establishment of elementary schools (in which Sarah played a large part); the formation of an efficient civil police; and the simplification of the appellate jurisdiction and the abolition of the offices of chief justice and attorney-general. Furthermore, when he became colonial secretary Russell was told by his predecessor that the changes in Malta 'seem to be proceeding with general concurrence and very great practical benefit,' and this included Austin's libel law, 'of which he heard so much at the early period of the Session and many of the provisions of which were so obnoxious to ridicule that it was no easy task to defend them; nevertheless [it] does not work ill. It prevents by its terms abuse, and by its enactment has secured greater liberty of the press than was ever dreamed of there before.'[46] This judgment was confirmed by the governor in Malta; after a trial of one year he reported that the law worked well and required no alterations, and consequently Russell submitted it to the Privy Council, where it was sanctioned.[47]

Austin could have felt vindicated by this outcome and by words of praise from Nassau Senior and James Stephen. Senior told Sarah Austin,

'All that I hear of your joint proceedings is admirable. I believe commissions to be the best instrument of government and yours to be the best of commissions.' Austin also heard that Stephen had expressed 'high admiration for Austin's commissionership.' All such praise, however, was communicated privately. There was no official expression of appreciation for his services, and this embittered Austin, as it did Sarah.[48] The greatest bitterness, however, came from Brougham's attack and the public humiliation it brought. This was made worse by Austin's pride in his clarity and precision, and by his belief that his special calling was drafting and codifying. To have had his drafts criticized by a former chancellor and the crown lawyers must have pained Austin, as did his awareness that the work on codification and other aspects of the law were among the few things he had left undone.

Unlike Lewis, who went to work at the Poor Law Commission shortly after his return to London and soon thereafter published his *Government of Dependencies* (1841), Austin had nowhere to turn. If he had hoped that his work in Malta would be a springboard to other government appointments, his disappointment must have been very great.[49] To Sarah, on the other hand, the Malta experience reinforced her awareness of inner strength, for she conducted herself courageously during the cholera epidemic, helped to foster primary education, organized the sale of Maltese crafts in England, and above all displayed sympathy and understanding for the Maltese. Moreover, she was eulogized in the *Malta Government Gazette* and was affectionately called 'La Signora Commissionaria,' and she must have sensed that she was widely regarded, as a quarantine guard put it, 'as a mother to us all.' Yet this hardly consoled her for what happened to her husband. 'I am surrounded by friends and acquaintances who esteem me,' she wrote in 1839, 'and I have my daughter, a handsome and talented girl; but I dare not think of the future.'[50]

6

'Rolling up the stone of Sisyphus'

IN OLD AGE Sarah Austin gave some self-revealing motherly advice to a younger woman, also a translator, who was about to marry the most studious of Lord William Russell's sons. 'So my dear Laura you must make Arthur distinguish himself, as he can. If anybody can enter into your *wifely* ambitions, my dear, I can. Whoever felt them more strongly than I? Whoever had more ground to do so? ... Stupid, selfish women want their husbands to be devoted to them – but your love will I am sure take a higher flight and will require that the object of it should be devoted to his country.'[1]

Sarah had approached marriage with a high pitch of idealism and fervour to serve principles and worthy ambitions beyond those of mere domestic felicity. She had tossed aside the conventional aspirations of the 'common herd of little Misses,' as Jane Welsh Carlyle called them, and had aspired by severe study and discipline to become 'worthy of being a wife' of no ordinary sort. The marriage she envisaged was to be one of intellectual companionship and partnership, and she prepared herself to participate in the achievements of a man of exceptional talent who would distinguish himself in serving mankind. All her qualities – her intensity, intellectual strength, supportiveness, and endurance – were eventually to be absorbed by this mission of helping Austin in his bid for fame.

In 1835 the Royal Academy of Arts exhibited two portraits of Sarah that are suggestive of different aspects of her character as woman and wife. John Linnell's portrayal of Sarah reveals a vivid, attractive woman – the appeal of the sitter is emphasized by the manner in which she leans forward, as if listening intently. This was the portrait commissioned in 1834 by Sarah's elderly admirer, Francis Jeffrey, with whom she had a playful, flirtatious relationship.[2] Even allowing for Linnell's conventional and idealized portrayal of femininity, the alert, gentle expression, the rounded outline of hair, shoulders, and arms leave little doubt that Linnell saw Sarah's distinguishing qualities to be sympathetic warmth and 'womanliness' in the traditional sense. The idea that a reputed bluestocking who had just brought out a book about Goethe could also be exceedingly attractive astonished young Sophy Horsley when she visited the exhibition. If Sarah Austin really resembled her portrait, she wrote, 'she must be a *sweet, charming* looking *woman*. Only fancy what an idea!'[3] The photograph of the portrait, which is all that remains available to us, gives a glimpse of the deep-set eyes (according to Carlyle, intense blue) and strong brows, but it does not suggest the shell-like complexion set off by dark hair that her granddaughter spoke of. It reveals, however, such an engaging beauty and responsiveness of manner that it is hardly surprising to find that a woman of this charm and ability should have won the interest of Francis Jeffrey and Sydney Smith and the admiration of so many eminent men, including Guizot, Victor Cousin, Barthélemy Saint-Hilaire, Alfred Vigny, and Auguste Barbier, and should have drawn to her young men, some with extraordinary talent, such as John Stuart Mill, John Sterling, and Charles Buller. Even to her sailor friends in Boulogne, Sarah was known as 'la belle anglaise.' The Linnell interpretation of her is entirely in keeping with the spirit in which she was described by many of her masculine admirers, and it was also this rendering of her personality that was the source of 'infinite pleasure' to her husband.[4]

If beauty, as Sarah once declared, was a sceptre bestowed by nature, she ruled for a long time. When Cousin met her in Bonn, when she was thirty-four years old, her striking appearance made a great impression on him. At forty she is said to have looked ten years younger. Even by the time she was in her sixties and had, as she admitted 'undergone ... amplification,' accounts of her mention that she was still a 'delightful-looking person,' whose handsome features and remarkable bearing attracted attention. Charles Sumner, an American visitor in London, spoke of her when she was forty-six as 'a fine person – tall, well-filled, with a bright countenance.' He also noted, not a shell-like complexion, but one that he thought 'slightly inclined to be red,' a decidedly unfashionable face colour in that era. He did not, however, mention another blemish that was a private joke among a couple of her friends, Francis Jeffrey especially, who called her 'bellissima Barbarata.' Thomas Carlyle, also discerning a moustache on the upper lip, assured his wife that it was one 'compared with which thine cannot name itself (mole and all) in the same week.'[5]

Sarah's admirers commented on her striking attractiveness, yet they dwelt more emphatically on another of her distinguishing qualities, her engaging manner and 'large heart.' Guizot referred to this when he told her, 'You possess the great qualities of your nation, and, in addition,' you are sympathetic and expansive, which are rare qualities in your country.' She differed from cold-blooded people, Sydney Smith noted, 'a tribe to which you have no relation.' And Santa Rosa, exiled and unhappy in London, found a great solace in her sympathy during this sombre period: 'I feel myself so well understood. The philosophy of Bentham has yet left you an excellent heart,' he told her.[6] This flow of warmth also drew Carlyle to her when they first met, and he reported to Jane Welsh Carlyle that he had found a potential friend for her, 'an exceedingly vivid person, not without insight'; and a few days later he confirmed that Sarah was 'an Enthusiast, whom I think you will like.' He described how Sarah's zeal for German thought matched her ardent and eager manner, which was evident in 'a pair of clearest, warm blue eyes (almost hectically intense).' She was also affectionate, understanding, and helpful. He gave such a convincing account of Sarah's appeal that he soon found himself explaining to his wife about 'the Austin (whom you need not fear *my* liking too well).' Even Mill, the former friend turned enemy, in the slighting account of Sarah that he wrote after quarrels had soured their relationship, reluctantly admitted her 'good nature,' which was, he acknowledged, 'to a certain extent genuine.'[7]

The Linnell portrait shows us Sarah as the beautiful, gracious, tender-hearted woman, which is how she struck so many men and how she liked to think of herself. Although in the first decade of her married life she had acquired a reputation as a bluestocking and, through her association with the Benthamites, as a radical, in keeping with the conventional expectations of her day she preferred to emphasize what she regarded as her 'feminine' qualities of feeling and sympathy. Charles Buller lightheartedly alluded to this when he planned to introduce her to Carlyle as the type of Benthamite that even he might find acceptable. As Buller explained, here was one of Bentham's disciples who yet has 'taken on herself human form and nature, and is a most delightful specimen of the union of Benthamite opinions and human feelings.' She might be an intellectual, but she was still enough of the conventional woman to please Carlyle's tastes. John Sterling came to the same reassuring conclusion. He had feared that she would resemble 'what I fancied of the German authors, bestowing your mind on books and embodying it in systems, but not keeping enough of it for the real world, and home consumption,' but on getting to know her better he could only laugh at his former absurdity, for she not only had 'abundant warm feeling and imaginative sympathy' but genuine understanding and insight. Auguste Comte in a similar vein related how when he met her in Paris, he was somewhat apprehensive about her reputed '*bluisme*,' but he found that she had much '*good nature*,' which, he added, was 'not a small asset ... above all in a woman.'[8] Sarah was aware that her accomplishments might create anxiety and antipathy even in her enlightened and gifted circle. She was careful not to present herself as competing with men, but preferred to stress that women were above all to inspire or be companions to gifted men – a notion that the young men of her circle were quite content to share with her.

Another side to Sarah's personality does not emerge from Linnell's smooth and graceful painting. A portrait painted by Henry P. Briggs, also shown in the Royal Academy exhibition of 1835, is a convenient symbol of a sterner aspect of her character. The oil painting is lost, but a lithograph of it shows a profile suggestive of a strong, imposing personality.[9] Sarah's head, with the hair scraped up severely into a tightly plaited chignon suggestive of a crown, rises regally above shoulders broadened by luxuriant balloon-type sleeves. She looks commandingly into the distance and her bearing is impressive, formidable. The emphatic lines of the face and the dimensions of the figure suggest a presence to be reckoned with, a woman with considerable will power and determination. Sarah obviously had qualities beyond those of beauty, warmth, and gracefulness of manner; she possessed great strength of character – courage, resourcefulness, stamina – and natural ability harnessed by years of study and self-discipline. Jane Welsh Carlyle sensed this instantly when she met Sarah. She thought her 'the best woman I have yet found here' and observed a 'refined and spiritualized' countenance and perhaps an intellectual rival as well: 'Her talk is all about books; and, tho' I should not imagine her a much cleverer person than myself, her command of what talent she has will I find give her quite the upper-hand of any intercourse we may have.' This was also the woman about whom the Earl of Carlisle noted in his diary, 'I sat by Sarah Austin, who is clever, [and] not wholly unassuming.' In the Briggs portrait one can glimpse the resemblance noted by contemporaries between Sarah's strong profile and emphatic chin and that of her independent and spirited daughter, whose features were said to resemble Napoleon's.[10] Sarah, however, though aware of her own ability and determination, often masked them, and did not dwell on the fact that she was an immensely competent woman with remarkable energy and drive, who managed to earn sizeable sums by professional work at a time when this was achieved by only a tiny minority.

Those who knew Sarah intimately were aware of her boundless energy and competence, and certain episodes in her life illustrate these qualities. The manner in which she tackled obstacles and took command is revealed in the account by her nephew Henry Reeve of a fire that broke out while the Austins were staying at an inn. It looked as if flames would consume the whole house, 'but they (i.e., the women – mother and daughter) exhibited their wonted energy and presence of mind, to the astonishment of admiring hostlers from the Star and Garter.' While Lucy manned a pump and 'raised a flood of water from the bowels of the earth,' Sarah 'pushed a man with a pail in his hand into the thickest smoke and then followed him with another.' Reeve reported that the two women soon got the fire under control, but his irritation with his uncle smouldered: 'Mr. A. of course, teeth chattering, knees shaking, paralysed. And then on the following day, he had the face to use big adjectives, and talk of energy.' The habitually restrained Reeve for once let down the family defences.[11]

Some years earlier, at the end of August 1833, during their visit to Boulogne-sur-Mer for John's health, Sarah had shown similar mettle when a ship sank within sight of the last house at the mouth of the harbour, a small British-owned hotel, where she and her husband and, it so happened, Heine were staying. Her resourcefulness and courage during this incident won her local acclaim, a diploma from the Humane Society (deserved even though the chairman of the society was a friend), Heine's praise for courage, and mention in *Le Temps*. A violent gale was raging in the channel when a British ship, the *Amphitrite*, ran aground in the sands about three-quarters of a mile off shore. Onlookers at the hotel and some local fishermen waited anxiously for some signal from the captain that he wished to disembark his crew, but none was forthcoming. One Pierre Hénin (who had taught swimming to Lucy) swam out to the ship and shouted to the captain that there was not a minute to lose: the tide was about to turn, and the rising surf would pulverize the vessel; a line had to be thrown immediately. But his warnings fell on deaf ears; the captain would not come ashore or land his crew even after some fishermen rowed out to repeat the warnings. As foreseen, when the tide came in the ship broke up. One hundred and thirty-five people perished needlessly and the only survivors were three crew members.

Sarah described the wild night and the agitation of those on shore, and the agonizing delay as the drama unfolded. The Marine Hotel, with its shutters closed against the danger of splintered glass, 'rocked sensibly with the violence of the wind.' Outside there was 'the ceaseless lashing of the sea, and the currents of the peculiar fine sand of the Boulogne beach, sweeping up the Port with blinding violence.' Only as the first insensible crew member was brought into the hotel and bodies of dead women were flung on the beach did she and others grasp the special character of the ship's passengers. This was no ordinary cargo vessel but a female transport bound for Botany Bay, its hold filled with women convicts, many of them very young girls held for offences such as prostitution. Later on some persons argued that the captain had acted not merely as a seaman but as a jailor, and that he had not dared to release his charges. It was also revealed that the captain was the owner of the ship and that hope of saving his vessel rather than fear of losing his charges may have played a part in his fatal misjudgment.[12]

There is an apocryphal story recounted by Sarah's granddaughter that Sarah saved a woman by pulling her out of the waves, but if a woman was saved it is unlikely that it took place in that manner. The wreck, like so many others in the early nineteenth century, invited brutality and rapaciousness, and it is improbable that Sarah, who accounted for her time that night, was on the beach itself. For as news of the disaster spread, great numbers of the Boulogne multitude assembled on the shore ready to assist or loot and pillage. On the beach also were French *douaniers* with bayonets fixed in order to impose the customs and sanitary laws of the time that were supposed to protect property and to guard against contact with disease carriers. A woman could have been saved and her rescue kept secret in a generous conspiracy of silence to save her from further deportation (as a French historian has suggested), but what is documented about Sarah's effort is that she put herself in charge of one room of the hotel whose corridors were filled with corpses and turned it into an improvised first-aid station. (Other victims were brought to the two-bed Humane Society shed and to another hotel room.) In the words of a witness, Sarah set 'aside that which would have been false delicacy on such an occasion, and with firmness of mind' applied resuscitating techniques to two of the crew members and tried to restore life to two women for whom there was thought to be some hope; but the efforts for them turned out to be in vain. The spirit in which she approached such crises is reflected in a letter she wrote to one of her brothers: as she put it, one lost 'the sense of the terrible when one is actively employed and has the hope of doing any good.'[13]

Heine, who caught a cold for his efforts that night, wrote a moving account of the scene – of the screams of the women above the noise of the storm; of the agonizing delay; of the beauty of some of the young women, and of one Aphrodite in particular (for some of the women discarded their clothing and strapped their children to them in an attempt to swim ashore): 'But the ocean was as pitiless as the laws of England, it showed them no mercy and interred them icily.' Another witness wrote a parallel account in *The Times*: 'I never saw so many fine and beautiful bodies in my life. Some of the women were the most perfectly made; and French and English wept together at such a horrible loss of life.'[14]

After the tragedy, Sarah, characteristically hoping 'to give something better than tears and sympathy to the unhappy beings whom England is, or believes herself to be, compelled to drive from her bosom,' gave evidence to an English naval officer who was sent to Boulogne to conduct a government enquiry into the behaviour of the British consul during this drawn-out ordeal. He was accused, among other things, of arriving hours after he was informed of the ship's plight, and it was said he appeared wearing evening clothes, having first gone to a party. Sarah appears to have given evidence against the consul, but interestingly the telling part of her story has been lost or removed from the records that were lodged in the Public Record Office. She also wrote a long, detailed account, which she took down from the sailors she had nursed, to the editor of *The Times* about the conditions and treatment of the women on board the convict ship. She pleaded for the segregation of the young prisoners from hardened criminals and for more humane conditions: 'There was cruelty and injustice in thus binding together half-extinguished virtue and inveterate vice in this fore-dooming of female infancy to foulness and destruction,' she wrote. The women, nearly half of whom were very young and quite a few under the age of fifteen, slept in the conventional convict ship arrangement, three to a bed, and even those with children (and there were pregnant women who gave birth on board and quite a few babies and very young children) still had two other women in their bunks. According to regulations, the ship's physician was in charge of the women, but he took no notice of them, and they were left to their own devices. When rioting broke out, the ringleaders were punished by being shut up for hours in a sort of locked sentry box. Even the two hardened sailors, one of whom had been at sea since he was five years old, told Sarah that 'nothing on earth would induce them to sail again on a female convict vessel.' Sarah's fact-filled letter was a telling indictment.[15]

More insidious danger, a pestilent epidemic, for example, also did not alarm her. When she found herself in the midst of the cholera epidemic in Malta, she faced it with tough but unscientific disdain. Cholera broke out on 9 June 1837 in an asylum for the aged. With terrifying fury the disease soon gripped the entire island, causing over 4200 deaths in three months, by which time the epidemic had finally run its course. Fear, gloom, rumours, general panic, and superstition unnerved the population; it was assumed by the populace that the disease was transmitted by contact with the sick, and even doctors were unwilling to approach the dead and dying. George Cornewall Lewis did not mince words about the doleful scene as he inveighed against the doctors cowardice, the 'pestilential race of miserable pauper nobles' who fled to the country and barricaded themselves in their houses, and the priests who went into hiding, especially the bishop, who 'put himself in quarantine and will not perform any of his ecclesiastical duties.'

Sarah, appalled by the spectacle around her, tried to stem the panic by making light of the danger. She opened her house to convalescents and commanded her servants not to desert their families, for 'contagious or not, the abandonment of friends and duties was, at all events, infamous.' She also had the notion that fear was the most predisposing cause of cholera and that she could save lives by prohibiting the ceaseless timorous discussions on the subject in her house. 'This feeble, abject terror, this inability to look death in the face, was always despicable to me; it is now odious. Under its influence I have seen mothers refuse to go near their children, husbands their wives.' She was as uncertain as the experts about the cause or the remedy for the disease. 'As to cure, it is anything, everything, nothing. Nobody knows. Everything succeeds – everything fails.' Taking advice from no one, she kept to her normal routine: ate the same foods as usual, rode as ever in the suspect calm evening hours, and bathed in the sea every day – 'prohibited most emphatically, I cannot guess why.' As always, she was valiant in the face of physical danger and uncomprehending of the 'degrading and brutalizing effect of fear.'[16]

She faced less palpable unpleasantness in the same spirit, and her strength of character often stood her husband in good stead. When they returned from Malta to face a political quagmire and a government that seemed to have forgotten that Austin was waiting to be paid, he, sick in body and heart, took to his bed and remained there. Sarah, however, rallied some powerful allies, including Glenelg, Lansdowne, Normanby, and Lewis, and put this anxiety to rest: 'I had to do strange things for a woman, *contro il nostro decoro*, certainly,' she wrote to a Maltese friend, 'but a woman fighting for her husband is always in the right.'[17]

Sarah's vitality and initiative were such that she continually attempted to spark her husband into activity. Despondency was vain and useless; he had a duty to serve society. When the future of his lecturership was uncertain, she cajoled him into enlarging his audience by publishing the most general of his lectures. This, his friends felt, would establish his reputation. The small volume, *The Province of Jurisprudence Determined*, became the only book published during his lifetime and the one by which he is best remembered: 'At first he quite rejected the idea; but on my placing before him many arguments which appeared to me weighty, he consented, only saying that he could incur no risk, neither could he send for a publisher, but that if I would find one and negotiate everything, he would print them. You may imagine I was not slow to undertake nor to accomplish this.' The publisher was John Murray, to whom she wrote, 'I shall consider myself your debtor as long as I live for your handsome and prompt compliance with my request ... if you should eventually find you have made a losing bargain, I shall feel myself pledged in honour to make the best atonement I can by translating for you some German novel which you shall accept as indemnification.'[18]

Sarah was proud of her tenacity, as was evident in her description of her ideal woman: 'Nature may now and then ... endow a woman with all the qualities that become her sex, and superadd rectitude of understanding, a steadiness of purpose, and firmness of principle that any man might envy.' This strength of character was well known to some of her closer French friends, especially Guizot, Barthélemy Saint-Hilaire, Cousin, and Vigny. Alfred de Vigny, whose sympathetic insight into Sarah's life may have been heightened by his own difficult marriage to a sickly wife, told the story about 'the beautiful, the brave, and energetic Madame Austin' who owned a letter holder with a Latin motto engraved on it, which he rendered as 'With energy and good spirit'; this, he felt, perfectly expressed her manner of working and living. Sarah's granddaughter, aware of the capable women in her family, by implication referred to this recurring feature in their make up; it was a case, she said, of 'the Taylor blood being strong.'[19]

THE TWO PORTRAITS BY LINNELL AND BRIGGS may be regarded as visual reminders of different facets of Sarah's compound personality. She held to the conventional ideal of the beautiful, responsive woman, but combined with this image was another that assumed the capacity, self-confidence, and strength to mould circumstances and initiate action. Sarah admired those she thought 'feminine' but who were also the 'antipode of *helpless*' – women who had equipped themselves to be independent if need be or were capable of being genuine 'helpmates' to their husbands. The image of the modest, supportive, and perhaps self-effacing wife thus merged, but not always comfortably, with the active, initiating, ambitious, and independent-minded woman who could summon all her worldly talent to shape her life and help her husband when he faltered. Yet how could this compound wifely image be sustained and justified in the face of John Austin's inclination to withdraw from all striving? The most devoted disciple, the most discreet supportive genius could hardly sustain such a part if the other performer vacated the stage entirely.

As time passed and John Austin increasingly seemed content to withdraw from an unappreciative world and resign himself to obscurity, Sarah's doubts about her assumptions increased. Disenchantment with marriage already lurked below the surface in the early 1820s, when she felt that her husband was so dejected that he seemed indifferent to her. She had gone to Norwich to be with her mother, who was dying with terrible suffering, and John had asked her to return to London. Santa Rosa now wrote to her about this 'painful conflict of affections and duties.' We have only his side of the correspondence, which indicates a troubled situation. Santa Rosa encouraged her to rededicate herself to her husband's care. She should be proud and happy to devote herself to such an extraordinary man. To make someone of John Austin's qualities unhappy would be doubly culpable; to make him happy was sublime work because it was arduous and required tender perseverance. Sarah followed his advice and returned from Norwich for the sublime work, but her doubts about her marriage emerged periodically during the next decades.

In the late twenties, in an aside to an unmarried acquaintance, she wrote: '*You* are an independent woman, what a miracle!' Despair drew her into the improbable Pückler episode in the mid-thirties: at that time a mirage had seemed preferable to facing reality. Work still offered some respite from rumination. Yet no amount of translating could banish brooding about her fate and that of other women, and her unhappy soliloquy about marriage at times overflowed into her work, where it surfaced in unexpected places, even in notes to her translations. For example, in a note there is this cry about marriage: 'How many a heart-ache, how many a misunderstanding, how much disgust and alienation, how much secret and black despair – nay, even despairing guilt – may be traced to the want of sane notions, chastised hopes, and rational expectations, at the beginning of married life!'[20] Marriage, she declared in another work, was 'an institution or estate pre-eminently requiring the perpetual presence of good sense, self-control, moderate expectations, and a firm and humble preparation for evil and weary hours.'[21]

Her attitude to her own marriage – her deep disenchantment but determination to cling to hope – is revealed in letters to other women with problematic marriages. Anna Jameson, for example, was a professional writer who, like Sarah, earned her livelihood from necessity, in her case created by estrangement from her husband. When, after years of separation, Robert Jameson peremptorily summoned her to join him in Canada, she wrote in distress to Sarah, who was also finding the path of married duty a thorny one. Sarah received the letter at a time when the failed professorship still left its aftertaste and while she as yet had no expectation of the Malta dispensation, as Sydney Smith was to call it, that would rescue them from their ignominious sojourn among English debtors in Boulogne. Sarah responded to Anna Jameson by commenting on marriage generally. With strong feeling she wrote: 'I have done with wondering at the injustice of men – at what they exact, in proportion to what they are prepared to give or to do. To make any impression on them, armed as they are with power, backed by opinion and absorbed in interests of ambition or of business, is hopeless. Would to God one could do any good by preaching to those women who have their destiny yet in their hands. Even *that* is hopeless.' What counsel could she give? 'My first impression was to say to you, Don't go – you are absolved from all obligation to make a sacrifice which has no requital.' Yet with so much invested in her own marriage she would not relinquish all hope for herself, nor would she do so for her friend. Thus after considering and rejecting defiance she offered the advice she also gave to herself – stoic acceptance. Life was a trial, 'a discipline, hard as any Spartan boy's.' It became

> tolerable and instructive exactly in proportion as we see it to be this, and *accept* evils as either chastisements or probations, looking with a steady eye for the result that may ensue upon them ... It is most important to satisfy one*self*. The injustice of others should never warp our views of what is our duty, independently of all reference to their conduct. It is an everlasting satisfaction to have it to say, at least I have done my part. They shall find no defense or palliation there.

Admittedly life in Boulogne with a depressed man and no prospects lacked zest and flavour; Mme Campan's observation that existence was worth little more than a glass of tepid water seemed true enough.[22] Yet, regardless of the cost, duty was the only path, and she and Anna Jameson would each have to bear their cross.

Although Sarah tried valiantly to make peace with her situation, she could not rid herself of her bitter disappointment that John had done so little to live up to his high hopes or to her expectations. Even after his teaching and the Malta experience had ended in disappointment, when she realized that he was unlikely to make further efforts to seek a position, she clung to the belief that he would return to the great work on jurisprudence that lay incomplete and which she felt he alone could write. When his spirits improved and he resumed writing, her hopes were raised; she grasped at any sign that he was rededicating himself to this task. Through the years she affirmed her faith in him: all would eventually be indemnified, she felt, 'believing him, as I do, capable of bequeathing an inestimable gift to posterity.' The idealism and ambition she had shown in her youth were never entirely exhausted; Austin's 'return to vigorous employment and ... some prospect of his accomplishing the great work he [had] set himself' and his ultimate distinction and public service would give meaning to her difficult life.[23] There is a tragic dimension to this aspect of the marriage – as if destiny had locked them into immutable positions, Austin frozen into unproductivity and Sarah unable to relinquish her ambition for them both. This tension between her aspirations and his inability to complete his work haunted them before and after Malta and during the 1840s as they moved to Germany, then to Paris, and finally back to England in 1848, and it was to cast a shadow on their last decade together in Weybridge before Austin's death in 1859.

The twenty months in Malta had been a brief respite for Sarah from financial anxieties, fears about her husband's health, and the burden of translation, but towards the end of their Malta stay and on the return to London, John Austin was 'more and more sick in mind and body,' and there was a re-enactment of their situation after the collapse of the professorship. With teaching, law, and government service foreclosed, his prospects were virtually non-existent, and during 1839-40 he was for much of the time so low and withdrawn that when in 1840 Lucy married Alexander Duff Gordon, a young man with 'nothing but a small *impiego* [job], his handsome person, excellent and sweet character, and his title (a great misfortune),' Sarah found great joy and comfort in the fact that he was well enough 'to accompany his dear girl to church.' During these years Sarah, once more faced with intense anxiety, and uncertainly about their future, took over the rudder of their lives and contracted to translate three volumes of Ranke's *Ecclesiastical and Political History of the Popes of Rome* – 'no trifle as to bulk or quantity.' Her life again was 'one of continual care, effort, and labour' – so much so that she explained, 'Often it is physically impossible for me to write letters be my heart or my head never so full.' The three years in London following their return from Malta, from mid-1838 to the summer of 1841, were ones of great strain, only somewhat alleviated when the three volumes of Ranke were published in 1840. John again wished to withdraw abroad, as he had done after his lectureship came to an end, while Sarah yearned to remain in England. Sydney Smith, very much Sarah's friend, revealed his irritation with him: 'I think Mr. Austin is the *Opprobrium Medicorum*. Nothing and Nobody seem to do him any good.'[24] In contrast to their pre-Malta uncertainties, there now seemed no necessity for such a move abroad, as their finances had improved. Apart from the £3000 for his services in Malta, Austin apparently received money from his father, from whom he had 'lately experienced extraordinary kindness.'[25] The assumption that they had more ample means is also borne out by Sarah's intention to offer financial assistance to Lucy. Austin's pride as much as financial need probably dictated his preference for living abroad. He would have been satisfied with the merest subsistence, Sarah explained, 'If he had been treated with the respect and deference he deserves.' A government discerning of true and rare merit would have found some way of utilizing his 'vast and peculiar powers.'[26]

Sarah's argument that they could afford to live in England was undermined when a financial calamity loomed that threatened their recently augmented fortunes. Together with George Grote, who as a banker was supposedly well versed in such matters, the Austins had invested a sizeable amount in Mississippi State bonds, but from the spring of 1841, when there was a default, they faced the possibility that their entire investment might be lost. Meanwhile the bonds paid no interest.[27]

These anxieties may have played into John's hands, and in the early summer of 1841 Sarah once more packed up their belongings. Still hoping for better news of their investment, they travelled to Carlsbad, where John had taken the waters during the previous summer. The regimen again appeared to be beneficial, and Sarah reported that her husband was 'being set up with a brand new intestinal workshop and laboratory, item, skin equal to new – by this same *sprudel*.' On hearing this Sydney Smith wrote pointedly: 'Nothing seems to do him good in England – everything when he leaves it.'[28] Thus they began what was to turn into a near seven-year sojourn abroad – first in Germany for two years until 1843 (where they spent the summers in Carlsbad and the rest of the year in Dresden, except for one winter in Berlin), and then in

France for four and a half years, until the revolution of 1848 drove them back to England.

While the outward circumstances of Sarah's life in Germany were 'easy and tranquil,' she was always haunted by the nagging uncertainty whether her husband would rally and set to work in earnest. Her attitude to Dresden should be understood in the light of this persistent concern. Initially she was delighted by the old and beautiful city – a German Florence, some said. Visitors flocked to it to enjoy its music and art, to promenade along the fine shady walks on the banks of the Elbe, and to gather in the little coffee shops and tea gardens. 'You walk home from the most charming opera ... you are greeted with the song of the nightingale and the odours of spring,' Sarah wrote. Dresden offered the 'kindest of friends – books and works of art, good music and the prettiest of scenes.' It was not far from Leipzig and a day's journey from Berlin, and it was cheap – the release from the iron yoke of penny-pinching was a great liberation. While they were on the way to Germany Sarah had written gleefully to Carlyle of the minimal cost for 'new lives or one "warranted as good."'[29] In the small world of Dresden she could satisfy not only her cultural but also her social tastes. John and she were treated as celebrities and visited the 'best society,' which of course included the prime minister and the royal family. Her delight at finding herself part of the social scene yet free of London expense is revealing: 'At Dresden we cut the same figure as the others. I indulge myself in all sorts of ways, and carry on as the other ladies do.' And what did all this cost? – 'The whole winter not the price of one London [gala] dinner!' While in Dresden Sarah wrote brief commentaries on art, travel, and literature for the *Athenaeum* and review articles for the quarterlies. Mill offered generous encouragement and praise: 'I think it [an article] is a kind of writing which suits you,' he wrote, and he felt it was probably 'a better speculation than translating.'[30]

Life in Dresden would have been agreeable to her if she could have seen an end to it, but John insisted they could not consider London, especially as news about their investment worsened. During their first winter abroad Sarah told Guizot, 'This exile, dear Sir, – it is hard to bear; but the Americans have stripped us to the bone.' Mill watched for news of the Mississippi affairs 'sedulously and interestedly' and continued to reassure Sarah that the debt '*must* ultimately be paid,' but he was to be proved wrong.[31] It is difficult to determine the amount they lost, but to judge by Sarah's calculation that £2000 in interest was owed to them by 1854, the principal lost must have been considerable, perhaps as much as £4000. To make matters worse, in 1843 a company in which once more both they and the Grotes had invested went bankrupt. News of financial misfortune pursued them during their years in Germany. 'No good news from America; to the contrary,' Sarah wrote from Berlin in 1843, and her hopes for an early return to England evaporated.[32]

Dresden's flaw was that while its tranquillity was beneficial to John – 'his misanthropy ... settled into a calm *contemptio rerum humanarum* [sic], which is more bearable to himself' – this did not allow him to write with greater ease.[33] In 1842 he produced an article for the *Edinburgh Review*, but he over-laboured the writing as much as ever, and there were the usual interruptions because of illness. Mill hoped that 'the consciousness of having *achieved* something' would have a good effect on his health, but the strain of the writing was such that Austin waited for five years to publish another article. Dresden in the long run, Sarah felt, was too lulling, too bereft of the stimulus of public debate for someone with Austin's temperament. 'If my husband proposes to return to Dresden,' she wrote from Bonn in 1842, 'I really think, for the first time in my life, I shall oppose his project. Is life so long that one can afford to throw away years? To vegetate, without any sphere of usefulness, any interchange of ideas, any society? Mr. Austin needs a different atmosphere.' As for their summers in Carlsbad, where Austin took the waters, they were wholesome enough but hardly a stimulus to work. Sarah agreed with Nassau Senior, who complained that he never found this watering place 'favourable to any part of the body except the stomach and the skin. It certainly does not stimulate the brain.'[34]

But in spite of wanting Austin to leave Germany Sarah remained an admirer of some aspects of German life: 'The religious toleration – the sentiments about art – the respect for science and literature – the simple frugal habits (in most parts), all these are qualities which so exactly accord with our tastes and opinions. Were Dresden but nearer to England.' Yet she longed for England, Lucy, and an end to her 'banishment.' She sighed 'to *rest* and [for] a cottage in England,' instead of roving from one watering place to another and alternating in Cinderella fashion between makeshift arrangements of sorts and being presented as a personage and a *Gelehrte* at provincial courts. Her nostalgia even for the 'suave and tranquil' landscape of her country filled some of the articles she wrote for the *Athenaeum* (ironically as its foreign correspondent). She extolled the English countryside, its villages and greens, its hawthorn hedges, winding roads, and even its 'moist and temperate' climate. 'Where can I find a Suffolk upland meadow, golden with cowslips?' she mourned, where on a hot day, 'the cattle ... standing under trees, or knee deep in the pond –

doing as they like – show me that here.' The salons had not obliterated memories of her East Anglian childhood. 'Never believe anybody who tells you that *anything* is *like* the idyllic beauty of England,' she declaimed. At times her yearning for home led to absurd dramatization: 'My children, my old friends, my country! with these I want to spend the rest of my days and to die!'[35]

John Austin, however, would not consider a return to England and decided on France – his favourite country – perhaps partly because his spoken French was so much better than his German, which on occasion he pretended not to speak at all.[36] Weary of 'new experiments on society, new ground to take up in life,' and anxious about the cost, Sarah approached Paris in 1843 with anxiety. Once settled, however, she discovered that it was far more agreeable than she had anticipated. The tradition of the salon offered an established place for an intellectual woman with strong political interests, and soon she became acquainted in varying degrees of intimacy with political and literary figures such as Mignet, Barthélemy Saint-Hilaire, Tocqueville, Thierry, Léon Faucher, Bastiat, Dunnoyer, Lavergne, Circourt, Lamartine, and Chevalier. Barthélemy Saint-Hilaire has described Sarah's salon: 'Though her means were very modest, her house was the meeting place of Frenchmen and notable foreigners who were passing through Paris. Lively intellectual conversation alone sustained these gatherings ... Managing a salon in such circumstances is an art given to few women.' A more detailed picture has been left by the German writer Heinrich Laube. In her rooms, he reported, Frenchmen, Germans, and English mingled and conversed about European literature and politics in three languages. When he was there Lord Normanby, the English Ambassador, a giant of a man, towered over the others in the small rooms. Also present were Ampère, Alfred de Vigny, Ary Scheffer, a nephew of Herder's, and shiploads of lean Britons en route from India. 'This tower of Babel,' he noted, 'the hostess dealt with admirably.' Obviously he was impressed by Sarah and her cosmopolitan circle. Not so Sydney Smith. He allowed that her visitors were 'very splendid,' but he chided, 'You seem to have too much talent in your drawing room'; he preferred more of a mixture.[37]

During these years in Paris, John and Sarah also became acquainted with Auguste Comte. John Austin had expressed a desire to meet him, and Mill arranged the introduction, explaining that Austin was an old friend of his father and himself and 'a man worthy of your sympathy, whose conversation is full of just and profound ideas.' He also praised his high intelligence and superior character: 'I could not name you a man whose friendship is more precious to me.' His comments about Sarah were more qualified; she had a reputation as a superior person – 'a reputation deserved in certain respects.' Comte, however, became fond of Sarah, who was an assiduous attendant at his Sunday gatherings.[38]

In contrast to Dresden, Paris offered nearly an excess of stimulation, both social and political. Sarah found the kaleidoscopic political scene so engrossing that she complained it was difficult for her 'to be tranquil and assiduous.' Long periods of intense concentration were essential, for, as she said, she came to Paris with 'a millstone round my neck – 1000 pages of closely printed German, very difficult in matter and style to put into English within a given time.' At the end of 1843 she had contracted with Longmans for her second major translation of Ranke – his *History of the Reformation* – 'no joke this,' she told Napier. Ranke apparently thought the same, for he told her he admired her courage in undertaking the book, and Sarah later said that it turned out to be 'as tough a job as, I think, I can ever encounter.' In addition to the length of the book (she published three volumes between 1845 and 1847), she was harassed by the speed with which the translation had to be done and by its difficult matter and style. The intense toil on this work, the weariness of hand and eyes it caused, remained a sore memory that she recalled as an old woman when she urged another translator 'not to overwork herself as I have done, when I translated 3000 large octavo printed pages of Ranke. I used to write eight and nine hours a day. It was killing and that was only one work out of many.' She also continued to write articles in Paris. In 1844 her pace may have helped bring on heart trouble. The fact that she had put on a great deal of weight also cannot have helped her health. 'If she were but five or six stone lighter,' James Stephen wrote while visiting Paris, 'but so much material bulk is an antidote to enthusiasm.' Sarah's heart condition led Madame Guizot's physician to prescribe a new regimen. 'I am condemned to *complete repose*,' she reported. 'This I *cannot* take – but I work slowly.' This translation of Ranke, 'my opus,' as she called it, was to go into repeated editions. Her hard work in Paris resulted in a translation that is still in use.[39]

Meanwhile John, as ever, lay fallow. When in 1846 he suddenly resumed work Sarah was overjoyed. She explained to the editor of the *Edinburgh Review* that his encouragement of the project brought tears to her eyes. The article he wrote, entitled 'Centralization,' appeared in 1847 and was the only work he published during the four and a half years in Paris.[40]

The time in Paris had special significance for Sarah, as they laid the foundation for an intimate friendship with François Guizot, which lasted for twenty-four years, that is, until her death. What led one of the most powerful men in France to become a close friend of a struggling English literary woman? Why would she turn to a man so preoccupied and known for his austere personality and cold, forbidding public demeanour? She undoubtedly provided him with an additional link to intellectual life in England, a country where his reputation was a matter of considerable pride to him, and Sarah, who was given to approaching eminent political figures in worshipful tones (as some of her less than attractive correspondence with Gladstone, Lansdowne, Grey, and Brougham shows), may have felt that in an age of patronage some good might redound to her husband from such an acquaintance. Although the relationship may have been furthered by such motives, in time it outgrew mere self-serving considerations and the tone between them became that of affectionate friends. Sarah came to revere the private man – the devoted son and father, the loyal friend, the politician who in defeat serenely returned to his scholarship and writing.

She had met Guizot at Lansdowne House in 1840 when he was ambassador to London (though he had sent her French government documents on education earlier); later she dined with him at the embassy, but typically Austin was not with her on either of these occasions. After a mere seven months in London, Guizot was recalled to Paris to direct Louis Philippe's ministry, and not long afterwards the Austins moved to Germany, from where Sarah sent him long letters filled with admiration for his statesmanship. She turned to Guizot as a confidant very early in their acquaintance. While still in London she wrote frankly of bearing 'the malice of fate' and revealed that she had 'not the slightest hope of tranquillity, or freedom from grinding anxiety and toil.'[41]

Once in Paris she was drawn into Guizot's orbit and developed great sympathy for the hard-pressed politician and boundless admiration for his personal character. The atmosphere of political acrimony in Paris – 'that vast cauldron of seething corruption' – appalled her and made Guizot's equanimity and aloofness appear all the more noble. He alone, she felt, stood above the rancour of a 'society full of vice,' and what some saw as disdain and arrogance she interpreted as contempt for demagogy. Her observation of his private virtues for the most part blinded her to his political failings. Soon she became a frequent visitor to the Guizot household in Paris and a friend to his mother and children. Guizot's mother still played a significant role in his life, for she headed his household and raised his children since he had twice been widowed.

There was affinity and sympathy between Madame Guizot, a Calvinistic, sorrow-laden woman with a veneration for learning and loyalty, and Sarah, schooled in the high-minded, moralistic, duty-bound gospel of the Octagon Chapel, and Sarah soon became an intimate of all the family.[42] The ease between them all became such that even John Austin joined his wife for a stay at Guizot's country estate in Normandy, as his only other guest. At this close range Sarah saw only the patriarch of a pious, cultivated, and affectionate family, the man of feeling and sentiment. 'I see him often and intimately, with only his mother and children, and I respect and love him more and more.'[43]

Guizot's embattled political situation during the 1840s made Sarah's companionship especially valuable. Her affection and interest were a refuge from the abrasiveness of political life. It was, after all, reassuring to be told that he embodied all the moral qualities of the dedicated statesman: 'As to the life you lead, I have the most lively conception of all its disgusts, which are a thousand times worse than its fatigues. But I have such a profound persuasion that there is nothing which can give so much value to life as the fulfilment of great duties, the conscious obedience to a high vocation, that I can hardly regret it for you.'[44] Such veneration was not a matter of indifference to a beleaguered man who yearned, as he said, less for physical rest than for rest of the spirit. Sarah knew precisely how to divert him by drawing his attention to subjects such as history and literature: 'The truth is, we do not talk much about politics. I think it is *humane* to Mr. Guizot to try to get him upon other topics.'[45] In her company Guizot could momentarily, as he put it, enjoy repose and refreshment midst all the rancour; her sympathy was a temporary shield against the abrasiveness around him. It was a role Sarah cherished and probably had hoped to play for her husband: in due course this debt of supportive friendship was to be repaid amply by Guizot.

THE CATACLYSMIC EVENTS OF 1848 ended Guizot's political career and gave Sarah what circumstances had until then denied – an end to exile and a home of her own near her daughter. She had hoped to live near Lucy in Kensington, and this seemed feasible, for their financial prospects were much brighter since Austin's aged father had drawn up an elaborate will in the summer of 1846 by which they became the beneficiaries of a trust that would add substantially, but not enormously, to their income. John Stuart Mill was presumably alluding to this when he noted that Austin's financial matters were now 'settled in the manner you desire.'[46]

The Austins' income was also augmented in 1848 when Sarah was granted a yearly pension of £100 on the civil list for her translations of German works. Such pensions were increasingly being given on grounds of distress rather than on merit alone, and she had some qualms about accepting it. That Harriet Martineau, amidst much publicity, had declined a similar pension on the principle that Parliament and not the crown should give such grants did not help Sarah's peace of mind. 'Miss Martineau is the last person with whom I wish to enter these or any lists,' she complained. Cousin, one of the friends to whom she voiced her doubts, was reassuring: 'It will come in useful,' he told her, 'and you are perfectly worthy of it.' Hallam told her that Harriet Martineau's refusal arose from false pride: it was arrogant of her to set up her own standards that were not in keeping with 'the etiquette of our constitution.' Sarah accepted this point of view and told Guizot, 'If I had been disposed to *faire effet* I should have rejected it with disdain like Miss Martineau, and called it robbing the people, etc. etc. But I have done no such thing. On the contrary, I told Lord John that though I could not have taken it on the score of *want*, I accepted it with pride and satisfaction, as a proof that my humble labours have been thought useful.'[47]

In spite of their more ample means, John Austin continued to object to a London residence. After a trial of a furnished house in Weybridge, they settled there into what Sarah described as two rambling old interconnecting cottages under one roof, in what was then, according to her, very wild country, with woods, commons, and heaths of fern and gorse, yet less than an hour by train from London. The substantial, fairly large house with its living room opening on a fine old lawn and garden still stands, though the garden was more extensive in Sarah's time. Even the name has hardly changed, though it is now more appropriately known as Nutfield House rather than Nutfield Cottage. Sarah liked to stress the humble cottage aspect of her home, a building of very ancient origin. She was obviously enchanted by their 'tiny retreat,' the fine pine woods, the fragrant heath: 'Mr. Austin and I shall be very happy to see you under the shade of our nut trees [where you can] steep your soul in the beautiful "green and blue" of which I am never weary.' She immersed herself in the half-forgotten pleasures of rural life. 'I am prodigiously busy and happy in a childish way, and not the least of my happiness is to find out how much of the child survives all the vain experiences of life. How the flowers and birds retain their old charm and are still as near to me as they were at six years old.'[48]

It was also a novel delight to have her family at hand. A favourite nephew, John Edward Taylor, lived in Weybridge with his family; in the summer of 1849 and 1850 Lucy and her children spent the summers in one part of Nutfield, and in 1851 Lucy gave up her London house and moved to Esher, only four miles away. There were great compensations for this end of their wandering existence. Sarah now savoured the humbler pleasures: 'When I am tired of writing I shall work in my garden, sew, or busy myself in the weighty minutia of my house.' She still travelled a good deal, sometimes with her husband (to the seaside at Cromer and Ventnor and to friends in country houses), but she was content to avoid London, though she did go occasionally – to prove to herself that she was not forgotten, she said. Mostly friends came to see her in Weybridge, and her arrangements for this were characteristically practical and well-suited to her heart ailment. As she told one visitor: 'I will be at the Station, *on the bridge*, in my pony chaise at the hour you mention. We will have some luncheon and a little drive ... then I will take you back to the *inevitable* train.' Driving about in the pony chaise, wearing what her granddaughter called a hideous poke-bonnet, became a daily diversion, and a friend thought that Sarah had found her master in the pony's strong will.[49]

Sarah's pleasure in their tranquil existence was enhanced by the obvious contrast with the state of affairs in France; and her domestic contentment mingled with her pride in England's political stability. We even have an unusual glimpse of Austin at one with the universe: 'All is so bright, so serene, so undisturbed. Under the large nut trees before my door sits the nursemaid with my grandson in her arms ... Janet busy gardening. My husband rolling the gravel walks. The birds singing in full chorus – all nature resplendent, tranquil, harmonious.'[50] Her return to England gratified a personal longing and a growing sense of national pride, which accompanied her move to conservatism. Whereas earlier she and John Austin had disdained English commercialism and narrowness, now she thought of herself as taking refuge in 'this our magnanimous Fatherland; in which daily prayers and daily thanksgiving seem all too little for one's sense of strength and the immunity [from revolution] God has given to it.' The letters from Paris did not tempt her to return there: 'I am too happy to be out of so unpromising and mortifying a scene,' she declared.[51] The suggestion that she might wish to move back elicited a page-long cry of outrage: 'And what should I, who have the honour and the happiness to be born an Englishwoman, and who am free to live in so peaceful, so strong, so noble a country in quiet and satisfaction; to watch rational progress and to contemplate the elevating spectacle of the force of steadfast will and the sanctity of venerable institutions, why should I abdicate my privileges and go to Paris?'[52] Sarah's life in the 'matchless nest' was more domestic than her former existence, but she was still energetic with 'superabundant employment for head and hand.'[53]

One of the things that occupied her after she settled down at Weybridge were translations for Guizot. She had translated an article for him in 1848 and his brief *Democracy in France*, and in the autumn of the following year she began translating another short work of his, *On the Causes of the Success of the English Revolution of 1640-1688*. As always there was a race to achieve the simultaneous French and English publication date, and Guizot and she planned that she should undertake the winter Channel crossing and stay with him at Val Richer to speed up the translation by working in tandem with him – as soon as he finished writing, she would begin translating. She would also use the trip as an opportunity to bring back the remnants of their Paris existence. Though Austin had been warmly invited by Guizot and promised a good library, no visitors, and tea instead of coffee, he declined the invitation; he did not wish to interrupt his work, he explained.[54] On Sarah's return, he did however help her with the translation, which, though it was short, was perplexing, because Guizot's style, according to Sarah, was not the best. It was always more difficult, she said, to translate French than German into good English because the use of large abstractions in French gave a terrifying vagueness to thought. On translating French, she complained, 'Cinderella's ball clothes drop off, and leave her dirty and ragged.' To her consternation she found that 'it is not only words, but ideas (that is, distinct ideas) that one has to furnish.'[55]

During the 1850s, Sarah, who had turned sixty in 1853, did no more major translations. The translation race was ill-suited to a weak heart. Instead she now preferred to write or edit – tasks she sometimes took on in loyalty to friends, as when she selected and edited a portion of the letters of Sydney Smith. Not surprisingly she ran into problems about his irreverent language.[56] 'It is difficult to write about the brave Sydney,' she told George Cornewall Lewis, 'because people will have him be what he was not – parsonic.' In 1854 she expanded and wrote connecting narrative for a series of reviews she had written in the forties about German history and published them under the title *Germany from 1760 to 1814, or Sketches of German Life*. In 1859 she wrote a long article about France in *Bentley's*, and during this decade she also wrote a variety of short pieces and articles, including some for the *Spectator* and the *Athenaeum*.

From 1848 onward she also sometimes worked for or with her daughter and granddaughter, and even her nephew Henry Reeve. Sarah could now pride herself not merely on having built up a career as a translator and reviewer for herself but also on having launched her daughter and grand-daughter on the same path, where they also earned laurels and supplemented their incomes. Sarah had founded a family industry of three generations of translators.[57] Her correspondence with editors in the fifties shows how she was also still proposing all sorts of schemes, but fewer than formerly came to fruition. Her reduced output was enforced when in the early 1850s she had a serious recurrence of heart trouble and suffered from liver and lung complaints. This, she explained, was 'all the fault of the heart – which poor thing cannot do its duty to its dependents.' For a brief while she was despondent and complained, I will never recover my power of action or endurance, and I only live by the aid of a thousand *tedious ménagements*,' but soon she declared, 'I am naturally *speranzosa*, I do not give up.'[58]

There remained, however, the old nagging worry about the effect on Austin of this atmosphere of domesticity and relative ease. As Sarah put it, there was always a 'but' in her life, and as ever it was Austin's unproductivity. As she had told Guizot, 'I would be content to live anywhere and anyhow if I could see that his great mind was leaving some worthy record of itself.' Paris had not stimulated him to write anything very considerable, any more than Dresden or Weybridge seemed to do: the inner conflicts that impeded him were beyond the reach of mere changes of locale. Austin read and pondered books, 'turning every part of his subject over a thousand times in his mind,' but he avoided the tension and difficulties of committing himself on paper; 'though the head works, the hand is absolutely inert.' Sarah had to face the intense mortification (the bitterest suffering of her life, she said) that all his learning and tortured thought and all her sacrifices and ceaseless efforts would be fruitless. She observed, 'He continually turns to what he *might* have done, what he *would* have produced, what he had mapped out in his head, had he received any support or encouragement – had even the barest pittance been offered him on which to live and continue his labours.'[59] Sarah poured out her anguish about all this to the ever-sympathetic Guizot: 'The trials of my life have been numerous, various, and I may say, some of them, hard to bear. But all the rest shrink into insignificance compared to the *despair* of contemplating day by day and year by year my husband's *resolute* neglect or suppression of the talents committed to his care, especially since he was one to whom the *ten* talents were given.'[60] She finally concluded that her husband would do nothing to vindicate his honour and her faith in him. His great faculties would remain veiled from the world. He was content to continue 'wearing away his life without devoting any part of his great power to the service of mankind, or leaving behind him any but the faintest trace of what he is.' His inability to resume his work, his reiteration of his bitter feelings, had 'become a sort of chronic malady, for which I see little hope of a cure.' Just before his death in 1859, Austin published the pamphlet *Plea for the Constitution*, and this was his final publication. In the previous twenty-seven years he had produced two essays – a pitiably meagre output for a man who had claimed to devote his life solely to intellectual effort and who had little other employment. In the last years of his life, Sarah found some measure of acceptance that all her striving had been in vain, but she never entirely made her peace with it. As she explained to Landsdowne, 'tho' resigned I was never reconciled to it.'[61]

NO MATTER HOW CONTENTED AND PLEASANT life in Weybridge often appeared, there was always the Austins' mutual suffering at this bitter failure. 'The thing goes on in the same manner,' is how Sarah put it. John Austin's despondency and inablity to set to work created a web of circumstances that warped both their lives. Obviously his withdrawal cast a terrible shadow on mundane and significant aspects of Sarah's existence, and she became 'his fellow sufferer.' She had told Carlyle, 'I so seldom hear the sound of a laugh,' and, according to one of her brothers, even a smile was not common.[62] Yet there was great variation in Austin's spirits. In 1853 George Grote, whose wife, Harriet, had stayed with John and Sarah, reported that all was 'tolerably well there. Austin in full force.' Other visitors might report him in very good form one day, holding forth vehemently on some favourite topic (while shoving pinches of snuff up his nose), yet shortly afterwards Sarah would report that he stayed in his room day after day, refusing 'almost all society, all movement, all recreation.' Nor did he grow more reconciled to the world with age, for Barthélemy Saint-Hilaire recalled that 'he loved solitude, and even in his own house no one saw him until dinner, at which he did not always assist.'[63] Even when his spirits were tolerable, he still usually refused to accompany Sarah to social events, and more often than not she went out alone or with her daughter. In accepting an invitation to visit Gladstone, for example, she explained that her husband, 'an incurable recluse,' would not be joining her. After his return to England, Austin continued to see little of his acquaintances; his relations even with those who esteemed him – Senior, Erle, Stephen, Mill, for example – were formal and distant. He lived outside the world, and his bitterness and *dégoûts* with mankind were nourished by this isolation. Well might Sarah repeat for decades that 'the great evil and burthen' of her life were her husband's 'bad health and worse spirits.'[64]

Austin's withdrawal and Sarah's reaction to it led to a complex relationship of interlocked needs and dependence. Unfortunately we have mostly Sarah's voice to give evidence, but her account is corroborated by contemporaries such as Harriet Grote, who knew the Austins intimately for about forty years. After John Austin's death she commented on how Sarah had moulded her life around Austin: 'It is clear to all who knew him well,' she wrote to Sarah, 'that to attempt to *serve* such a man was to roll up the stone of Sisyphus – nothing short of your indomitable zeal, activity, and tact, would have carried your husband forward in any form of professional enterprise.'[65]

The relationship between wife and husband had been anticipated in the unusual tone of John Austin's engagement letter. He had asked Sarah to be his companion, helpmate, and psychological support, and she had been eager to lend him her strength, to play a part, and become a genuine participant in a noble ambition. Soon, however, she also became his agent, protector, apologist, nurse, and secretary. From the start his bouts of nervous collapse led to a pattern of care and pampering that never ceased. There were times when she was reluctant to leave him alone. 'My life has been one continual and anxious nursing,' she said. The nursing included physical care as well as extreme psychological protection – perhaps well beyond what his condition required. Her determined effort to smooth his path included continuous efforts to circumvent the nervous fussiness, 'the 10,000 Umstände,' and the excessive scruples that characterized almost everything he did.[66]

In the early decades of their marriage she attempted to find appointments for him; later she struggled to induce him to return to writing. It was a delicate task to promote Austin, to allow for his sensitivity and work habits, to ensure that he would meet his commitments. She made herself not only his caretaker and amanuensis, but also his interpreter and mouthpiece. Nothing better illustrates Sarah's persistent efforts on her husband's behalf than her striving to get him to resume his work. If there was any indication that he might resume his writing, she was available to outline his ideas and to seek a publisher. She wrote as his surrogate: 'He would have written himself,' she explained on one occasion, 'but he has the bad habit of thinking I can express his meaning, and he has a sort of scruple about troubling you.' At another time she explained: 'His ill health and all its train of incapacitating consequences unfit him for being his own interpreter.' In another instance she explained, 'Partly at my own desire, partly at my husband's, I take upon myself ...': there is no doubt that Sarah took a great deal upon herself. She outlined articles and sent pleading letters to elicit interest, to the point where it seemed she could well have written the article herself – something she eventually did in the 1859 article on France.[67]

This smoothing of the path for Austin so that he might return to work and receive some intellectual recognition that would sweeten his life is revealed most strikingly in Sarah's approach to Macvey Napier, the editor of the *Edinburgh Review*. When Austin was pondering a review article on Charles Dunnoyer's book *De la Liberté du Travail* she initiated overtures to Napier. Apologizing for her husband's previous failure to deliver articles, she explained she was 'well aware how capricious his conduct must have appeared.' Napier was 'to forget his omissions for [her] sake' and make allowances by recalling 'the occasional state of his health and spirits ... the calamities and cares by which [they had] been bent for so long.' Meanwhile she assured him, 'This time you would not have to fear disappointment ... for his heart is very much in the work.' Her pleading left out no chord: if Napier could incite him to work she would regard him 'without the least exaggeration as the greatest benefactor.'[68]

She also tried to foresee some of the hurdles that might trip Austin up on the way to meeting publishers' deadlines. Her anxious watchfulness that there should be the generous margin of time that he needed is clear in her tortuous negotiations with Napier: 'The article would not, of course, be ready before the October number, perhaps not in time for that. I suppose you must have it earlier in September. Perhaps it w[oul]d be safer to promise it only for the January No.' When it became clear that Napier would go to great lengths to be considerate, the effusiveness of her thanks were poignant and revealing: she told Napier, 'You have guessed all that I have to feel about my dear and honoured husband, whom nature and fortune have so unequally endowed.' Nothing he could do for her elicited her gratitude as much as 'any stimulus or encouragement given to *him* to employ his great power.'[69]

Another ally Sarah sought in her crusade to bring Austin back to his 'mission' was John Murray, the publisher of *The Province of Jurisprudence*, which by the 1840s was out of print. She wrote repeatedly to Murray that he should 'urge [Austin] to go to work immediately,' and her negotiations with him on this subject continued for years.[70] In her effort to find an audience for her husband she cast her net wide among their friends. Thus Lansdowne was also requested to show some curiosity about Austin's efforts: 'A word or two of interest and encouragment now and then from your Lordship would be above all price – and to be permitted to give you occasionally some report of his progress is all I ask.' Brougham was similarly asked to offer some words of encouragement 'to one most worthy of them,' and Guizot was also nudged to do the same, and presumably their inquiries were passed on.[71] Such managerial efforts (however gracefully formulated) on behalf of a retiring, fastidious, fiercely proud man could border on disloyalty and betrayal, as Sarah at times recognized. This was evident in her plea to Lansdowne: 'I entreat ... that you will keep the secret of my imprudence – above all from the subject of it'; but it appears she felt driven to manoeuvre and manipulate behind his back in a manner he would have abhorred. Already in 1831 she had sent Brougham the syllabus for Austin's course of lectures, enclosing the statement that it was an act of 'conjugal disobedience'; it was not the only one.[72]

Sarah's zealous efforts on her husband's behalf were combined with an extreme protectiveness – a constant caretaking that may have helped him less than she intended. In her efforts to protect him from the abrasiveness of the world – from major aggravations as well as the most minor awkwardnesses which might disturb him – she sometimes sifted news and correspondence and withheld information. For example, when Brougham complained about Henry Reeve, she concealed Brougham's letter from her husband, explaining, 'I have not mentioned your Lordship's letter to my husband. I have my own notions of conjugal duty, and one is, not to throw upon him any part of the responsibility of an act that may possibly give offence. I lose the advantage of his advice, but on the other hand I bear all the blame – if blame there be.' When news of one more financial loss reached her in Carlsbad she delayed informing Austin: 'I think it would only put his mind in an unhealthy train, and he is not well, and it is important, while he drinks the water, not to agitate him.' Her willingness to step forward and take charge left John Austin with few responsibilities and made it easy for him to regard her as his shield against the world. He became so dependent (Sarah herself used the word) on her that he became unwilling to carry out most of the ordinary demands of life, such as writing a letter. Meanwhile she reiterated proudly, 'Here is one to whom I am of use.'[73]

She also made him psychologically comfortable by outwardly deferring to his opinion. She might secretly arrange and negotiate on his behalf, but she was determined not to agitate him by crossing his express wishes. Her deference to his opinions in the early days of their marriage is illustrated by a note to her printer brother, Richard, about an unknown matter: 'Austin thinks it better not to meddle with the subject. It must therefore go out. I am sorry I sent it.'[74] Similar compliance with John's preferences, even whims, continued later. When in the mid-fifties he 'silently but inflexibly' dropped relations (which later were restored) with their old friend (and relative, through Lucy's marriage), George Cornewall Lewis, over some unrecorded dispute, Sarah said, 'I lament this. I am his wife. It is my duty to find him right; even were he wrong.' Under the influence of his unstable health and spirits she allowed her deference and supportiveness to merge into an unwholesome submissiveness.[75]

Sarah's accommodation to her husband appears to have included a self-limiting approach to her own professional ambitions. She may have curbed her own ambitions as a writer not only to ensure a steady supplementary income from translation, but also to save his pride. His failure to complete his work and publish it might have been more anguishing for him if Sarah, who wrote with facility, had led the way to the publisher with books bearing their name. Controversy that might upset his tightly strung nerves was also to be avoided. When she was a young woman it had seemed appropriate to her friends that she should help launch an intellectual giant by her earnings from translations and reviews, but she remained reluctant to assume independent authorship and to publish her outspoken opinions, though it was evident to her and to others that she could write. After her successes in the 1830s, Mill, Lewis, Jeffrey, Barthélemy Saint-Hilaire, and Murray repeatedly encouraged her to give her talents freer reign, for example, on the subject of Germany, but she remained for the most part reticent. Her decision to subordinate her own ambitions to those she had for Austin undercut outspoken authorship, as did her terror of the press, which was reinforced by an attack on her by the tory critic John Wilson Croker and by the aftermath of their Malta service. Translating, editing, annotating – such discreet occupations seemed suitable to her as Austin's 'helpmate.' 'If I can interpret and illustrate, it is something,' she wrote in 1832 to Jane Welsh Carlyle, another 'loyal wife,' when she was beginning to break into professional work, 'and I have the advantage of remaining, what a remnant of womanly superstition about me makes me think best for us – a woman. These are "auld world notions." You know that word in my vocabulary excludes no particle of strength, courage, or activity.' Eight years later she still spoke of being as yet 'a mere expositor,' and she continued to be reluctant to assume the risks of authorship in signed articles. Better by far to subdue her talent, she felt, especially as John Austin's potential contribution to human betterment always had priority. She thus told Napier when she was arranging for Austin's article to be published, 'Think nothing about my trifles, I have enough in hand at present,' and she emphasized the same to Murray. Harriet Martineau, unmarried and by no means afraid of notoriety, could thus accusingly say of Sarah that her vanity starved her ability. She was correct at least in part – Sarah's talent was kept within carefully self-imposed bounds.[76]

Yet if Sarah curbed her talent with her husband's needs in mind, it was not without side glances at what might have been, as is revealed in a comment where she refers to 'voluntary abnegations of what [she] might perhaps have attained.' There is also the extraordinary statement, in an article she wrote after John Austin's death, that Madame Récamier's relations with Chateaubriand proved that 'every woman, sooner or later, feels the necessity of making herself a slave.'[77]

Sarah's determination to serve Austin at all costs had unwholesome consequences for them both. Since she had nursed, cosseted, and protected him, it is hardly surprising that her attitude appears to have fostered some unfortunate characteristics in him, including a selfishness of which Sarah herself became the victim. Austin became so dependent on his wife that it seems she was barely allowed to grow old, suffer from overwork, or be vulnerable like other mortals. In the opinion of Madame Guizot's physician, the sedentary life of translating played a part in inducing the heart condition that became acute in 1844. (Sarah had earlier ignored heart palpitations on climbing stairs.) John Austin, according to his brother Charles, was 'a little frightened' by her illness, and in a letter to Mill he revealed his 'mental distress' about it; but he reassured himself she was on the road to recovery, while not going as far as Charles, who thought Sarah impervious to illness. 'I can hardly believe she can ever be [fragile],' Charles Austin told Harriet Grote, 'like you and me.' When Sarah later recovered from another serious heart episode in which her life, she felt, had hung by a thread for five days, she spoke of 'the warnings' she had received: 'My reprieve does not blind me to my precarious tenure of existence. Indeed I have long felt and known it to be very uncertain, but I was not believed.' Perhaps for similar reasons she was not permitted to age in Austin's eyes, for one learns that although his hair had gone white when he was twenty-four, Sarah, in deference to his wishes, dyed hers in middle age, something she apparently did very clumsily and ceased to do after his death.[78]

In some of the rare glimpses we have of their day-to-day relationship, John Austin appears less than the lofty personality that Sarah described after his death. Indeed, he may well have been a quite tiresome, demanding, semi-invalid given to watching his health with intense self-absorption: the scraps of personal letters that were extant till recently were apparently largely about his health, regimens, and symptoms. One is bound to wonder whether his sister Charlotte Austin, who inherited Sarah's letters to her husband and daughter, destroyed them in their entirety because they might have detracted from the portrait of the high-thinking philosopher she wished to have perpetuated.[79]

Some small, less than attractive glimpses of John Austin are revealed by Santa Rosa. When Sarah was away from home, Santa Rosa invited John, but was afraid his offer would be met by 'di gelata riposta,' although in the event Austin received it with pleasure. He also appeared in an unappealing light in an incident at Boulogne when Sarah wished to make an extended visit to London to negotiate with publishers and see her daughter, whereas he wished her visit to be brief. Afraid that she would be hurried back by him, she arranged with his sister to keep house for him in Boulogne until she returned. Yet he silently but effectively objected, and Sarah explained, 'He is less willing than ever to be left, and he has never spoken a word about my going.' Nor on one occasion did Christmas lure him out of his room, for Sarah wrote, 'My husband is poorly in bed, and the once joyous table exchanged for a solitary mutton chop on a tray by my fireside. But so it must be.' With the egoism of the chronic invalid, John may have subtly exploited and dominated Sarah. She seems to have entertained a suspicion of this. To Harriet Grote she wrote, 'You know ... *my* will never passed for much. I think nobody ever had less the talent of making it heard or minded. These are things of which it is useless now to speak. *Elles ont pris leur pli*; and for the short time I have to live it is not worth while either to complain or revolt. Nor, indeed, would it do any good. For as my existence and happiness are not separable from his, we must live where *he* can be best content.' Two years before she died, she summed up this aspect of her marriage by referring to the watchful and tender care she had bestowed on her husband. 'Nearly the whole of my married life was passed ... in rendering such offices, and a very small portion of it in receiving them.'[80]

One can speculate as to the effect of Sarah's supportiveness and management on Austin's personality. Would he have been better off without her enveloping care and support? Harriet Grote asked the question after his death but failed to answer it. However, Sarah had thought about it herself. 'I often think it would be well for him if I were gone altogether,' she once mused to Guizot; 'he *must* then [exert] himself.' She spoke to friends about his 'inert ease' and revealed her doubts about ascribing his failure to work solely to his health. She told Guizot that it was 'partly from a constitutional indolence arising from ill health, [that] he dislikes all effort, and is glad to take refuge in a retirement when[?] none is necesary.' Shortly before his death she once more stated that his paralysed will was to be explained not only by ill health but by lassitude, weakness, and misplaced pride:

> What reason can he give to me or to himself? Health? But to *me*, he can hardly urge *that* [since her own health was so poor]. The truth is, that many causes, and among them some very sufficient ones, long ago conspired to disgust him with men and their judgments and their affairs; and he, poor fellow, has made this an excuse to himself for obeying his own reluctance to set about work ... It is true he was shamefully treated; but you and I know that there is another way of avenging oneself on the injustice of men.[81]

SARAH EVIDENTLY NEEDED to justify the past even to herself. When Henry Taylor sent her a volume of his maxims counselling duty, endurance, self-sacrifice, submission, and humility, she wrote to him that nobody valued his writings more than she did. His books were 'a great prop and solace to the soul of those who had deviated at all from the world's ways, and judged things according to a standard wh[ich] is not the received one.' It did her good to see his views set forth, for they led her to congratulate herself on many things that might look like misfortunes, deprivations, or renunciatons.[82] In the last part of her life Sarah was searching for justification of what she often regarded as decades of sacrifice.

Sarah's suffering in this tragic marriage of mismatched temperaments was perceived especially by French friends, to whom she felt more free to unburden herself. Barthélemy Saint-Hilaire concluded that Sarah's attitude to life, which he thought rivalled that of the Stoics, was derived not from the study of learned works but from the trials of her life. That sad thoughts often preoccupied her is also evident from her common-place book in which the longest passage she copied is one that described how suffering could only be consoled by those who had themselves experienced it.[83] With this belief, it is not surprising that one of those she turned to for 'solace to the soul' was Guizot; and once again emotional sustenance came by post.

At a period when John Austin's undeniable failure jeopardized all the assumptions on which her life had been built, Guizot, to whom she had revealed her anguish about her husband, offered her reassurance that her lifelong dedication had not been wasted. He was particularly well suited to a consolatory role, for the tragedies of his own family – the death of his father by guillotine, his mother's ceaseless mourning, and the loss of his first and second wives through illness and that of his gifted son at the age of twenty-one – had attuned him to grief. He told Sarah that life had no sorrows that had been spared him, and he had forgotten none of them. Strangely enough, the reconciling message that he offered Sarah was embedded in long letters (near-lectures) analysing French political developments. Politics were of intense interest to her, but she cherished the words of Guizot the man even more than those of Guizot the politician. In Guizot, she declared, she had found 'a son, a father, and a friend'; he was 'one of those to whom, morally and intellectually, [she] owe[d] most.' Guizot, in gallant French phrases that lose their flavour in English, endorsed her character, attitudes, and ideals. He could distil esteem, affection, and consolation: 'There are few souls and hearts with which I feel myself in such complete sympathy ... I feel so entirely *at home* with you,' he told her. When she was contemplating visiting him, he wrote: 'You have a place in my past life, at times of my greatest trials and my most cherished memories ... We will talk together – at length, gently.' The words varied, but the sentiments did not: 'You are with me, as the Catholics put it, in a *state of grace.*' This sort of soothing, all-embracing acceptance stemmed from a sympathetic insight into her situation.[84]

His most significant reassurance lay in endorsing Sarah's attitudes as a woman. At a time when she faced a reality that mocked decades of struggle, Guizot with all the authority of his character upheld values that mirrored those by which she had lived. Directly and indirectly he reassured her that he understood her life and its trials and that he admired her courage and resilience. While he esteemed intelligence and strength of character, he also put great value on the side of her personality depicted in the Linnell portrait. She gave affection unstintingly and had the talent, energy, and dedication he expected of women of quality. She was also congenial to him as the antithesis of the new emancipated woman exemplified by George Sand, who as an apostle of love had loved too little, he said, to understand or depict its reality. Sarah's intellectualism had not driven away 'tenderness of the heart.' She combined political and intellectual interest without giving up the traditional qualities of woman-hood; she had that 'dual intelligence of the mind and the heart' that he prized in women.[85] This sort of sympathetic understanding of her ideals was balm to Sarah's spirit.

Guizot's endorsement of her as a woman extended specifically to her role as a wife. He entirely approved of her wifely devotion to Austin. His own marriages had brought him a felicity that he liked to recall, and the ideal of marriage had deep significance for him. He now was able to convey to Sarah that her service as a wife had been noble and worthwhile. After Austin's death he told her, 'Not to be solitary one must absolutely possess, entirely to oneself, a human creature, and belong exclusively to her (or him.) This is the power of marriage, even for those who meet with many imperfections.'[86]

In the last part of her life Guizot's idealization of wifely supportiveness, his belief in devotion, fidelity of affection, and constancy in the face of all life's hardships, helped to reassure Sarah in the part she had played. After reading her biographical preface to the posthumous edition of *The Province of Jurisprudence Determined*, Guizot told her, 'Austin must have been proud to have inspired in a soul such as yours a tenderness so profound, so respectful, so enduring.'[87]

With Guizot's consoling and affirming attitudes to help guide her, Sarah struggled to find some measure of reconciliation. She echoed his sentiments and reiterated the constancy of her devotion to her husband: 'It is necessary for the safety and repose of one's soul to have been heartily in love, and with whom, but with one's husband? I allow for all *contretemps* and disappointments; spite of them all, there remain the embers of the *sacred fire* which the breath of misfortune, illness, or a thousand accidents can always wake into fresh life.' She even claimed that it had all been worthwhile: 'Much as I have suffered and still suffer from what is called adversity, were I to begin again, I should choose the same lot.'[88]

As Sarah and John Austin gave up some of their ambitions, they each found a measure of tranquillity. After her husband's death Sarah declared that, 'since he had given up the conflict with fortune,' his state of mind had become 'so gentle and noble, so without all alloy of unsatisfied cravings, or vain repinings, or harsh passion, or low desires ... In this blessed frame of mind all his youthful passionate love for me seemed to return, mingled with a confidence and intimacy which only a life passed together can produce.' A friend also said that the last years of their marriage were the happiest in their lives – 'a deferred and long honeymoon.' Such statements put too high a benedictory gloss on their final years together, but there seems to have been some acceptance. Sarah, again retrospectively trying to stress the greater harmony of those last years together, as ever found the appropriate words: 'The midday of our lives was cloudy and stormy, full of cares and disappointments; but the sunset was bright and serene – as bright as the morning, and *more* serene.'[89]

Her greater acceptance of the past was accompanied by a softening in her feelings about her husband's failings. Her discontent was tempered by pity and tenderness for him. In spite of all her frustrated ambitions, she became more reluctant to prod him: 'For the few years we have to live, I do not care to disturb the tranquillity of mind he has attained.' For her he was 'sometimes as a god, sometimes as a sick and wayward child – an immense, powerful, beautiful machine, without the balance-wheel, which should keep it going constantly, evenly, and justly.' She now accepted what she had recognized for so long, that he was not suited to the demands of the everyday world, and she wondered whether destiny did not owe him some heavenly recompense:

> In my heart I continually commend him to God, and pray that his great and noble soul may find a sphere more fitted to its development. With this hope I am obliged to console myself for my *bitter* disappointment – not, believe me, that he has not coined his talents into gold or risen upon them to power or greatness, but that he will depart out of the world without having done for the great cause of Law and Order, of Reason and Justice, what he might have done. To enable him to do this I should have been proud and happy to share a garret and a crust with him. But God knows our ambitions, and checks them.[90]

She even entertained the thought that she had been destined to be humbled for her pride and her worldly aspirations, and this eased the way for her to forgive Austin for his failings.

If Sarah's idealism, ambition, and self-deception seem at times to have been extreme, it is worth recalling that George Eliot in *Middlemarch* depicted a fictional heroine whom readers have for decades recognized as reflecting some observed truth about one type of Victorian woman. Like Sarah, Dorothea embarked on marriage with ardour, idealism, submissive affection, and unrealistic visions of her husband's and her own character. She wanted to devote herself to him and share and promote all his great ends. Austin's work fortunately was more substantial than Casaubon's, but there are similarities in Sarah's and Dorothea's temperaments, and their effects on their timid, constrained, diffident husbands may have been similar. Dorothea's suggestion to Casaubon that he take his volumes of notes 'and begin to write the book which will make your vast knowledge useful to the world' and her offer to write it down at his dictation may have been as cruelly irritating to him as Sarah's submission, manipulation, and constant sacrifices, which, she made clear, were made so that her husband could deliver himself of his great work. Dorothea, in the early part of her marriage, 'was as blind to Casaubon's inward trouble as he to hers,' and she had 'not yet learned those hidden conflicts in her husband which claim our pity.' Like Dorothea, in the final part of her marriage Sarah no longer struggled against the unchangeable reality: 'Now when she looked steadily at [her] husband's failure, still more at his possible consciousness of failure, she seemed to be looking along the one track where duty became tenderness.'[91] Such sentiments may now appear unlikely and highflown, but they had their roots in values with which George Eliot was very familiar and that Sarah had imbibed in Unitarian Norwich.

7

'The relation between the sexes ... the insoluble problem'

SARAH AUSTIN FACED A CRUEL SITUATION with remarkable courage and tenacity, and she retained some pity for her husband, but her character did not emerge unmarred from the experience. After years of struggle, supported by conventional assumptions about the role of women and wives, she tended to the vanity of seeing herself in heroic terms as the embodiment of abnegation and self-effacing martyrdom. The stirring of the feminist movement posed a threat to this self-image, and she reacted with a defensive antagonism and self-congratulation that are in painful contrast to some of her earlier attitudes. From late middle age onwards she abandoned many of the liberal sentiments of her younger days and became an exponent of the most traditional ideas about women. Yet she never went so far as to put her ideas into an anti-feminist manifesto to complement her husband's anti-democratic *Plea for the Constitution*. The woman question was unsettling, but she refused to meet it head on. Instead she revealed her opinions in a somewhat furtive manner in books and articles on other subjects, and in occasional outbursts in notes to translated works. It is thus not surprising that a suggestion of radicalism on this issue has clung to her – an inference perhaps drawn from her close association for so many years with John Stuart Mill.[1] In fact she became that not unheard-of phenomenon, an intellectual woman of liberal background who by the middle of the century opposed the main thrust of the movement for greater equality of the sexes: she thus justified the position she had taken in her own life and kept in step with her husband's increasing conservatism. The traditionalism of her old age is above all autobiographically revealing; it lost her a place in the history of changing ideas but gave her a social and political viewpoint compatible with her personal situation.

It might well have been otherwise – at least much of her background and early beliefs pointed in another direction. The Unitarians were among those who pleaded for wider horizons for women, and Sarah's outlook and ambitions had been cast in their mould. She had begun married life equipped with an unusual education for a woman at that time and committed to a radical cause, which for some of her close friends such as Bentham and John Stuart Mill included women's suffrage. This background combined with her strong personality, sensitive social conscience, and an ardent interest in politics seemed to prepare her for a role in the women's reform movement. She had shown that the compass of a woman's mind did not need to be confined to the narrow range of petty 'accomplishments,' and it thus appeared entirely appropriate that one of the first issues she addressed should have been education. Basing herself on Cousin's report on Prussian education, which she had translated, she became an ardent advocate of a system of compulsory national primary education, very much a minority view at that time. She also proposed that education should become as universal for girls as for boys and that the two sexes should be taught alongside one another in the same classroom, as had been the practice in Norwich in her youth. The anxiety to segregate mere children was 'one of the very suspicious refinements of later times.'[2] She also shared Austin's view that married women should be capable of enjoying property apart from their husbands, and in the early decades of her marriage she would have endorsed his condemning verdict that 'the rules of the English Common Law in this respect are in every way worthy of the savage and stupid ages in which that chaos arose.'[3]

Her enlightened views were apparent in her exasperation with German attitudes to women. In 1827 during her first visit to Germany she wrote with disdain about 'this land of dowdiness, insipidity, and slavish, base prejudice as to all that regards our sex.'[4] The education of middle-class women in Germany was deplorable. She was struck by the 'extraordinary inferiority of German female education, in proportion to the high superiority of that of men.' The intellectual place assigned to women even by the great German writers was 'the barbarian spot on the high civilization of Germany.' Men required of women that they should possess 'the virtues rather of attached and industrious servants, than of equal, intelligent, and sympathizing friends'; they sought above all to possess 'a thorough cook or a contented drudge.'[5] In Germany, she complained to Guizot, 'no man thinks of talking to a lady.' She, who had conversed with the most distinguished men of her day, did not value the parochial conversation of minor German officials, 'but my English blood boils at seeing myself so degraded. We in England are *oppressed*, – but not condemned.'[6] Nor was she to change her mind on this score, for in 1840 she wrote to Ottilie von Goethe, the poet's daughter-in-law, 'In Germany (if I mistake not) public opinion condemns women to a far more animal and menial life even than in England. Were I educating a daughter in Germany I would not consent to her stooping to court the lowest appetites of men by skill in cookery, nor their still meaner vanity and jealousy by an ostentatious abdication of all power of thinking, or right to think.' By 1854 she still felt that German women were not treated with 'the tone of frank, respectful equality – the civility neither of condescension nor adoration – which characterizes the best society in England.'[7]

Yet in time concern for women's position was to be submerged by personal preoccupations and fear of too rapid social change. The thought that women were oppressed – even partially – receded in her mind. She had been born at the end of the eighteenth century, when women's position for a brief interlude became a matter of interest and debate, but the pressure for wider spheres did not become a sustained movement till fifty years later, and by this time the pattern of Sarah's thought was set. When she was a young married woman in the 1820s the political rights of men had been the cause that stirred enlightened opinion; by the time the women's issue came to the forefront again, Sarah's personal circumstances made the topic disturbing to her. By 1857 when the Matrimonial Causes Act made divorce slightly less difficult, though still practically inaccessible to middle-class women, Sarah was sixty-four – it was late to refashion assumptions. Not that she abandoned her old beliefs in intellectual equality, but she would not join the demands for wider opportunities. By now she was entirely out of step with the progressive ideas of her time. The new attitudes seemed to touch raw nerves, for she responded with indignant cries of outrage. Her declarations about wifely duties, humility, and sacrifice became extreme even for her own day and so rhetorical that she often sounded (though she was not) as if she were an exponent of the cult of true womanhood. It was a sad, poignant reversal of the promise of her youth. She, like John Austin, was 'out of time and place.'

Sarah's traditional image of women emerged most explicitly in her writing after 1848, though she first approached the theme in the early years of that decade. The composite image of woman's place as depicted in her letters and late work leaves no doubt about her position, though of course she never contemplated a verbal collage on a subject on which she expressed herself privately or incidentally in reviews and translations. She was, however, forthright enough in letters. To Dilke she wrote that her views, 'especially regarding women, [were] diametrically opposed' to those of her relative Harriet Martineau. Women's struggle 'to force an unnatural *resemblance*' to men was part of the wider conflict 'of those who have, with those who want to have, power, which is now stirring society.'[8] In the remnants of the pre-revolutionary salons of Paris into which Guizot and Vigny had taken her, she had observed women playing a significant role, but the cost of such social equality between men and women had seemed too high for her, and she came to think that the position of women in French salon society resulted from the looseness of conjugal ties.[9] In England, fortunately, things were different; there men managed the world and domestic life was the province of most women, 'indissolubly linked with the privileges, pleasures and duties of maternity.' A woman's first and most sacred duty was as wife and mother. Women should be 'gentle, kind, loving, anxious to please and fearful to offend.' They should lead unobtrusive and reserved lives; theirs was to endure 'the monotony and obscurity of domestic life.' It was 'incalculable what comfort and encouragement a kind and wise woman may give to timid merit, what support to uncertain virtue, what wings to noble ambitions.'[10] The ostensible subject of this remark was Madame Récamier, yet it strongly recalls some of her own aspirations when she married John Austin with the hope of assisting him in his high purposes.

The personal dimension of Sarah's traditionalism is noticeable in her latter-day heroines. Sarah the woman is never far below the surface in her later work. Those she admired most were depicted as gifted women of virtue, courage, and humility who dedicated themselves to serving noble men striving for greatness. Unfortunately, suffering and the capacity for endurance frequently accompanied such a calling. Outstanding among such heroines was the Duchess of Orleans, widow of the heir to the French throne who was killed in an accident in 1842. She had fled France with her children in 1848 and became Lucy's neighbour at Claremont. Sarah's boundless admiration for her arose partly from political sympathies, but this alone hardly seems to account for the high-pitched veneration with which she wrote of this woman's 'courageous resignation' and 'womanly patience' and 'a mind made up to all the consequences of duty.' The duchess had been her husband's companion in his high duties: 'Her ambition was, to cheer him on to all great aims; to console him under the disappointments ... to surround him with an atmosphere of virtue and intelligence; to aid him by every faculty of a tender, devoted, and heroic woman, in the performance of the highest most arduous tasks that can be imposed upon man.' When misfortune struck, 'what a front she had opposed to all strokes of calamity.'[11]

Lady Lansdowne was another admired woman: 'the most perfect example of the womanly character in its truest and highest form ... in nothing greater than in her matchless humility.'[12] The wife of Rev. Whitwell Elwin, editor of the *Quarterly Review*, was also held up as an example: 'She has five children, whom she educates and attends to. She does four times as much as most active women without any fuss; with all this she is the companion of her husband, and to-day I heard her discussing the translation of an Ode of Horace with him.' Among the figures of the past she extolled Caroline, the wife of Frederick Perthes, the Hamburg patriot and bookseller, who resisted the French invasion in 1806: 'Never for an instant did she quail before danger, or cease to encourage or cheer her husband.'[13] The women she admired were those whose sense of duty, humility, and dedication to their husbands matched her own. The theme recurs in her later letters and work, and she repeatedly lauds those who in this spirit urged their husbands on to onerous but important public duties.

Sarah's traditional attitudes from the late forties onwards were nowhere more explicit than in her views on women's suffrage. Politics was an absorbing interest throughout her life, but as she succumbed to fears about 'the inexorable march of democracy,' she came to support the masculine orthodoxy that the management of national affairs belonged solely to men. The extension of the suffrage would increase electoral irresponsibility. Women's 'determination to maintain established rights with a passionate sense of supposed wrongs' and their demand for political power were part of the pervasive radicalism that was stirring society.[14] She approved of a view she attributed to Sydney Smith that it was 'vain [to] attempt to create for [women] a new and independent position in Society.'[15] She looked forward to the time when 'the world will hear no more of the "emancipation of women," or of preposterous schemes for bringing them into a sort of competition with men − God knows at what disadvantage.'[16] Women generally, with rare exceptions, were poorly equipped emotionally to participate in public affairs and made 'dangerous advisers in political matters.'[17] They were incapable of the calm deliberation needed for politics, and their judgment was bound to be ruled by their affections and passions. As for the notion of women in Parliament, such 'nonsense,' she told Brougham, was 'preposterous' and fit only for ridicule.[18] It so happened that he may have needed little convincing, for in 1835 during a debate on the rebuilding of Parliament he objected to the provision of accommodation for the admission of ladies even as spectators, saying that they 'would be infinitely better employed in almost any other way.' He felt 'entire devotion to the sex; but he wished also always to see them in their proper place.'[19] As the agitation for women's political rights spread, Sarah became more emphatic. When in 1857 she was invited to join in the founding of the National Association for the Promotion of Social Science, which included among its purposes an improvement in the position of women, especially working women, she 'desired it to be distinctly understood that she belonged not to the party, however estimable in many respects, who maintained what were termed the rights of women, especially in respect to political influence.'[20]

Sarah was fighting a rearguard action. While John Austin was making his last appeal to ward off any extension of democracy, she bemoaned the rapid torrent of change that was sweeping away traditional marital and parental relationships and the duties she regarded as basic for her sex and for social tranquillity. Women's desire for work outside the home appeared as threatening to traditional ways as their clamour for political participation. 'Society is going at such a pace in the direction of what your friend Miss [Bessie] Parkes and her allies call *non-domestic* employments, that our successors will have to go about with a lanthern [sic] in search of ... a *Hausmutter*,'[21] she told Brougham, who incongruously was the recipient of her most exalted rhetoric about domestic virtues: 'My own opinion is that the desertion of their posts as *centre* of the family by women is at the bottom of most of our worst mischiefs ... the question seems to me no less than this. Is domestic life to *exist*.'[22] What would make women return to their 'most sacred duties,' i.e., those of domestic life, when the whole current of modern society appeared set against 'that consummation of womanhood, the Housewife.' Economic forces were leading working-class girls, ignorant of domestic skills, to be employed by the thousands in factories while there was no corresponding occupation for men. Meanwhile some of the middle and higher classes affected superiority to domestic tasks and disdained even the essential domestic management that was their duty. Some were clamouring for the right to enter professions, preferring 'public and showy, over private and obscure duties.'[23] On this topic Sarah even differed with such an old friend and relatively guarded advocate of women's rights as Anna Jameson: 'All this business of *women's work* seems to me in a strange state and quite out of joint. They cannot and will not do their own work, and they want to do other people's.'[24] At times she sensed a lost cause and recognized that it was useless regretting what was inevitable, but soon enough she was once more declaiming to Brougham about changes that were 'taking away all meaning and appropriateness from the title which it is woman's highest glory to wear – Housewife.'[25]

At best there were only artificial and partial remedies for bringing women back to 'their natural place and their natural duties' and for stemming 'the torrent that was sweeping away domestic life among the humbler classes of England.' One expedient was to restore domestic talent among the poorer classes by emphasizing more practical training in schools for working women. Sarah confessed that since 1834, when she had advocated wider book learning for the masses, her opinions on the subject had 'undergone considerable modifications.'[26] She now saw that there were 'things more important for working class girls to learn than the river system of Hindostan [sic].' A false direction had been given to aspirations, and it was necessary 'to recall the young women of the working classes to a sense of their true vocation.' This theme became a favourite of her old age, and a tone of high-wrought emotionalism tended to accompany it: 'Something, may, perhaps, yet be done to protect and uphold the sacred edifice of Home.'[27] Again there was a personal dimension to her harangues about the lack of domestic skills. From the early years of her marriage when she made over a pair of her father's silk breeches, probably to embellish her household furnishings in some way, she had overcome narrow means by domestic contrivance and ingenuity.[28] She always stressed how she did as much in the way of 'normal weibliche Geschäfte [women's tasks]' as those who made 'a great parade of it.' When she was an old woman a visitor to her house commented on the impeccable order of her household. He reported that, although she was devoted to literature, she was not 'the least *blue*, but [was] very keen on the subject of housekeeping.' She had little sympathy for untrained working girls who could not cope as she had done: 'She is useless as most girls of her class are,' she wrote disdainfully of one such girl: '*She* could not paper a room ... I have done many such things, and so has my Janet [her granddaughter], but the girls who have neither birth beauty money nor education, seem to me never to ask themselves how they are *to live*.'[29]

The autobiographical element in Sarah's traditionalism can be discerned in her statements about marriage and the relations of the sexes. Though her own marriage had led her to harbour doubts about the institution, in old age she generally suppressed such thoughts and reiterated the old orthodoxies. Marriage was the most momentous event in life, 'involving obligations of all others the most grave and sacred.'[30] It was to be approached with very great caution, for after marriage there was no turning back. There had to be 'scrupulous and self-denying adherence to rules which are based on reason or to engagements voluntarily undertaken.'[31] As the law stood in the 1840s, separation was to her mind hardly an alternative for women. 'I mean to write one Chapter on Divorce, about which much nonsense is talked here,' she wrote from Paris; 'I have seen how it *works*.'[32] Women who 'desire[d] to be freed from the marital authority [would have to] be content to bear an equal share of the ruder conflict with life.' Individuals might experience 'impatience, restless hopes, and exaggerated expectations' in marriage, but 'human institution and divine command' came to their aid and relieved them 'from the burden of liberty too heavy for man to bear.'[33] She was dogmatic about the nature of the family: 'I cannot too loudly and emphatically utter my protest against every project for disturbing the great relation between Man and Woman which began at the creation and underlies the whole fabric of society,' and late in her life she spoke about her own marriage in parallel exalted terms: 'I have always felt that my highest honour, my greatest privilege, was to be the servant (I am not afraid of the name) of a noble hearted, great minded and not very fortunate man; and all schemes that would emancipate me from that servitude, are to me odious and shameful.'[34]

Yet Sarah continued to be drawn to the subject of marriage, and she revealed uncertainty and doubt about it even at the time of her most emphatic statements against liberated literary women who defiantly violated conventional morality. For example, to Ottilie von Goethe she wrote, 'It is impossible for me to say how much I wish to see you and talk with you de coeur en coeur on the subject which occupies so much of both our minds – the condition of our sex. Every where there is going on a [work?] of Klährung [sic] which must have *some* results,' but whether these would be desirable or not would depend on the moderation of the leaders. She agreed with Ottilie's statement, though she did not expand on it, that 'society crams us with fictions,' and she added, 'All that *must go* and will go in time.' Although she had considered writing on the woman question, she desisted because, as she explained, 'I have resolved *not* to publish anything on a matter on which I cannot say what I think, i.e., all I think. Halftruths will do no good and might attract unpleasant attention to myself.'[35]

Muted doubts about marriage and the relations of the sexes continued to occupy her. She complained that people who 'let their daughters read the most (fundamentally) licentious novels, are "shocked" at any serious, dispassionate enquiry into the grounds of our opinions on all that relates [to] the gravest of all subjects – the relation between the sexes – which my husband used to call the "insoluble problem." '36 There are hints that she thought marriage should cease to be regarded as the path for all women, yet she acknowledged that there was a problem of reconciling sexual passion in women with her belief in moral imperatives. Those such as Harriet Martineau who had 'omitted in their calculations *one female* item, *sex* and all that it brings with it' did not understand 'the unconquerable force of the physical relations of women.'37 Her interest in such issues in her younger days was reflected in her fascination in the mid-1830s with Goethe's *Wahlverwandschaften* (Elective affinities), a novella about marriage, convention, passion, and duty that she hoped to translate but which Ottilie von Goethe warned her against by saying that it was an audacious idea but would bring an uproar around her ears.38 Had she done so, she might have been drawn into more explicit statements on a subject that she repeatedly referred to as the most interesting of all social questions, yet on which she confined herself to vague allusions. For example, when she was editing Lucy's letters, she again stated that 'of all the problems which society seeks in vain to solve, the most difficult by far are those which regard the relations between the sexes.' In an article late in life she reflected about such relationships in Goethe's time: 'There was (and when and where has there *not* been?) so much to condemn and to deplore, so much of injustice and falsehood, of corrupting license and corrupting restraint.' Here were to be found 'unfathomed sources of the most poignant sorrows of human life!'39

If Sarah's experience engendered some uneasiness about marriage as an institution, it also led her to recoil from German avant-garde women writers whose emancipated views often mirrored their lives. 'I know the German women,' she wrote, 'and am prepared for any conceivable aberration and extravagance on their part.'40 Though the conventional attitudes to women in Germany had led her to exclaim, 'God forbid that I should bring up a daughter here,' the excesses and histrionic romanticism of some of the German women writers of her day led her to be suspicious of any movement endorsed by such advocates.41

The unconventional, even libertine ideas of some of the women intellectuals made them especially suspect. For example, there was that mercurial child of nature Ottilie von Goethe, with whom she began corresponding when she was preparing *Characteristics of Goethe*. Temperamentally they had little enough in common, but the woman question was a theme of mutual interest. Sarah tried to bridge differences, but the gulf between them should have been apparent to both. Ottilie's illegitimate child by an Englishman was no secret to Sarah, whose friend Anna Jameson had helped secrete Ottilie away at the time of the child's birth. In correspondence with Ottilie, Sarah seems to allude to her own former passion in the most oblique of ways: 'This is what we who have *lived* come to!' Yet having long ago tamed her own wayward feelings, she was not going to condone Ottilie's behaviour. She counselled Ottilie, always on the brink of some new infatuation, to 'submit to all actual and peremptory laws of society – but not one which can with safety to your engagements, to your selfrespect, and to your reputation be disregarded and which you believe to be mischievous and false.' Of course the qualifications permitted little flexibility, and in any case Ottilie was not likely to be moved by prudential maxims.[42]

Ottilie was not the only target of Sarah's criticism. There were the extravagances of Ida Hahn-Hahn and, outside Germany, the mischief of 'those who like Mme. Dudevant [George Sand] have stained a holy cause with even a suspicion of dissoluteness.'[43] Ida Hahn's 'erotic-psychological' novels and her personal life provoked Sarah to moral outrage. Hahn, whom Sarah saw as a German George Sand, wrote with impassioned subjectivism and disregard for conventional restraints, often about a romantic triangle of lover, heroine, and a devoted, forgiving friend and protector in an exclusively aristocratic setting. Her disregard for the conventions of marriage, her admiration for Byron, and the high emotionalism and exaltation of her characters aroused 'effusions of disgust' in Sarah. She condemned the self-absorption of the heroines who, unmoved by the restraint and obligations to others that Sarah thought essential, concentrated solely on the swells of sentiment within: 'As to your Mme. Hahns and *ad hoc genus omne* – you must excuse me – ce n'est pas mon genre.' She would not translate Hahn: 'I can never lend my hand – even in my humble and subordinate way, to the task of exalting the narrowest and most impenetrable selfishness, veiled under the name of love, passion, sentiment and the like, into a virtue and heroism.' The absorption of 'these sublime egoists' in their feelings for one individual and their total indifference to the destiny and suffering of the mass of mankind seemed to her 'the last corruption of the human heart and understanding, worse than open debauchery.' Plain debauchery might be recognized for what it was, whereas Hahn's passions were dressed up to sound like idealism. Furthermore, Hahn's 'unverschämte [shameless] vanity and egotism, this claim to boundless freedom for herself, and insolent assumption of superiority over us of the Bürgerstand [middle class], this taste for everything that is *schief* [irregular] in the relations of women' put Sarah out of patience. The woman's heart, in her view, should 'keep alive the sacred and eternal fire of *Charity*,' but Hahn let such feelings be 'burnt out in *passion*, and nothing [was] left but the dirt and ashes of disappointment and apathy.' It was 'a miserable and contemptible spectacle.'[44]

Sarah not only had little sympathy for the free spirits of the contemporary German literary world, but she condemned some of the earlier eighteenth-century romantic literature, with its 'odious race of sentimental novels.'[45] The 'speculative sentimentalists' of that period used unwholesome models and by concentrating on the 'small world of self' encouraged an image of women that was inconsistent with nature and society. Thus Frederick Schlegel's controversial novel *Lucinda*, which was implicitly critical of the relations of the sexes, marriage, and conventional values, struck her as 'notoriously immoral.' She was eloquent in denouncing another novel of that time, Jacobi's *Woldemar*, hardly read in our day, which pictured 'a passion, miscalled friendship, which absorbs the whole being, and renders life intolerable out of sight of its object.' The assumption that such an ideal could be 'entertained without prejudice to conjugal fidelity or to maiden freedom and purity is the thing which renders this book peculiarly absurd, mischievous, and, at the same time, characteristic.'[46] The perversion of wholesome ideas, the confusion created between virtue and vice, and the garrulous self-display reflected in such enervating literature had enfeebled the whole nation and prepared the way for its bitter defeat by Napoleon.

German literary women and the sentiments generated by the romantic movement undermined women's roles and threatened social values. It is ironic that Sarah, who is known for her promotion of a wider appreciation of German literature, should have shown so little sympathy for German romanticism. She acknowledged its liberating influence in a country where any 'sober superiority' on the part of women was given so little recognition, but she discerned its social implications and felt bound to condemn the 'speculative dissoluteness which tried all the props of human society.' By 'reducing aberrations of the affections to a system, and philosophizing upon them in the most elaborate manner,' the movement threatened basic beliefs about women, morality, and society:

> In Germany, from the time that all the conditions of social life were brought under discussion, the relations between the sexes became the subject of passionate reverie, refined analysis, and intrepid theory. Writers and readers

shrank from no novelty and no paradox. The imagination and feelings were systematically withdrawn from the control of reason, whose jurisdiction in 'affairs of the heart' was denied altogether; and from traditionary [sic] morality, which was regarded as blind and narrow prejudice.[47]

Even Goethe, Sarah's *Abgott* (idol) in the 1830s, was partially dethroned, not on poetic but on political and moral grounds, even though she knew she would be 'hotly attacked' for this irreverence. Goethe showed moral indifference, even obtuseness, she complained, in his early love affairs and in his neutral attitude to his country's conqueror, Napoleon. Also his wide-ranging speculations about great social issues such as the relations of the sexes were left without satisfactory conclusions; they tended towards 'a vague discontent with things as they are' and brought 'great social questions into a state of doubt, confusion or indifference, and left them there.' Thus his ruminations were 'among the most active dissolvents of society.'[48]

Sarah's opposition to the ideals of emancipation may have played a part in sundering her friendship with Mill. The sudden and permanent rift between them remains something of an enigma. Mill had known her since he was fourteen years old; he had found a second home in the Austins' household and as a boy had briefly been an 'eccentric lodger' in her mother's household. For years he called her 'Mütterlein' and sometimes signed himself as her 'Söhnchen.' The relationship was sufficiently intimate for Sarah to write to Mill in 1837 telling him he was 'too important a piece of ourselves.'[49] As Austin's career faltered, Mill's affectionate concern about Sarah's anxieties and Austin's misfortune was evident in letters through two decades, till the break came in the late 1840s. Yet Mill continued to esteem Austin even after *The Plea for the Constitution* (1859) left no uncertainty about Austin's politics. The rupture with Sarah, however, was nearly complete. The feelings involved in this estrangement were so strong that when the Austins took temporary lodgings in Weybridge in 1848, the threat of their permanent presence was one of the inducements for Harriet Taylor to move away from the area.[50] Even after Austin's death, Mill could not bring himself to write a letter of condolence to Sarah directly but addressed it instead to her grand-daughter, who was then seventeen and staying with Sarah. This 'evidently intentional slight cut [Sarah] to the heart.'[51]

There have been various explanations for why these friends became enemies – political differences, Sarah's imprudent gossip about Mill's relationship with Harriet Taylor before their marriage, and Harriet's envy of another attractive woman who had known Mill well. Sarah's attitude to the woman question may also have played a part, since emancipation was a crucial issue for both Mills. Sarah's publication of an article in 1849 with a decided anti-feminist tone may have confirmed the Mills' suspicion about her opinions.[52] Mill had observed Sarah's inclination to cast off the mantle of intellectual woman and ascend the pedestal of sacrificing, devoted wifehood. Discussing the Austins with Comte, he hinted at Sarah's posturing: 'As for her inclination to be *blue*, I think she would defend herself against this most vigorously. Her type of vanity seems to me to take another form.'[53] After the break Sarah usually spoke of 'our poor friend Mill' and declared that his conduct towards them had been 'strange and deplorable.' She could not have been unaware that her views on the position of women would have offended him beyond reconciliation. In Mill's *Autobiography* that was published only after his death, Mill threw some final barbs at Sarah, but meanwhile she directed some at him. She told Grey that while she greatly admired Mill's speech on the malt tax, she had 'a great distrust of his judgment and appreciation of *premises*. His *inferences* will be correct enough.'[54] The woman's issue certainly had been a matter of premises.

If Sarah's attitudes to the woman question can be ascribed to self-justification and anxiety about social change in the last part of her life, her family background, which was liberal on political and educational issues but conventional socially, also played a part. The woman who left Norwich dissenting circles so far behind remained loyal to many of their values. Sarah's mother had been fascinated by the gossip and ideas relayed to her about Mary Wollstonecraft, but she would have agreed with her friend Amelia Opie, who thought of herself as 'more a wife of the *old* than the *new* school.'[55] Susanna Taylor was a clever woman animated by considerable social and moral idealism, but she was no rebel. The language of equality applied to women's intellectual and moral capacities only. The model that she held out to her daughter was Anna Letitia Barbauld, who had declined to associate herself with the more strident writers on either side of the feminist arguments of the 1790s. 'Mrs Hannah More would not write along with you or me,' Mrs Barbauld told a friend, 'and we should probably hesitate at joining Miss Hays or, if she were living, Mrs. Godwin [Mary Wollstonecraft].'[56] The issues were different by Sarah's time, and yet there is a remarkable continuity between the values of mother and daughter. Sarah's conventional ideas about women were also reinforced by her admiration for Guizot, who implicitly supported her tendency to see her role in Austin's life in idealized terms. She thus changed her self-image from that of a long-suffering wife into that of a valiant woman with a noble purpose, and this interpretation was consoling and reconciling. She felt she had devoted herself to supporting and serving a gifted and unfortunate man: to have permitted herself to entertain notions about emancipation would have made a mockery of this dedication.

8

'Out of time and place'

AFTER AN ENCOUNTER with John Austin in 1854 Macaulay reported that Austin 'was wonderfully fluent and wonderfully conservative. He seems to have lost his taciturnity and his radicalism together.' Sarah had also changed: she 'had become rather Tory,' according to Victor Cousin.[1]

The shift to outspoken conservatism in the last period of their lives did not bring the Austins closer to the main stream of opinion. In 1859 Austin published a statement of his political beliefs, recalling the days of his early radicalism when liberal opinions 'exposed the few who professed them to political and social proscription.' Now that public opinion had become more liberal, Austin, as a conservative, expected similar treatment. His new opinions were likely to be as unpopular among some of his contemporaries as his old ones had been, and he foresaw that they might 'possibly expose [him] to some obloquy.' He seemed destined to run against the tide; as he said, 'I was born out of time and place.'[2]

The Austins' conservatism became most evident after the revolutionary year, 1848, but there were anticipations of it during the 1840s. In 1839 John Austin had in his polemical way argued in conversation that the Reformation had been an evil for mankind, and he was equally sceptical about the French Revolution, saying that he doubted 'whether the world would not have advanced more quickly without it.' During the 1840s, when noting the increasing class conflict in England and in France, he feared that he was living in a revolutionary period, and in 1846 he contemplated writing an article on the antecedents of the French Revolution in order to apply 'all the reflections suggested by those events and their causes to the actual state of society, and more especially to England.'[3]

His inclination towards conservatism can be discerned in such statements, but it was not until 1848, when he observed the revolution in Paris, that Austin turned into an emphatic conservative. The Austins were in Paris when the first blow fell, but he could hardly have been surprised by the revolution, for before it broke out he pointed to the prevalence of 'communist and anarchical opinions' and warned, 'The great danger is, that France may fall into anarchy.' What did surprise him, however, was the moderation of Paris working men immediately following the outbeak in February. He reported the absence of pillage or destruction except by thieves and *gamins* and a remarkable deference to those in the better-off classes who appeared to sympathize with the workers. Sarah also noted that at first the people 'exhibited great moderation and absence of sanguinary vindictive and rapacious passions,' but she also observed the torrent of wild placards that covered every conceivable empty space and the processions of drunken and armed mobs. When the Austins decided to leave Paris it was to escape not imminent personal danger, but the spectacle of misery and the potentially explosive passions which they discerned in the populace. The people, they claimed, on the whole, had behaved like lambs but could turn into tigers; if Lamartine's feeble hold on power were lost, he might be succeeded by those 'most verging on Communism'; the smallest wrong move would make the 'heated mass ... burst into a flame.' Austin forecast that Lamartine's government would fall, and although he was momentarily reassured by the suppression of the radical workers on 15 May, his expectations of anarchy, which were shaped by his historical memory of the great revolution, were fulfilled.[4]

Sarah departed from Paris in March, and her husband followed in late May. Thereafter they looked back on the events of 1848 as a turning point in the development of their political opinions, although Austin, in retrospect, 'reserve[d] his execrations for those who prepared 48 ... rather than towards the wild beasts who consummated their work.' Sarah attributed Austin's firm disapproval of democracy to 'the example of France,' and after 1848 when thinking of France she said, 'an *Ahnung* [apprehension] of a terrible future comes over me!' After returning to England she wanted to publish letters from France so 'that people here might see the *innere Wirkung* of revolutions.' They had 'lived too long and too much out of England,' she explained, and had been 'too near witnesses of terrific political convulsions, not to have modified many opinions and questioned many axioms.'[5]

The turn to conservatism was evident in many ways. Austin's opposition to democracy became more extreme, and he regarded parliamentary reform as a 'perilous experiment' which would lead to a democratic regime and ultimately to socialism. He was opposed to egalitarianism and complained about the spread of socialist opinion in England: 'A great majority of the working classes are imbued with principles essentially socialist.' Socialist schemes 'were big with deception, disaffection, and anarchy,' and from Paris he wrote, 'My fears of Socialism, of Communism, are anything but fanciful.'[6] Sarah shared these views and called the wish for equality 'one of the prevalent diseases of the time.' She was even deeply suspicious of Cobden and Bright and thought the latter 'a powerful demagogue,' even a kind of anarchist. She also watched 'the rise of the democratic tide with anxiety, not to say alarm,' and both of them were very criticial of American democracy. Revolution was even more objectionable, as it unleashed 'the low prejudices and passions and the adoration of brute force which are among the motive powers in all revolutions.'[7] These opinions were combined with support for free trade, which perhaps justified Austin's calling himself liberal conservative, a label that was consistent with his admiration for Peel and his approval of the Aberdeen ministry in 1852. But despite this label and Sarah's denials that he was a Tory and his efforts to dissociate himself from legitimists and other ultra-conservatives in France, he acquired a reputation for being 'a high Tory.' His conservatism was revealed in many ways during the 1850s, but it became most explicit in 1859, in *A Plea for the Constitution*.[8] Meanwhile Sarah's conservatism was expressed in her complaints about the subversiveness of the *hommes de lettres* and those whose poor judgment she thought a consequence of their liberalism. She became increasingly gloomy about politics. The future of France, she said, was dim and doubtful, and she expected she would 'not die easy about [her] country.' She even confessed that she and her friends did 'nothing but condole and help one another to visions of evil.'[9]

With this shift to conservatism, John Austin also experienced changes in his religious convictions. He was said to have shared the agnosticism common among Benthamite radicals, but by the time he gave the lectures on jurisprudence he combined a theological position with his political and legal views; soon afterwards his daughter denied he was an atheist and attributed to him a belief in the importance of religion as a source of morality. He seems to have moved further in this direction, however, for late in life he said (according to Henry Reeve), 'I think, if I live long enough, I too shall be a Christian.'[10] That he did just that is revealed in a surprising condolence letter written to Sarah Austin by James Stephen in 1853 after hearing what proved to be a false report of Austin's death:

I can never forget the seriousness and the eloquence with which many years ago he explained to me the path which he had travelled through his enquiries as a jurist to the admission of the excellence and the truth of the gospel. It is a topic to which I have since repeatedly heard him refer, with that fertility and power of discourse in which he was unrivalled, and from him such language came with the sacred impress of truth; for the very infirmities as well as the strength of his nature rescued him from the slightest alloy of cant or hypocrisy or pretention when speaking on such subjects. A man so profoundly wise and so severely upright could not have admitted to his soul the convictions which he avowed without also cherishing there the germs of that hidden life of which as you and I believe the fruits are imperishable.

Such views, which were also confirmed by Barthélemy Saint-Hilaire, who undoubtedly relied on Sarah Austin for this information, reinforced Austin's conservative diagnosis of the world's ills and also pointed to the remedies he would use to relieve them.[11]

The Austins' conservatism on constitutional issues went beyond most contemporary opinion. Their unyielding resistance to constitutional change put them out of step with both the Whig party, which still practised a policy of concession and trimming, and much of the Tory party, which had adopted flexible approaches to parliamentary reform and an extension of the suffrage. Such was Austin's reputation that when the conservative *Quarterly Review* rejected his *Plea for the Constitution*, which had been written as an article reviewing Grey's *Parliamentary Government*, Henry Reeve suggested: 'There is some apprehension his views may be too conservative for the modern Tories!'[12]

Although the Austins' conservatism was extreme, it was not unique, for there were others who shared their fear of revolution and their opposition to democracy. Their outlook, however, was made somewhat unusual by their great concern with what they called attachment, by which they meant the feelings and sentiments that produced loyalty to institutions and to society as a whole. Sarah emphasized the non-rational, unthinking character of attachment, which, she said, was 'unreasoning, inasmuch as those who feel it would be unable to give a clear and precise reason for their preference of those institutions.' The German states, especially since their regeneration after the defeat of Napoleon, exemplified one kind of attachment – the loyal support of a regime as a consequence of attachment to the person of the monarch. England exemplified another and more sophisticated kind, which involved attachment to institutions as well as to the monarch. In this case, John Austin said, 'the attachment to the form of government [is enhanced] by attachment to the individual who prominently represents it.' When he applied the concept to Britain he called it the 'sentiment of constitutionality,' a notion he introduced in his *Plea for the Constitution*. He welcomed the sentiment of constitutionality because it made the government 'an object of love and veneration' and bound the people to it as a matter of authority and habit.[13] Since such feelings of attachment were habitual and unthinking, they were not easily undermined; and when, as in England, they were widely shared, they made for unity of opinion and thus prevented the divisiveness which was the germ of anarchy.

In contrast to England, France demonstrated how attachment could be undermined. Frequent changes and especially revolution destroyed the sentiments that made attachment possible. In France some attachment to the monarchy had survived until it was destroyed by the Revolution, and the many subsequent revolutions and counter-revolutions had prevented the slow growth of a new kind of attachment. Observation of French politics 'confirmed [Austin] in his opinion of the difficulty, if not the impossibility, of reconstructing a society which has once been completely shattered.' When he returned from Paris he described 'the state of mind of the French as one of perfect political scepticism and indifference ... They have no confidence in any public man, and no attachment to any political institution.' Thus it was all the more important to protect the foundation of attachments where they existed, as in England. Consequently, proposals for change in the constitution had to be resisted.[14]

It was clear that attachment was valued because it provided stability, but it gained its greatest value by serving as an obstacle to certain undesirable conditions. With the erosion of attachment individuals became self-oriented, sceptical about public affairs and unwilling to take part in them, and they lost confidence and conviction. The selfishness that was unleashed was allied to an envy which was given respectability by egalitarian ideas. Faced with such conditions, Sarah said, society ceased to be a 'well-ordered and decorous procession' and became 'a chaotic and struggling crowd.' This picture of society as a crowd resembled Tocqueville's description at the end of *Democracy in America* of the conditions that led to the undesirable democratic regime in which individualism replaced communal attachments and liberty was sacrificed to comfort and equality. In France, which Tocqueville also had in mind, Sarah sensed 'the decomposition of society' and commented, 'The whole thing seems to me utterly ... if I may make an awkward word, cementless.'[15]

Such conditions were distasteful because they were associated with dissatisfaction and restlessness, but the most serious objection to them was the likelihood that they would lead to despotism. When attachments disappeared and society became a 'cementless crowd,' there was an inclination to look to a centralized authority as the appropriate instrument of government and to submit to it even when it became absolute and despotic. The Austins evidently had an apprehension of this phenomenon, but their description of it lacked the penetration of Tocqueville's analysis and the clarity that can be found in more recent theories of mass society. Recalling the example of France, especially the egalitarianism of 1848 and the success of Louis Napoleon, Sarah described 'the mixture of insubordination towards regular and mild authority, and of submission to brutal tyranny,' and she forecast that in a democracy 'the mass of the people ... [would] find it impossible to wield this [democratic] power for any long period, and [would] hand it over to, or suffer it to be usurped by, some man who knows how to gain their confidence, or to work on their fears.' Democracy, she feared, could 'easily [be] used as an instrument of oppression.'[16]

French history since 1789 was interpreted by the Austins in the light of their belief in the close connection between popular, democratic regimes and despotism. Typically, revolutionary regimes (which the Austins chose to call democratic) gave way to despotism, and this process produced the first Napoleonic regime. Under Napoleon there was 'the same political impotence, the same habit of looking from all points and on all emergencies to the centre, as the sole source of political life and force, which had prevailed before the Revolution.'[17]

The regimes that followed Napoleon – the Restoration, Louis Philippe's, and the second Republic under Cavaignac – were not admired by the Austins, but they were defended as preferable to either revolution or despotism, which seemed the only alternatives. Thus the Bourbon Restoration was approved because it 'promised ... some security from such enormous evils' as civil convulsions, domestic tyranny, and external wars. Although the Restoration was an improvement on what preceded it, it was very defective, and consequently the Revolution of 1830 was not regarded as objectionable, for 'the provocation was real, the conflict without ferocity, and the victory used with moderation.' During Louis Philippe's reign the Austins were highly critical of him but feared something worse if he should fall. The same tone of settling for something far less than even second best in order to avoid a worse alternative was evident in Austin's nervous toleration of the Republic in April 1848, so long as 'no pretext for a civil war be given to the evil-disposed'; in Sarah's approval of Lamartine's feeble government on the ground that 'the next step, *inevitably* and *certainly*, is the party of the National and those most verging on communism'; and in her uneasy support for General Cavaignac on the ground that 'he is the best they have ... He *does* maintain some sort of order. If he goes, what have you behind?'[18] These varied regimes, although acceptable in the very difficult circumstances, were 'cementless' and unstable and thus vulnerable to revolution and despotism.

When Louis Napoleon took over he represented the despotism they had feared. Much of what the Austins wrote about France was written from the perspective gained by observing his reign, and this allowed them to emphasize the connection between democracy and despotism. This second Napoleonic regime confirmed their belief in the connection between tyranny and the democratic spirit in France, for Louis Napoleon succeeded to a revolutionary regime and gained and confirmed his power by universal suffrage. He was a 'revolutionary despot, the instrument and the representative of the lowest passions of the populace.' The French elections, according to Sarah, demonstrated that universal suffrage not only had '*no* effect whatever in securing popular rights, but that it is easily used as an instrument of oppression, as well as corruption.' To John Austin Napoleon III was 'an especial object of aversion'; he refused to visit Paris, as he was 'afraid of being ill from pure vexation.' Decades later his 'vehement denunciations of Louis Napoleon' were recalled by his granddaughter. In Sarah's view the emperor was responsible for a brutal tyranny, and his was an 'iron heel that is upon [French] intelligence and freedom.' France in the 1850s, Sarah held, was a reflection of a condition that was endemic – 'the absence of political convictions and political attachments; the absence of every kind of political power except what emanates either from the central government for the time being, or from the populace.'[19]

The Austins' newly acquired conservative outlook released a flood of proud boasts about the British constitution. The title of Austin's pamphlet indicated how much he now valued it. In Sarah's estimate, England had 'the oldest and most stable constitutional government in the world' and was 'its cradle and its mighty nurse.' Although she understood that English institutions could not be imitated easily, she was 'entirely convinced that no man can be qualified to legislate for what is called a free country (or a country aspiring to be so), without a very attentive and profound study of England. England is the most *suggestive* of all countries to a legislator.' She was so emphatic about this that one can be confident it would have been one of the themes in the book she planned at this time, but did not complete, to be entitled *Contrasts of Foreign and English Society; or, Records of a Residence in Various Parts of the Continent and England*. It was not that the Austins were blind to difficulties in England – there was a growing spirit of insubordination, class conflict, and a great need to educate the working classes – but, on the whole, both stability and liberty did exist. Sarah's pride in British government was boosted by the outcome of the Chartist demonstration on 10 April 1848. She was nervous before the event, but after witnessing the Chartists' failure and thinking of the large numbers of citizens who volunteered as special constables, she boasted that the English 'stood up like men, and said at once what was their determination.'[20] She was keenly aware of the contrast with the events at Paris, where the propertied class defended itself with great difficulty; to Sarah, this contrast illustrated the weakness of attachment to a constitution in France and its strength in England.

Since John Austin wished to preserve existing attachments, he upheld the aristocracy as the source from which leading politicians should be drawn. In his later years he and Sarah identified all political good with a responsible aristocracy and with veneration of the aristocracy by the people at large. They argued that in order to support and preserve skilled leadership, respect for historical aristocracy was necessary. John Austin's conception of aristocracy was not narrow, however, for he insisted that it was not an exclusive caste and that it included the higher commonality, that is, those who acquired wealth by industry and whose conduct and manners were those of gentlemen. While this loosely defined class required independent means, he did not approve of plutocracy and was horrified by the prospect of a 'regime of parvenus,' or, as Sarah put it, 'a parliament of railway kings,' which might result from a 'deification of money by a whole people.' What was wanted, he said, was 'a class of *gentlemen*, diffusing gentlemanly feelings.' In spite of their veneration of the institution of aristocracy, the Austins' estimate of English aristocracy was mixed: as a governing class it wanted judgment and confidence, but they admired particular members of it and thought the institution capable of improvement. At its best, English aristocracy only approximated their ideal.[21]

John Austin linked his wish for aristocratic political leadership to his belief that a talent for compromise was essential for political stability – a belief he held despite his reluctance to consider a compromise with those demanding an extension of the suffrage. Only through compromise, he said, could there be coexistence and 'internal quiet' among those with different opinions and goals. Compromise permitted a minimum level of co-operation in an inevitably varied society, and the aristocracy, he argued, produced politicians with the requisite skills, which were acquired through experience made possible by privilege. Independent gentlemen could afford to give their attention to public affairs; from 'the peculiar influences acting upon them from the cradle, they are naturally restrained ... by the sentiment of gentlemanly honour'; more than others they were responsible to public opinion; and they had 'habitual moderation ... which tempers and sets a measure to their hottest contentions.' Austin even thought their moderation had mainly arisen from their 'breeding.' The gentlemanly class would apply the principle of utility, but they would do this, in a sense, instinctively, without self-consciously knowing about it as a principle, but rather as a result (in Professor Michael Oakeshott's phrase) of 'a tradition of conduct.' Thus they had 'more capacity for statesmanship than public men of less elevated classes.' They (including untitled gentlemen) constituted a class which was 'a *political aristocracy* on account of its special vocation to practical politics.' Sarah, who in her correspondence was even more extravagant than her husband in pointing to the importance of an aristocracy, said one of his 'deepest and most earnest convictions [was] the absolute necessity for a patrician class, devoted to the business of legislation.'[22]

An indication of how far Austin had changed is revealed in John Stuart Mill's disagreements with him. Mill had found much to approve in Austin's jurisprudence, but the experiences of 1848 brought their political differences to the surface. Mill, who knew of Austin's critique of revolutionary developments in France from Austin's letter in *The Times* and from correspondence, told Sarah, 'I never thought I should have differed from him so widely in feeling on any public event as it appears I do on this ... My hopes rise instead of sinking as the state of things in France unfolds itself.' The Austins, on the other hand, had a clear picture of Mill's opinions on French affairs, for his long article vindicating the provisional government appeared in April 1849. What Austin thought of it can be inferred from his general statement, made before Mill's article appeared, that he could not think with patience of any Englishman exulting in the awful ruin of revolution. In a clear allusion to Mill, Sarah Austin confessed her dismay that 'so-called "Liberals" in England expressed great satisfaction at the over-throw of the constitutional monarchy, and warm sympathy with the revolutionary government so reluctantly accepted by France.' She also recalled her amazement when she returned from Paris to find 'men of the educated classes rejoicing in this disastrous overthrow of all hope of good government in France, as a triumph of liberty.'[23] The *Plea for the Constitution* was an occasion for additional disagreements. In his review of it Mill mainly differed about the aristocracy, arguing that it was not responsible for the effective working of the constitution, that it was not the only source of statesmen with a talent for compromise, and that it did not produce talented legislators.

Despite the differences that separated them, Mill was not acrimonious in his review; however, privately, in conversation and in his still unpublished autobiography, his disdain was apparent, but with Sarah as the target. His hostile observations partly reflected Harriet Taylor's dislike of Sarah, but political differences also played a part, as indicated by Mill's observation that Sarah Austin 'slid into the opinions agreeable to the well-to-do classes.' John Austin, however, was spared. Perhaps recalling their former closeness and his intellectual debt, Mill emphasized points of agreement and the prudence of Austin's warnings, and he also included flattering observations and rejoiced that Austin had 'resumed the pen, even on a question on which we differ with him, if it authorizes us to hope that we may yet see the completion of his great book.'[24] Mill's sympathies were important to Austin's reputation, for his reviews of *The Province of Jurisprudence* (in 1832) and *A Plea for the Constitution* (in 1859) were the only notable contemporary reviews of these works, and the reputation of these publications owes something to Mill's attentions.

9

Did Austin remain an Austinian?

WHEN AUSTIN STOPPED LECTURING at the University of London he
intended to complete and publish his full course of lectures on jurisprudence. Periodically during the troubled years that followed he set to work
on this task, yet he never finished it, and in the end it was only through
Sarah Austin's efforts that the book was published posthumously,
although as an incomplete work. Entitled *Lectures on Jurisprudence or the
Philosophy of Positive Law* (1863), it consisted of a reprint of *The Province of
Jurisprudence Determined* (first published 1832, reprinted 1861), an additional forty-six lectures which had been given at the university, and
supplementary material which Sarah found among her husband's papers.

Various explanations have been offered for Austin's failure to finish
the work in which he had invested so much labour and hope. His friends
attributed his failure to ill health, lassitude, and depression, and Sarah
stressed his discouragement in the face of misfortune. These undoubtedly played a part, but there was also an intellectual component to his
reluctance to resume the work. After the publication of *The Province of
Jurisprudence* Austin changed many of his ideas and beliefs, and this may
have been the stumbling block that impeded his plans. The impetus for
these changes was an altered political outlook that eventually led to
important revisions in his jurisprudential ideas, including his assessment
of the role of the principle of utility. The implications of his new political
beliefs became apparent only gradually in his work, but as his conservatism became more explicit, it became evident that it would be difficult to
make his new political views compatible with his jurisprudence. This erosion of Austin's early confidence in the validity of his jurisprudence may
also have been an obstacle to his completing the work. His awareness of
the crumbling intellectual foundations on which he had built his hopes

can hardly have helped him overcome his inclination to self-doubt and depression.

Austin's dissatisfaction with his jurisprudence did not set in immediately after the London lectures. His appointments to the Criminal Law Commission (1833-6) and the Malta Commission (1836-9) allowed him to do work, including codifying and drafting, that was perfectly compatible with the purposes and the conceptualizations of his jurisprudence. It was only after the Malta experience and while living on the Continent that indications of intellectual dissatisfaction appeared. Various persons had urged a second edition of *The Province of Jurisprudence*, and twice during the 1840s he received proposals from his publisher John Murray to reprint it, as the book was out of print (only 500 copies had been printed) and was fetching high prices in the second-hand market. Yet Austin refused to republish, despite flattering appeals, such as one from his former pupil and Malta colleague George Cornewall Lewis, who told him, 'If you would unlock your stores, you would find that your teaching would gradually make its due impression.'[1] There appears to have been some planning during the 1840s for a revised and expanded volume, but nothing came of it. Sarah said he did 'little more than ex-cogitate his book. I wish,' she added, 'I could see the pen at work.' This condition continued, and just before Austin died she reported that although he planned a revised version of his book, 'he has never touched it, and *never will*.'[2]

Austin's understanding of the inadequacies in *The Province of Jurisprudence* developed slowly, and his ideas about the necessary revisions took shape gradually. The first indications of uneasiness appeared in 1843-4. George Cornewall Lewis understood, from what Sarah Austin had written, that Austin was 'meditating the publication of something more upon jurisprudential subjects'; and in early 1845 Mill knew there might be 'a reprint of [the] former book, with the second volume which he projected.'[3] Austin at this stage seemed to think that he could reprint *The Province of Jurisprudence* and add the unpublished lectures or new material. The prospect of having to rewrite the book does not yet seem to have occurred, for he used the concepts and distinctions laid out in that book in his 1847 article, 'Centralization' (written in 1846).[4] The continued use of some language and ideas from *The Province of Jurisprudence* could not continue, however, for after Austin felt the rumblings of revolution – in 1847 he contemplated writing on the antecedents of revolution – and after the outbreak in Paris, he appears to have realized that some of the ideas in that book had been undermined. Thus in 1849 when John Murray proposed reprinting the 1832 volume and asked if there were corrections or additions, John Austin responded that revisions would require considerable time: 'To meet my present views, a recast of the present volume, with the addition of one or two more, would be necessary.' At the same time he told Mill that he was going to 'prepare a new edition of his book on jurisprudence on a much enlarged plan.'[5]

When Austin began working on the book, he warned Murray that his life or health might not last long enough to allow for the completion of so laborious a task, but he did make preliminary plans. Although nothing came of them, we know the kind of revision he would have made, for he prepared for Murray a printed prospectus or advertisement for the new book. If he had revised, Austin would have added ethical inquiries and integrated them with his science of jurisprudence. Whereas *The Province of Jurisprudence* dealt with the science of positive law, only tangentially bringing in the science of positive morality (that is, moral rules without legal sanction as they actually existed) and the science of ethics (the standards for judging law and morality as they ought to be), the revision was to put equal emphasis on positive morality and ethics and positive law. Also, whereas in the published work the science of positive law was treated as if it could be isolated from positive morality and ethics, in the revision Austin intended to recognize that the three sciences were 'inseparably connected parts of a vast organized whole.' The revision, then, was to discuss ethics as a source of moral standards as well as the actual ethical notions that prevailed in contemporary society: 'His opinion [Sarah said] of the necessity of an entire *refonte* of his book arose, in great measure, from the conviction, which had continually been gaining strength in his mind, that until the ethical notions of men were more clear and consistent, no considerable improvement could be hoped for in legal or political science, nor, consequently, in legal or political institutions.' The title of the new book was to be *The Principles and Relations of Jurisprudence and Ethics*.[6]

Austin did not recognize the full extent of the changes until after he came to terms with the revolution of 1848, and this strongly suggests that it was his recently developed conservatism that undermined his belief in the validity of *The Province of Jurisprudence*. There were related influences, however, that might also have contributed to this result – for example, his experience in Malta. Since one important ingredient of his conservatism was a recognition of the importance of custom and 'unthinking feelings' as sources of attachment and loyalty, one may speculate that his observation of the strong grip of tradition and religion on the Maltese people contributed to his recognition of the tenacity and importance of such feelings. Experience in India had just such an effect on the legal scholar Henry Sumner Maine, and perhaps Austin was affected in the same way. One might also speculate about his failure in Malta to revise the draft code that had been prepared by a commission of Maltese lawyers. This was surprising in view of his strong belief in codification, and it is possible that this experience contributed to his doubts.

Another influence might have been John Stuart Mill's *Logic*, which was published in 1843, shortly before the possibility of reprinting *The Province of Jurisprudence* was discussed for the first time. Austin certainly read Mill's book and appears to have read parts of it in 1842 before it was published, and he told Mill he would like to review it sympathetically in the *Edinburgh Review*. These facts are suggestive only because Mill's book could have stirred Austin's doubts about certain themes in *The Province of Jurisprudence*. There is a parallel between Mill's observations about the necessary conditions of political stability and Austin's new thoughts on this matter, which were expressed as observations about attachment and the sentiment of constitutionality and which were at the core of his new conservative outlook. In the *Logic* Mill described as one of the conditions of permanent political society the existence of allegiance or loyalty, including a feeling 'that there be in the constitution of the state *something* which is settled, something permanent, and not to be called into question ... some fixed point: something which people agreed in holding sacred.' Although such a feeling, according to Mill, was compatible with freedom of discussion, it was, except in moments of crisis, 'in the common estimation placed beyond discussion.' Mill was acknowledging (using the terminology of *The Province of Jurisprudence*) that positive morality might be founded in custom instead of a science of ethics, and his observations have a striking affinity with Austin's post-1848 emphasis on the sentiment of constitutionality based on unthinking feelings.[7] Mill's influence – and that of experience in Malta – must remain a matter for speculation; but whatever their importance, they were subsidiary to that conservatism which came not from books such as Mill's but from alarm about the divisiveness and the revolutionary currents of the 1840s.

MANY OF THE INCOMPATIBILITIES between Austin's conservatism and *The Province of Jurisprudence* flowed from his new emphasis on attachment and the sentiment of constitutionality. Once he adopted the belief that the bond between subject and sovereign ought to be based on custom and unthinking feelings, he could no longer uphold the principle affirmed in *The Province of Jurisprudence* that that bond ought to be based on rational appreciation of the superior knowledge of those who enjoyed political authority. Whereas earlier he thought deference to authority would originate in an understanding of the 'leading principles' of such sciences as political economy and ethics, after 1848 Austin regarded this as unrealistic because such sciences could not generate the sentiments and loyalties which were necessary for the stable support of authority. His conservative recognition of the importance of traditional sentiment as a source of attachment undermined his belief in the possibility of a scientifically based positive morality that would be the source of attachment to a sovereign authority guided by the principle of utility. The consequence was that he could no longer uphold the political ideas found in *The Province of Jurisprudence*. He continued to ask the same questions as he had earlier, both when he was a radical and when he was lecturing on jurisprudence – who should govern, how are subjects made to obey? – but once again the answers were different.

Another discrepancy between Austin's post-1848 conservatism and *The Province of Jurisprudence* concerned the class to which he looked for political leadership. The emphasis on existing attachments led to admiration for the aristocracy, whereas in *The Province of Jurisprudence* Austin had not identified in class terms those who would or should exercise sovereignty, and he had mentioned aristocracy merely to define it but never to hold it up as an estimable class. The exercise of sovereignty in that book was a matter of having skill at making laws and at arranging compromises, and these functions required an understanding of the principle of utility. Thus sovereignty belonged to those qualified by knowledge of this principle and the sciences associated with it. Now, however, 'one of his deepest and most earnest convictions [was] the absolute necessity for a particular class devoted to the business of legislation.'[8] The scientific élitism that was Austin's preference in *The Province of Jurisprudence* was abandoned.

The erosion of his position in *The Province of Jurisprudence* went further, for doubts about the principle of utility itself also crept into his thinking. Austin recognized both in *The Province* and after 1848 that authority had to be upheld by generally accepted beliefs among the populace, but whereas in the earlier work it was assumed that such beliefs would be in accord with the principle of utility, after 1848 he discovered that the principle of utility produced anything but general agreement about authority. In *The Province of Jurisprudence* the principle of utility was regarded as the foundation for the moral and political sciences which commanded agreement, not only from those who understood them, but also from the partially educated multitude whose understanding of the 'leading principles' of these sciences made it possible for them to accept the authority of those who were experts. In *A Plea for the Constitution*, however, Austin asserted that 'the principle of public utility, applied to so vast a subject as the constitution of a sovereign government, leads generally to an invincible diversity of views.'[9]

This meant that during his last decade Austin thought the only foundation for the political order was a shared belief which originated independently of utility. In contrast to utility, he said, 'the only opinion or sentiment favourable to the constitution, which the great majority of a people can generally hold in common, is the sentiment of constitutionality.' Austin went through contortions trying to make the principle of utility compatible with his new belief that sentiments originating in veneration and tradition rather than utility were the foundation of the political order. In the *Plea* he continued to pay lip service to the principle of utility as the ultimate principle which in extraordinary cases might silence the sentiment of constitutionality, and he noted that this sentiment was a 'feeling [which] is not rejected by that ultimate test' and which was 'sanctioned by public utility.' Yet he also said it was 'not reposing directly and exclusively on considerations of public utility'; indeed, it was a feeling '*in and for itself*,' that is, it existed independently of calculations of benefits and consequences.[10]

Evidently he had lost conviction about the applicability of the principle of utility in the realm of the constitution and therefore of positive morality, but he was unable entirely to cast aside the language of utilitarianism. If this was not an abandonment of his earlier position, at least it was a major retreat. It may be noted that John Stuart Mill, in his review of *A Plea for the Constitution*, did not mention Austin's equivocation about the principle of utility, although at this period he was preparing to publish his own deviation from orthodox utilitarianism, which was to appear only two years later (first in *Fraser's Magazine* in 1861, then in book form, *Utilitarianism*, in 1863). Indeed, despite what Mill read in the *Plea*, he did not change the passage in his *Autobiography* that claimed, 'Like me, [Austin] never ceased to be an utilitarian.'[11]

Austin's conservatism also brought a change in his estimate of the value of liberty. In *A Plea for the Constitution* he urged that the constitution should be sustained because it provided liberty, but in *The Province of Jurisprudence* he had insisted that liberty was not the end of government; the end was the general good, and liberty, like restraint, was merely a means: 'Political or civil liberty, like political or legal restraint, may be generally useful, or generally pernicious; and it is not as being liberty, but as conducting to the general good, that political or civil liberty is an object deserving applause.' Previously, liberty was regarded as less useful than restraint as a means for promoting the general good. He had even argued that there could be too much freedom and had been impatient with the 'ignorant and bawling fanatics who stun you with their pother about liberty'; and he noted with disapproval that 'they who distinguish governments into free and despotic are ... lovers of democracy.' In his last work, however, Austin, although not a lover of democracy, made just such a distinction. Whereas formerly he had said despotism was a misused word and that it was a characteristic of all truly sovereign governments, in his last decade he used the word to condemn oppressive governments such as Louis Napoleon's, and he warned that an extension of the suffrage would 'turn our tempered and emphatically *free* government into an uncontrolled and tyrannical democracy.' With pride and 'without exaggeration,' he said that British government was 'the freest of all governments past and present.' Indeed, because he had observed political conditions in Germany and France, he could 'appreciate the matchless union of order and liberty for which we are indebted to our present incomparable Constitution.'[12]

Admiration for the English constitution was allied to an appreciation of tradition which would have been alien to Austin in 1832. He now thought the feudal origins of the constitution essential to the loyalties that persisted into the nineteenth century. The constitution enjoyed popular support because it 'has been preserved and ameliorated during a long succession of ages and changes.' Sounding like Burke, he said a government was 'a work for generations' which no individual intelligence could create according to a design.'[13] Sarah also argued that such institutions were 'the offspring of slowly developed circumstances.'[14] This high regard for tradition was in sharp contrast to Austin's opinion, not only during his radical years, but also during the period exemplified by the book on jurisprudence. During the radical years he berated communities which were 'the slaves of custom' for being 'bloated with an absurd conceit of their own institutions and manners,' and in the book on jurisprudence he held that love of things ancient was adverse to the rapid development of science, and he noted with disapproval that 'brute custom' rather than 'manly reason' was the basis for many legal and moral rules.[15]

The new reliance on tradition led him to alter his views on education. Whereas in the 1830s he had spurned tradition as a source of attachment and instead looked forward to education as the source of convictions that authority was justified, now that the 'sentiment of constitutionality' and tradition were relied upon, education ceased to have its earlier political significance.[16] Sarah added a footnote to the posthumous republication of *The Province of Jurisprudence* in which she sadly confessed that the passage of thirty years did 'not seem to justify the author's sanguine anticipations of the effects of the spread of education among the people.'[17] After considering the recent events in France and Germany she rhetorically asked what was the result of the seemingly excellent educational systems in those countries, and she told Gladstone that asking the question was 'a voluntary recantation on the part of the zealous translator of Cousin.'[18] (Sarah was critical not only of German education but also of German policy, especially German nationalism, but she continued to admire the simplicity of life and cultural taste in Germany.)[19] It was not that she ceased to appreciate support for authority based on reasoned judgment, and therefore education, but she now thought it an inaccessible goal: 'Until the reason of the masses can be appealed to with some chance of success, the tutelary force of habit and sentiment can ill be dispensed with.'[20]

Centralization was another issue on which Austin now had a changed outlook. In *The Province of Jurisprudence* centralization – although the word was not used – was assumed to be a feature of the indivisible sovereignty that was inherently a part of the modern state; and in the article 'Centralization' Austin argued that the existence of rival authorities, such as local governments or the constituent parts of a federal government, diminished sovereign authority, and therefore was a 'structural defect.' His purpose was to define and defend the claims of the state, and although he believed in free trade and opposed excessive regulation, protection, meddling, and the unnecessary multiplication of functionaries, he regarded the article as a critique of extreme laissez-faire policies which denied the state its proper authority. He did, however, pay obeisance to conventional opinion, which tended to regard centralization as unconstitutional, by acknowledging that local government, if limited in its functions, was beneficial and compatible with centralization, although he said that it was to be denied any significant authority and not allowed to undermine 'the indispensable power and influence of the central authority.'[21]

Austin countered the argument that centralization, while it might be an instrument of good in the hands of a good government, might well become an instrument of evil in the hands of a bad government, by asserting that it had a beneficent effect, regardless of the quality of the government with which it was associated. He upheld this surprising view by asserting that since centralization presupposed a civilized, enlightened people, a centralized government, whether good or bad, 'will aim at the ends sanctioned by a commanding opinion.' Thus 'if the form of the government be good, centralization, with the causes from which it springs, will enhance its good tendencies; if the form of the government be bad, they will go far to correct its bad ones.'[22] This opinion was consistent with his argument in *The Province of Jurisprudence* that forms of government were a matter of indifference, but it contradicted the entire tradition of constitutionalism.

These views of centralization were fundamentally changed after 1848. Austin's defence of centralization crumbled with the discovery that it undermined attachment. Having been made aware of the vulnerability of centralized systems to both revolution and despotism, Sarah (who shared opinions with Austin on such matters) remarked on the French 'feeling of incapacity to combine for public business' and their 'absolute reliance on the central authority.' This condition not only denied the French the benefits of private initiative, but it was 'suffered to pervade the whole region of internal political life ... [creating] a society which cannot defend itself, and must submit without a struggle to force, from whatever side 'force may come; – whether from a despot ... or ... a mob.' She also complained about 'the paralyzing difficulties of a people enfeebled by ages of centralization.' In England, by comparison, there was an 'absence of all visible intervention by the government' and an immense variety of local powers and a people acquainted with the use of those powers. The result was a 'quiet and (as it seems) self-regulating movement of the whole complex machine ... [and an] almost unconstrained and rarely-abused individual liberty.'[23]

The drastic reversal in the Austins' opinion about centralization – from strong defence before 1848 to criticism afterwards – calls for comparison with Tocqueville, for the author of *Democracy in America* was the most notable critic of centralization at that time, and the Austins were familiar with his views. The contrast between them before 1848 is noteworthy in the light of their acquaintance, which may have begun during Tocqueville's visit to England in 1835, when they could have been introduced by Mill or Nassau Senior or perhaps by Sarah's nephew Henry Reeve, who was then translating *Democracy in America*; and it certainly developed in Paris after 1843. The Austins knew Tocqueville's book, for Sarah referrred to it in 1835, and John Austin mentioned the 'tyranny of the majority' in his article 'Centralization,' although only to ridicule the notion.[24] Austin's disagreement before 1848 with Tocqueville's well-known position on centralization is so great that possibly he had Tocqueville in mind when he wrote the article in order to counter prevailing opinion on the subject.

For Tocqueville in the *Democracy* the supreme task was to preserve individual liberty, especially under a popular or democratic government. Since despotism was the greatest political evil, Tocqueville valued all institutions and circumstances that were obstacles to despotic power. Thus he welcomed decentralization, and although this theme became especially prominent in his thinking after the publication of *Democracy in America* (part one in 1835, part two in 1840), it was already present in this work, as his discussions of town meetings and federalism made evident. Tocqueville, like Austin, recognized the need to maintain the authority of central governments, but he allowed considerable autonomy to local governments, including legislative authority, whereas Austin before 1848 emphasized their subordinate and dependent status. Whereas Tocqueville welcomed federal arrangements as an obstacle to despotic power, Austin regarded them as anomalous and redefined them to make them compatible with his understanding of sovereignty as residing in only one body. Whereas Tocqueville looked back with appreciation of the localism in France that was historically linked to aristocratic privileges, Austin regarded its abolition by the French Revolution as 'a great good' and felt 'contempt of the silly regrets for the former provinces and their privileges.' For Tocqueville, those provinces and their privileges prevented the excessive encroachments of despotism, while for Austin they were obstacles to the development of the modern state.[25]

This vast difference between Austin and Tocqueville disappeared when the Austins recognized a connection between strong central authority in France and many of the country's political problems. Their newly discovered scepticism about centralizatiion during the 1850s obviously had affinities with Tocqueville's. Whether they arrived at their new understanding of the problem without Tocqueville's help is not clear, but it is difficult to believe they were not influenced by him. They enjoyed cordial relations with him during their five years in Paris, and these relations continued even during the disturbed days of early 1848.[26] Both Sarah and John Austin read his *Ancien Régime* (1856), in which the centralization theme was even more prominent than in *Democracy in America*. Just before the publication in 1859 of her long article on France, in which her agreement with Tocqueville about the dangers of centralization was most evident, Sarah reported that she and Austin were reading

Tocqueville's *Ancien Régime* with great interest, although she did not acknowledge it as a source for their most recent opinions. The book, she said, would 'suggest to the mass of readers many considerations which are familiar to you [Guizot] and not wholly new to us.'[27]

After 1848 there were, of course, other affinities with Tocqueville which were related to the centralization theme: the emphasis on the threat that society would become 'masses of unorganized individuals,' the concern with the decline of 'habits of corporate action,' the vision of the unorganized populace acting as if in a 'sheepfold,' and the belief that between an absolute ruler and the people 'there remained nothing – not even a voice.' All these concerns had parallels in Tocqueville's writings, and there is even some similarity in language, especially in the use of the sheepfold simile. Together with the centralization theme, and in view of the differences between Austin and Tocqueville before 1848, these parallels signify the drastic changes in the Austins' political outlook.[28]

If Austin had made revisions in his work on jurisprudence that took into account his many altered views – about positive morality, the principle of utility, tradition, education, the importance of aristocracy, centralization, liberty, and the constitution – the changes would not have been mere additions or small corrections but substantial modifications. No wonder Sarah could report that he 'had discovered defects ... which had escaped the criticism of others,' and that he said, apparently quite often, 'that the book must be entirely recast and rewritten.'[29]

Sarah Austin attributed her husband's reluctance to reprint *The Province of Jurisprudence* to a variety of reasons but mainly to his fastidiousness, perhaps without realizing the full extent of his dissatisfaction with the original work. But his failure to revise and complete the work can be attributed at least partially to the conflict between his new beliefs and the assumptions and substance of *The Province of Jurisprudence*. When in the 1840s he first shifted his interest to positive morality and ethics, and especially after 1848, when his conservatism led him to look to tradition and custom and non-rational attachments, such as the sentiment of constitutionality, the new beliefs were a direct challenge to his earlier conceptualization and ideas. In this connection it is worth noting that once he gave free rein to his conservative convictions, as he did in *A Plea for the Constitution*, he had no difficulty in writing. Sarah reported 'great – immense – news ... *My husband is writing* ... He is working – not laboriously and slowly, but with more energy and rapidity than I ever saw in him ... I never in my life knew him to write with such rapidity, ease and *verve* as he has this time.'[30] With the conflict put aside and perhaps resolved, there was a great release of energy. Macaulay seems to have recognized this when he noted that Austin had simultaneously become fluent and conservative. In view of the contrast with the earlier period, it seems plausible to point to his second thoughts and the ensuing conflict as a major source of Austin's inert pen.

THE EXTENT OF THE CHANGES in Austin's outlook since he had published *The Province of Jurisprudence* can be indicated by making the suggestion that he was moving in the direction of the historical school, which emphasized the importance of continuity and tradition – that he was ceasing to be an Austinian. This is suggested by the clear affinity between certain themes in *A Plea for the Constitution* and the distinctive characteristics of historical jurisprudence. In the *Plea*, of course, he did not consider every topic taken up in *The Province of Jurisprudence*, but he was sufficiently close to the historical school on matters of government and the constitution to make it very unlikely that during his last years he could have written on jurisprudence as he had done earlier.

The idea of common law, with its emphasis on custom and tradition and the belief that a sense of the past sustained the legal tradition, was an important part of historical jurisprudence. Austinian jurisprudence, as Vinogradoff has said, had displayed contempt for the historical tradition of common law, but in about 1849 Austin established a special place and gave enhanced significance to positive morality, which was composed of custom and moral beliefs, and which greatly overlapped with the notion of common law.[31] In the *Plea* he praised the British constitution and the general idea of constitutionality which exemplified what he had called positive morality, and he did this by using language that had also been used by those who eulogized the common law tradition and by identifying as virtues of the constitution the qualities that were claimed for the common law by the historical school.

The historical school held that the common law allowed for adaptations to new circumstances and for gradual improvements without revolution. Austin's move towards this outlook was evident in his appreciation for tradition after 1848, and in the *Plea* where he argued that so complex an institution as government was 'a work for generations' and that the constitution was 'preserved and ameliorated during a long succession of ages and changes.'[32]

Austin also came close to adopting the historical school's view that law was descended from the past, from history, and that its virtues and advantages could not exist without that history. Referring not to law but to government, including the constitutional rules regulating it, he said:

> It has arisen insensibly from the past states of the country, and has been adapted insensibly to its present situation. There are, moreover, important parts of the system which have arisen from usage and not from positive institutions; and owing to the subtlety of their operation, as well as to the obscurity of their origin and growth, it is difficult to appreciate their importance or even to apprehend them accurately.

He also said that the object of loyalty by the British people was 'not a constitution of recent origin, but one which has descended to them from preceding generations.' The constitution had ancient origins, and Austin appreciated the survival of feudal sentiments which allowed loyalty to 'free governments grafted on feudal institutions.' Thus freedom in Britain depended on historical traditions which other countries unfortunately did not possess.[33]

There was also a resemblance between his great emphasis on feelings, sentiments, and attachments that provided support for the constitution and an argument that was an important part of Savigny's contribution to the historical school's position; Savigny argued that law, like the constitution and language, had no independent existence, but was subtly and organically connected with all aspects of national culture and history. In this view the cultural and social basis of law was associated with what was later called the *Volksgeist*. Although Austin traced sentiments and attachments to love and veneration and habit, he also regarded them as existing by virtue of a particular historical experience and independently of acts of the sovereign, and in this they became similiar to the *Volksgeist*.[34] Indeed, the resemblance is so marked that one wonders about the effect of Austin's conversations with Savigny in Berlin in 1842-3. There are hints of mutual sympathy in the report that Savigny praised the Austins and in Sarah's appreciative observations about him.[35] However, it is not necessary to trace this development to a specific intellectual influence, for it was closely connected to Austin's conservative recognition of the importance of social bonds which gave attachment and loyalty. This recognition led him to an appreciation of the social basis of law, which was also part of the historical school's position. This theme was reflected in the Burkean ingredients in the *Plea*, whereas Hobbes, with whose philosophy Austin had such close affinity when he wrote *The Province of Jurisprudence*, would have been quite alien to the spirit of the later work. It may also be noted that Austin, who once thought of himself as having a special vocation for untying intellectual knots and who was regarded as being skilled at 'precisionizing,' now lost much of the crispness of style and clarity on which he had prided himself.[36]

Evidently Austin did not reveal to Sarah the distance he had travelled since writing *The Province of Jurisprudence*, thus belying Sarah's confidence that she was 'the person with whom he had no reserves.'[37] It must have been a terrible thing for him to realize that his early confidence had been unfounded and that he had sacrificed decades of thought and labour to a science of jurisprudence whose foundations he now recognized to be feeble. Perhaps this was why he had an 'aversion to the subject of his labours' and why he reacted to suggestions that he revise and republish *The Province of Jurisprudence* with a 'look as if anybody had hit him a blow.'[38] But for Sarah, who had made sacrifices of her own, had she known, it would also have been a grievous blow. Recalling her relation with Pückler, one might say that each guarded a secret which if revealed would have been devastating to the other. Sarah at least acted as if she did not appreciate the significance of the changes in Austin's views, for after his death she ignored his long record of refusal to republish *The Province of Jurisprudence* and immediately reprinted the 1832 volume; soon thereafter she also brought out the remaining extant University of London lectures which he had repeatedly declined to publish. Her venture was successful. There were two editions in her lifetime, and four by 1885. Thus she perpetuated his reputation as one of the founders of analytical jurisprudence long after he ceased to believe in it.

10

Helpmate to fame

WHEN JOHN AUSTIN DIED on 17 December 1859 his doubts about the value of his jurisprudence died with him. Sarah occupied the seven and a half years that remained to her making a prodigious effort to secure her husband the reputation as a legal philosopher that had eluded him during his lifetime. The first step in this mission to rescue him from obscurity was to place his work before the public. She republished the lectures which he had refused to reprint and boldly published the manuscripts that he had refused to publish. Amidst solitude and gloom, despite ill health, and while enduring terrible anxieties about Lucy's heroic struggle with consumption, Sarah, with her usual determination, went about constructing her husband's monument. The result of her determination was to make him famous as the founder of Austinian jurisprudence. Her achievement was not so much to perpetuate his reputation as to establish it.

Sarah chose mourning stationery with three-eighths of an inch black borders, surely among the widest of such borders available from London stationers. The cult of mourning could not have had a more zealous devotee. She made a shrine of his room: everything remained as he left it, and Sarah lived there, leaving it only for solitary meals and her daily drive in her pony chaise. She experienced 'convulsions of sorrow,' and even wallowed in grief:

> I think it is not possible for grief and desolation to be deeper and more settled than mine. How can it be otherwise? Every link in our early love had been rivetted by common adversity and suffering, by mutual cares and services, by profound humble reverence on my part, and tender indulgent approbation on

his – lastly by a community of thought and feeling more rare than all the rest, and enjoyed in an almost unbroken tête à tête for years. You may understand the void is *entire* and incurable.

Of course, in recalling the past Sarah glossed over the frustrations that had been the source of so much unhappiness. Aware of the darker side of the Austin marriage, Harriet Grote ridiculed Sarah's conspicuous mourning and called her Artemesia, after the widow renowned in ancient Greece for her extraordinary grief at the death of her husband, King Mausolus. Artemesia mixed her husband's ashes in her daily drink and built a monument (remembered in the word mausoleum) to perpetuate his memory. Sarah's behaviour in building a monument for Austin seemed no less excessive to Mrs Grote.[1]

Sarah had declared that she thought her husband was dependent on her, but now she discovered that she needed him to justify her existence, which without him seemed directionless: 'Everything I read, or heard, or saw, or thought, came *from* him or tended *to* him as the centre of my inward being.' The refrain was endless: she had merely been his reflection; his word had been her law; she was without a compass, and her mind drifted; her feelings and ideas were drawn from him, so that 'now I feel that I am nothing.' The emptiness left in her life was made greater by the peculiarity of their relationship. Now that the object of her devotion, sacrifice, and support was taken from her, she faced a purposeless existence, as she called it, a divided life, a life broken in halves, a void.[2] She had lost not only her husband but also her mission.

Sarah continued to grieve, but she soon recovered a sense of purpose. She decided to serve Austin, although he was dead, as she had done while he lived. She told herself that he had failed to revise and complete his book on jurisprudence and ethics because he lacked the will and the energy to struggle for a reputation; but since she did not lack these strengths, she would lend them to him even after his death. First she would reprint *The Province of Jurisprudence*, and she planned to bring out the lectures and fragments that were not included in the original publication of 1832. These latter writings might be imperfect – Austin had thought them so – but she was convinced that nevertheless they were valuable and would vindicate him.

Publishing would serve several purposes. First of all it would force the legal profession, which had neglected Austin, to recognize the usefulness of his work and the quality of his mind. She would 'render [the work]

useful to the ungrateful world, who did not know how to appreciate *him*.'
His talents had been concealed from the world. 'It sometimes grieves me,'
she wrote a year before his death, 'to think how imperfectly he is known to
any one but his wife, how few traces he will leave of his great faculties and
acquirements, of his greater virtues; how completely the poverty and
obscurity ... veil him from the world.' While achieving recognition for her
husband, publication would also confer benefits on the public. She always
believed he was 'capable of bequeathing an inestimable gift to posterity,'
and she suffered to see him 'wearing away his life without devoting any
part of his great power to the service of mankind.' Now she would save
what might otherwise be wasted. One also recalls that when Sarah
complained about Austin's failure to write and publish, she said there was
'another way of avenging oneself on the injustice of men,' and now, it
seems, she planned revenge on his behalf.[3]

There was yet another, highly personal dimension of Sarah's plan,
which was to satisfy her '*wifely* ambition.' To achieve recognition for him
would at last allow her to be the successful helpmate to a man whose life
was ennobled by a wish to serve the public and discover useful truths.
Although her hopes for him had 'all ended in disappointment and failure,
yet you see,' she wrote, 'now when he is in his grave, *that* survives or rather
*re*vives, and my young ambition was not more fervent than that which is
now the sole unextinguished passion of my old age – the sole gleam of
light in my darkness. It is this which enables me to bear solitude and keeps
me from utter despondency.' By gaining worldly recognition of Austin's
talent and achievement Sarah would also gain confirmation that he was
indeed a great man and that her devotion and sacrifices had not been
made in vain. She would serve herself as well as her husband by making
famous the name they shared; as she said, it was the 'name I sought to
exalt.' Sarah thus found a renewed sense of dedication; she knew the work
would be long and laborious, but it would be 'the main object of [her]
remaining life.'[4]

Sarah's vigilance for Austin's reputation was evident in her efforts to
secure him a worthy obituary. Soon after his death she sent Lord
Brougham information about Austin that he might incorporate in his
forthcoming obituary, for the former Lord Chancellor and leading
spokesman for law reform could provide valuable publicity. Brougham
acknowledged that her letter was invaluable, and he 'inserted her very
words in more instances than one.' After the obituary article appeared in
the *Law Magazine* Sarah showered him with gratitude: 'You have made
prominent,' she wrote, 'those qualities so great, so lofty, so rare which

peculiarly distinguished him ... I am satisfied, touched, grateful ... I bless you for what you have done.'⁵ Brougham's generally laudatory obituary was one of the very few that appeared.

Even before Austin's death, Sarah had cultivated good relations with Brougham. Her flattery and sycophancy, in the light of the Malta dispute and her memory of Brougham's 'wild and unaccountable hostility,' including his public humiliation of Austin, show how much pride she was willing to swallow for her purposes. She visited Brougham, sent him Austin's Malta papers so that he might reconsider his judgment on that matter, and told him that Austin's esteem for him was boundless. She also contrived to have her own and supposedly Austin's admiring statements reach him through third parties. After the obituary appeared she spoke of Brougham's 'overflowing with zeal for my dear husband's fame' and how this had the effect of 'more than obliterating all the past.'⁶ Such was her zeal to gain recognition for her husband.

Sarah began by publishing in 1861 a new edition of *The Province of Jurisprudence*. She introduced it with a long and moving preface, which tried to explain her husband's unproductive life. Yet she did not regard it as a biographical memoir. 'It is not the life of a man,' she said, 'but the history of a book.' Her purpose was to 'vindicate ... him from the charge of indolence or indifference to truth.'⁷

The next task was to edit the previously unpublished manuscripts. At first these were bewildering to her, for, in addition to the University of London and Inner Temple lectures, they included tables, fragments, insertions, and notes. The subject seemed strange and difficult, and Sarah was diffident, especially as she did not wish to appear presumptuous or irreverent. She spoke about the bitterness of seeing noble ruins falling into her feeble hands. She consulted Austin's old friend Sir William Erle, now a judge, and James Fitzjames Stephen, the author of an appreciative article on Austin and the son of Austin's close friend James Stephen, who had been under-secretary in the Colonial Office when the Austins were in Malta. She also was advised by former students, including George Cornewall Lewis and Sir John Romilly. William Whewell, the Master of Trinity College, was consulted about particular points of information, and her nephew Henry Reeve was generally helpful.⁸

As she worked on her husband's manuscripts Sarah's confidence in their importance increased. Brougham recommended *The Province of Jurisprudence* as a university text, and Sarah was delighted to hear about the interest it excited: 'And *he* thought nobody would ever appreciate him!' Such recognition spurred her on. Now she called her editing a sacred work, and she referred to the manuscripts as 'beloved relics.' When she survived another serious episode of heart disease she thought God had spared her so that she could labour for her husband. She confessed, 'I have even a superstitious fear of dying before I have finished and could say to him, "I have done my best that your great thoughts might not perish."' She also regarded the manuscripts as a mine from which future thinkers would extract great riches. The work, she explained, 'gives an interest to life I could find nowhere else ... I am never weary of it, for I see in a future (so remote that I *can* see it only with the eye of faith) my husband's fame and usefulness increasing with every page I finish.' When in 1863 she completed the *Lectures on Jurisprudence*, which, in addition to *The Province of Jurisprudence*, included forty-six lectures and supplementary essays that had not been available before, she declared, 'It does not signify what becomes of me. I may die, the house may be burned, and the MSS. and I in it; my dear husband's labours and thoughts are safe.' With Austin's thoughts 'beyond the reach of destruction or of oblivion,' it was 'as if [her] life were done,' and her 'business in this world ... over.'[9]

Sarah's performance as an editor of the lectures was, on the whole, satisfactory. 'I alter *nothing* but what I find marked by my *husband's own hand*,' she told the publisher; 'I shall add a few notes, left by him, and marked for insertion, but I will take *no* liberties with his text ... that is sacred in *my* eyes.' It was not difficult for her to meet this high editorial standard for the lectures, as the manuscripts were left in good order.[10] She fell far short of her standard, however, in dealing with the notes, fragments, and miscellaneous essays, which were in part 'a chaos of disjointed fragments.' These parts of the book were based on 'the merest *jottings*' which 'rather show[ed] what he meant to do, than what he had done.' Sarah published all these in their entirety, but despite 'the difficulties of combining and arranging these precious fragments,' she imposed an order on the material that Austin might not have approved.[11]

Sarah's achievement was not the editing of Austin's work but its publication. This was a matter of her determination and energy, and perhaps, also, her insensitivity to the extent of Austin's difficulty in reconciling his jurisprudence with his later ideas about liberty, constitutionalism, tradition, and the principle of utility. Although the posthumous publications did not provide accurate and full statements of Austin's ideas during the last decade of his life, they did stimulate interest in jurisprudence in the legal profession and in the universities. Sarah did not live long enough to witness the full impact of her work, which included a third edition in 1869, a fourth in 1873, and a fifth in 1885. An abridged

Student's Edition appeared in 1875; and *An Analysis* (that is, a précis) in 1877. Henry Sumner Maine in 1884 said Austin's book 'must always, or for a long time to come, be the mainstay of the studies prosecuted in [the Jurisprudence] Department [at Oxford].' Sheldon Amos, Austin's successor at the University of London, in 1877 called him 'the true founder of the science of law,' and A.V. Dicey, who 'spoke the language of the law with a decidedly Austinian accent,' testified to Austin's revival of speculative study of the law.[12]

Sarah did witness, however, the first signs of her success, and she was deeply gratified. The 1861 reprint of *The Province of Jurisprudence* quickly became an examination book at both Cambridge and Oxford, and she could report:

> His book is daily rising into fame and authority to a degree which I never hoped to live to witness, and which he would never have believed ... I am assured by barristers that there is a perfect enthusiasm about it among *young* lawyers – men among whom it was unknown till since [sic] I published the second edition. So I have lived for something.

When Sarah visited Oxford with Barthélemy Saint-Hilaire, she 'had the great satisfaction of hearing [her] husband spoken of with the utmost admiration and reverence.'[13]

John Stuart Mill played a part in resurrecting Austin's name. When the forbidding three-volume work first came out, Sarah was disappointed that, except for a few brief notices, one of them (in the *Athenaeum*) published on her own initiative, it was 'received ... with total silence.' Mill attracted the attention of serious readers with his long and appreciative essay on the work in the *Edinburgh Review* for October 1863. Although Sarah realized that such a review in so notable a journal was important to her enterprise, it must have aroused bitter recollections. In 1860 she had been angered by Mill's reluctance to help; she had applied to him as Austin's 'former friend, almost "son," and élève in logic and in law,' but he was '*too much occupied!*' Of course, she also recalled what she regarded as Mill's cruelty to her at the time of Austin's death. In spite of these recollections – she often criticized Mill during her last years – his forty-four page favourable review must have been welcome. Austin's was 'a most remarkable mind,' Mill wrote; not only was his jurisprudence an organon for certain faculties of the intellect, but the three-volume work had 'a claim to a place in the education of statesmen, publicists, and students of the human mind.'[14]

Sarah may have been thinking of Mill's review, along with the use made of the book at Oxford and Cambridge, when she realized that Austin's place in history was being established:

> Proofs of the tardy recognition of his supreme excellence as a Jurist are almost daily coming to me and bringing with them a tide of mingled joy and grief in which first one and then the other predominates. I should however be unworthy to bear his name if I did not feel that his most earnest and constant desire – to be of use to his country – had been accomplished.

She continually affirmed this consoling belief: 'The book is evidently *taking root*'; 'My husband's influence grows.' Eventually she thought his work and his reputation imperishable.[15]

APART FROM THIS CONSOLATION, Sarah's last years were sad, and they were also lonely. She continued to suffer from heart trouble (in June 1860 her doctor thought she was on the verge of death); in 1861 she had a fall while visiting Guizot and never fully recovered; and she suffered from fainting fits and gout in the right hand. Two brothers died within two months in 1863, and her sister, Susan Reeve, died the following year. She travelled to Ventnor and Wales, and to the seaside at Cromer in Norfolk; she also went to Bonn, Boulogne, and Paris to see friends and visit once again places where she had lived. In Weybridge, however, she was rather isolated, especially after her granddaughter Janet's marriage in 1860 and Lucy's departure the next year to the Cape of Good Hope (and a year later to Egypt) in search of a benign climate while waiting to die from her tuberculosis. Sarah worried continuously about Lucy's health, and this was made worse by the month-long wait for letters from Egypt. The danger, she said, although not present, was always near, and she complained of the 'corroding anxiety' and asked only to be spared 'a second death-blow.' She met Lucy in 1865 at Soden, near Frankfurt, and realized it would be their last meeting. Although distraught, she managed to edit and publish the letters Lucy sent to her family from Egypt and the Cape. Alone and unwell, she complained of being 'companionless' and of suffering from insomnia, 'distressing restlessness,' and 'settled gloom,' and she spoke about 'recurring fits of illness which destroy my living soul before they put an end to my body.'

Amidst her many sadnesses she was able to note, 'The only ray of sunshine in my life is the success my book has had.' The success was valuable for what it indicated about Austin: 'The rise of my husband's reputation and authority is the one bright spot in my dark life.'[16] Whereas Austin when he died was hardly known outside a small circle, now, because of her enterprise, his fame was established. Her own stake in this outcome was great. Throughout a difficult life she had clung to the belief that he was capable of great achievement, and by boldly producing evidence of it after his death, she was vindicating her sacrifices and her faith.

Sarah Austin died on 8 August 1867, at the age of seventy-four, from heart and kidney disease. At the time she was preparing yet another edition of her husband's book. She lies buried beside him in Weybridge beneath a stone bearing the Latin inscription she had composed for him:

> Here is buried John Austin. A man equally distinguished by intellect and worth, not allured by the hope either of profit or of fame, he earnestly dedicated the marvellous keenness of his intellect and the powers of his lofty mind to the pursuit of truth justice and honour. Especially he unravelled the principles of jurisprudence by his subtle reason, and clearly expounded them by his speech and writings. This memorial, little as it is, of her regret and love has been placed by his sorrowing wife.

She had written this with great care and had it cut in polished granite 'as the most durable stone.' Practical as ever, she also seems to have composed her own inscription: 'Sarah, who in her bereavement had placed this monument to her much lamented husband John Austin, after painfully surviving him for 8 years, at last gladly rests beneath the same stone.'[17] Although weathering of the gravestone has obscured her eulogy, she would have been gratified to know that by virtue of her more durable monument the Austin name has survived.

Abbreviations

AT	Authors' translation
BL	British Library, London
Blakiston	Mrs Georgiana Blakiston
Bowood	Bowood House: Papers of the Marquess of Lansdowne
'Centralization'	John Austin 'Centralization' *Edinburgh Review* 85 (January 1847) 221-58
CLC	*The Collected Letters of Thomas and Jane Welsh Carlyle* Duke-Edinburgh edition, ed. Charles Richard Sanders and Kenneth J. Fielding (Durham, N.C., 1976-)
CO	Colonial Office Papers at PRO
CW	*Collected Works of John Stuart Mill*, ed. J.M. Robson (Toronto 1963-)
Durham	Durham University, Department of Paleography and Diplomatic
EL	*The Earlier Letters of John Stuart Mill 1812-1848* ed. Francis E. Mineka, in *CW* XII-XIII (Toronto 1963)
Fragments	*Fragments from German Prose Writers*, translated by Sarah Austin, illustrated with notes (London 1841)
GCL	George Cornewall Lewis
Germany	Sarah Austin *Germany, from 1760 to 1814; or, Sketches of German Life, from the Decay of the Empire to the Expulsion of the French* (London 1854)
GP	Guizot Papers, Archives Privées, Archives Nationales, Paris
Hansard	*Hansard's Parliamentary Debates* 3rd series
JA	John Austin
LDG	Gordon Waterfield *Lucie Duff Gordon in England, South Africa and Egypt* (New York 1937)

Lect. Juris.	John Austin *Lectures on Jurisprudence or the Philosophy of Positive Law* ed. Robert Campbell (4th ed. London 1873)
Letters of GCL	*Letters of the Right Hon. Sir George Cornewall Lewis, Bart. to Various Friends* ed. Gilbert Frankland Lewis (London 1870)
LL	*The Later Letters of John Stuart Mill 1849-1873* ed. Francis E. Mineka and Dwight N. Lindley, in *CW* XIV-XVII (Toronto 1972)
MA	Archives of John Murray, Publisher, London
Murray	John Murray II and John Murray III: all letters dated before 27 June 1843 were addresssed to John Murray II; all letters dated after 27 June 1843 were addressed to John Murray III
NLS	National Library of Scotland, Edinburgh
Plea	John Austin *A Plea for the Constitution* (2nd ed. London 1859)
PP	*Parliamentary Papers*
PRO	Public Record Office
Prov. Juris.	John Austin *The Province of Jurisprudence Determined* (1832), as reprinted in *Lect. Juris.*
Reports	*Copies or Extracts of Reports of the Commissioners Appointed to Inquire into the Affairs of the Island of Malta, and of Correspondence Thereupon*, in *PP*
SA	Sarah Austin
SA, Preface	Sarah Austin, Preface to *The Province of Jurisprudence Determined* (2nd ed. London 1861) as reprinted in *Lect. Juris.*
St Bride	St Bride Printing Library, London
TG	Janet Ross *Three Generations of English Women, Memoirs and Correspondence of Susannah Taylor, Sarah Austin, and Lady Duff Gordon* (revised ed. London 1893)
TP	E.M. Butler *The Tempestuous Prince, Hermann Pückler-Muskau* (London 1929)
UCL	University College, London
UCLA	University of California, Los Angeles
Wales	National Library of Wales, Aberystwyth
Waterfield	Mr Gordon Waterfield
Weimar	Nationale Forschungs- und Gedenkstätten der Klassischen Deutschen Literatur in Weimar
WO	War Office Papers at PRO
Yale	Yale University Library

Notes

Chapter 1

1 Sarah Taylor was born on 1 April 1793 and John Austin on 3 March 1790. Sally was the name by which Sarah was known in her childhood, which, she said later, 'the rest of my family have suffered to drop into the more respectable form of Sarah': SA's endorsement to Henry Taylor, on letter of Edward Taylor to SA, 3 April 1849, Bodleian Library, Oxford, MS Autog. d 23, f. 111.

2 Janet Ross *Early Days Recalled* (London 1891) 69, 107; Janet Ross *Fourth Generation* (London 1912) 21; *Memoir of Mrs. Eliza Fox* ed. Franklin Fox (London 1869) 65; *Dictionary of National Biography* I 739; John Knox Laughton *Memoirs of the Life and Correspondence of Henry Reeve* (London 1898) II 323

3 *TG* 46

4 *LDG* 31; *A Concise History and Directory of the City of Norwich* (Norwich 1810) 51; John Taylor (continued by Edward Taylor) *History of the Octagon Chapel, Norwich* (London 1848) 59. John Rising Staff seems to have been a Unitarian and a member of the Octagon Chapel.

5 *TG* 44

6 *Army List, 1808* 199; *Army List, 1809* 202; *LDG* 13; R. Wilson to Col. J.W. Gordon, 6 February 1807, WO 31/222.

7 Lt. Col. Robert Gardens to Gen. Rainsford, 8 January 1808, WO 31/245

8 On Austin's move to Sicily, see 'Statement of the Pay and Daily Allowances of the Commissioned Officers of the 1st Battalion 44th Regiment of Infantry from the 25th September to the 24th of December 1808' WO 12/5646. Austin received £1.0.6 while on board ship from 10 August to 30 October 1808. On the military situation facing Austin's battalion, see Thomas Carter, ed. *Historical Record of the Forty Fourth, or the East Essex Regiment of Foot* (London

1864) 52-63; John W. Burrows *The Essex Regiment: 1st Battalion (44th)* (2nd ed., Southend-on Sea 1931) 36.

9 Gen. Sir John Stuart to Liverpool, 9 October 1810, WO 1/309, f. 228. The Faro Point was regarded as the key to the entire island. Austin was detached to the grenadier battalion from July 1809 until July 1811 and again in January 1812: Monthly Returns of 1st Battalion 44th Regiment, WO 17/156. This grenadier battalion was different from the 1st Regiment of [Grenadier] Guards, for whom the term 'grenadiers' is conventionally used. A historian of the regiment reports that the grenadiers 'were a fine body of men, and there existed great pride and jealousy among the several companies to keep up the credit of each corps': Carter *Historical Record* 47n. As a consequence of being detached to the grenadiers, Austin was removed from the scene of a minor engagement that took place in September 1810 when Murat landed a small force at Milo, seven miles south of Messina. Austin's regiment was at Messina when this occurred. The landing, which was easily repulsed, was the only one accomplished by the enemy. Apparently it was a diversion from a larger invasion north of Messina which was called off when the diversionary landing failed: Gen. J. Campbell to Stuart, 18 September 1810, WO 1/309, ff. 209-14; Carter *Historical Record* 49; Bunbury *Narratives* 400-3.

10 The one occasion when the war of waiting was interrupted occurred when the 44th regiment participated in an attack against Murat's army on the mainland, and therefore it is highly probable that Austin also took part. An expedition set off to harass the enemy coast in June 1809. Part of it attacked the castle at Scylla, and the islands of Ischia and Procida in the Bay of Naples were seized and occupied. Austin's battalion was relegated to the reserve brigade and occupied the island of Procida, where the defenders mutinied; other battalions either attacked Ischia, where fighting did take place, although on a small scale, or landed at Scylla, where the attack was unsuccessful. After a month the entire British force, including Austin's regiment, was withdrawn to Sicily, as it was decided that the ships in the Bay of Naples and Sicily itself were vulnerable to attack by the French fleet from Toulon. Thus Austin's regiment resumed its defensive position on the east coast of Sicily. J.W. Fortescue *A History of the British Army* (London 1912) VII 245; Carter *Historical Record* 47-9; Henry Bunbury *Narratives of Some Passages in the Great War with France, from 1799 to 1810* (London 1854) 364-75, 380-3, 461; Stuart to Castlereagh, 9 June 1809, 5 July 1809, 2 August 1809, WO 1/307, ff. 169-71, 181-91, 251-3; Monthly Returns for 1 June, 1 July 1809, WO 17/156.

11 *LDG* 13. The diary was among papers belonging to Mrs Aubrey Waterfield which were lost in Italy in 1945. Therefore the only passages that survive are those in *LDG* and in *Encyclopaedia Britannica* (11th ed., London 1910-11) II

938-40. The first entry in the diary was 31 December 1811, only two months before Austin's return to England, and it was not kept while he was in Sicily. On the move to Malta, see Monthly Returns, WO 17/156.

12 *LDG* 13-15. Austin also complained in his diary about a tailor's bill; this was understandable in view of the required uniform, which included a large cocked hat, leather breeches, and long boots above the knee. Powdered hair with a curl at the back was required. In the Malta garrison officers on duty were inspected to determine that their swords and their twenty-five silver buttons were bright. To appear out of barracks without being in regimentals and wearing swords 'was never dreamt of': Carter *Historical Record* 47-8. Austin probably had a servant; it was common for officers to have as many as five to seven soldiers as menial servants until an order in 1811 limited the number to one: WO 1/310, ff. 211-15.

13 *LDG* 16

14 *LDG* 15-16; JA to Gen. Sir Thomas Trigge, Ipswich 25 August 1812, WO 31/354; Monthly Returns, WO 17/156. Austin's mixed feelings and indecisiveness were also evident in his letter of resignation: 'This measure is on my part involuntary only in as far as it has been forced from me by the concurring wishes of my whole family.' Had Austin not resigned, he would have gone with his battalion to fight in Spain and America (Bladensburg, New Orleans, and Mobile).

15 Betsy Rodgers *Georgian Chronicle: Mrs. Barbauld and Her Family* (London 1958) 236

16 Rodgers *Georgian Chronicle* 235; Susan Reeve to Richard Taylor, 22 November [n.y]; Susanna Taylor to Richard Taylor, 4 December 1814, St Bride

17 Susanna Taylor to Richard Taylor, 4 December 1814, St Bride; *TG* 41, 42

18 Susanna Taylor to Richard Taylor, 4 December 1814, St Bride

19 Edward Taylor 'Obituary – Mr John Taylor' *Monthly Repository* 21 (August 1826) 482; R.K. Webb *Harriet Martineau* (New York 1960) 58-9

20 John Taylor to SA, 16 June 1824, Osborn Collection, Yale; Brian Hayes 'Politics in Norfolk, 1750-1832' Ph.D. dissertation, Cambridge University 1957, 87; Taylor family pride was later exhibited in a family tree drawn up by a John Taylor in 1897 on a scroll that is approximately twenty feet long: Manchester College Library, Oxford.

21 Dr John Taylor to his daughter, 1 January 1745, St Bride

22 John Taylor 'History of Norwich Manufacturers' *Monthly Magazine* 6 (December 1798) 415

23 John Taylor to SA, 31 May 1825, Osborn Collection, Yale; document dated 25 December 1813, St Bride

24 John Taylor to SA, 31 May 1825, Osborn Collection, Yale

25 Janet Ross *Fourth Generation* 22; Henry Reeve to Janet Ross, 17 January 1873, Waterfield

26 Mr Wallace Morfey of Woodbridge, Suffolk, kindly supplied information about the Austin family's connection with Ipswich School; *TG* 49.

27 JA to Bentham, 20 July 1819, UCL. Margaret C.W. Wicks *The Italian Exiles in London, 1816-1848* (Manchester 1937) 252

28 John Taylor to Richard Taylor, 14 September 1819; John Taylor to Richard Taylor, 17 November 1814; Susanna Taylor to Richard Taylor, 4 December 1814, St Bride; John Taylor to SA, 16 June 1824, Osborn Collection, Yale

29 *TG* 56, 364; Susanna Taylor to Richard Taylor, 4 December 1814, St Bride

30 *LDG* 25-9; SA, Preface 3

31 *LDG* 24-5; JA to Nassau Senior [c. 1820], copy, misdated November 1818, Wales

32 Sarah Taylor to Richard Taylor, 30 December 1814, St Bride

33 *LDG*, 30-1; Sarah Taylor to Richard Taylor, 30 December 1814, St Bride

34 Susan Reeve to Richard Taylor, 26 October 1814, St Bride; *Memoir of Mrs. Eliza Fox* 75

35 *LDG* 13-15

36 *TG* 373

37 Susan Reeve to Richard Taylor, 22 November [1814], St Bride

38 Austin was religious, at least until he came under Bentham's influence. As a child he is said to have read the Bible to his religious mother, and during his courtship he requested that Sarah give him a Bible: *LDG*, 30. There is a statement by Lucy at age fourteen that indicates unawareness of her father's Unitarian background (Lucy Austin to Alice Spring-Rice, 15-21 September [1835] Bodleian Library); but the evidence of the Austin family's Unitarianism is strong: see Janet Ross 'Lady Duff Gordon' *Macmillan's Magazine* 30 (October 1894) 531; 'Death of Charles Austin, Esq.' *Suffolk Chronicle* 26 December 1874, 5. See also Lina Waterfield *Castles in Italy: An Autobiography* (New York 1961) 8; A.D.E. Lewis 'John Austin, Pupil of Bentham' *Bentham Newsletter* No. 2 (March 1979) 23.

39 Sarah Taylor to Richard Taylor, 30 December 1814, St Bride

40 *The New Schaff-Herzog Encyclopedia of Religious Knowledge* (Michigan 1960) XI 285; Dr John Taylor to his daughter, 8 November 1756, St Bride

41 John Taylor 'Some account of the origin and progress of the Congregation of Protestant Dissenters ... at the Octagon Chapel in the City of Norwich' (1796), Local History Library, Norwich; *The Principles and Pursuits of an English Presbyterian Minister of the Eighteenth Century; Exemplified in a Selection from the Writings of Dr. John Taylor of Norwich* (London 1843) 16-17.

42 Susanna Taylor to Richard Taylor, 1 February 1807, St Bride; John Taylor,

D.D. *Value of a Child, or Motives to Good Education of Children, in a Letter to a Daughter* (2nd ed., London 1816) 4

43 Richard Taylor (SA's grandfather) to his aunt [c. 1745], St Bride; Lucy Aikin *Memoir of John Aikin* (London 1823) I 301; Edward Taylor 'Obituary – Mr John Taylor' 488

44 Dr John Taylor 'Sermon Preached at the Opening of the New Chapel in St. George's Colgate, May 12, 1756' in *Principles and Pursuits* 6; Joseph Hunter 'Notice of Taylor Family of Norwich' BL Add. 36527, f. 71; *TG* 25, 31, 43

45 Harriet Martineau *Autobiography* ed. Maria Weston Chapman (Boston 1877) I 20

46 *TG* 34, 39-40; SA to Blackwoods, 12 November [1848], NLS

47 Henry Reeve *The Times* 12 August 1867; SA to Richard Taylor, n.d. [c. 1810], St Bride; *Anna Jameson, Letters and Friendships (1812-1860)* ed. Beatrice [Mrs Steuart] Erskine (London 1915) 166

48 Anna Letitia Le Breton, ed. *Correspondence of William Ellery Channing, D.D. and Lucy Aikin from 1826 to 1842* (London 1874) 414, 28-9

49 Harriet Martineau *Autobiography* I 301; Mary Wollstonecraft *A Vindication of the Rights of Woman* ed. Carol H. Poston (New York 1975) 4-8, 29; JA to SA, 15 December [1819], Trinity College Cambridge; JA to SA, n.d., William L. Clements Library, University of Michigan. Wollstonecraft's ideas are reflected in one of Harriet Martineau's first articles, written from Norwich: 'On Female Education' *Monthly Repository* 18 (February 1823) 80. See also Lawrence Stone *The Family, Sex and Marriage in England 1500-1800* (London 1977) chap. 8.

50 Susanna Taylor to Richard Taylor, 4 December 1814, St Bride; *LDG* 28

51 *TG* 364

52 *TG* 364

53 John Taylor to Richard Taylor, 14 September 1819, St Bride; Philip H. Le Breton, ed. *Memoirs, Miscellanies, and Letters of the Late Lucy Aikin* (London 1864) 147; Rodgers *Georgian Chronicle* 235

54 Philip Taylor 'Address' 3 August 1819, 1-7, printed by Richard Taylor and bound-in with John Taylor *Hymns and Miscellaneous Poems* (London 1818), Yale.

55 Le Breton *Memoirs ... of ... Lucy Aikin* 147

56 John Taylor to Richard Taylor, 14 September 1819, St Bride

57 Susanna Taylor to Richard Taylor, 17 July 1819; John Taylor to Richard Taylor, 14 September 1819; John Taylor (SA's brother) to Richard Taylor, 17 November 1814, St Bride; wedding announcement in *The Norwich Mercury* 28 August 1819

58 Henry Reeve to Janet Ross, 17 January [1873], Waterfield; Lina Waterfield *Castles in Italy* 229

Chapter 2

1 *TG* 283-4, 381; *LDG* 12-13, 15-16; 'Disposition of Property by Will – Primogeniture' *Westminster Review* 2 (October 1824) 548

2 Mill *Autobiography* in *CW* I 77

3 Mill 'Reorganization of the Reform Party' (April 1839) in *CW* VI 469, 476; Burke *Works* (London 1887) VII 57. Although Unitarians dominated the Whig party in Norwich, the Taylors, according to Richard W. Davis, were one of the leading families among the young, so-called New Unitarians, who were more radical than previous generations of Unitarians: *Dissent in Politics 1780-1830; The Political Life of William Smith, MP* (London 1971) 121, 124, 207, 210. See also R.K. Webb *Harriet Martineau* (New York 1960) 66.

4 *The Cabinet* (Norwich 1795) 317; *Memorials of the Life of Amelia Opie* ed. Cecilia L. Brightwell (Norwich 1854) 47; Warren Derry *Dr. Parr* (Oxford 1966) 128; Brian Hayes 'Politics in Norfolk, 1750-1832' Ph.D. dissertation, Cambridge University 1957, 87, chap. 6, passim; Davis *Dissent in Politics* 28-52; George Thomas, Earl of Albemarle *Fifty Years of My Life* (New York 1876) 152-3. The 'Trumpet of Liberty' appeared in *The Norwich Chronicle*, 16 July 1791.

5 Philip Taylor to Richard Taylor, 9 August 1830, printed fragment, St Bride

6 'Memoir of the Late Edward Taylor, Esq., Gresham Professor of Music, Died at Brentwood, March 12, 1863' 8-9, 12-13, from *Norfolk News*, 28 March and 4 April 1863, in *Biographical Memoirs*, at Local History Library, Norwich; Philip Meadows Taylor *A Memoir of the Family of Taylor of Norwich* (privately printed 1886) 26; Hayes 'Politics in Norfolk' 290, 315. When the Austins took young J.S. Mill to Norwich in 1822 he reported to his father that he had 'seen of Radicals many; of clear-headed men not one': *EL* 13. Edward Taylor was one of the two leading radical politicians in Norwich: Davis *Dissent in Politics* 145.

7 JA to Bentham, 20 July 1819, UCL. Sarah's mother approved of the connection: 'It is a fine thing to know a man like Mr. Bentham, who will speak out and expose such a farrago of mystery and absurdity as the Church Catechism, and all its foolish formularies': *TG* 49, 381. On affinities between Unitarianism and utilitarianism, see Francis Mineka *The Dissidence of Dissent* (Chapel Hill 1944) 145-9; Webb *Martineau* 88.

8 George Bentham, Autobiography, vol. 2, ff. 364, 404-5, Library, Royal Botanic Gardens, Kew. Bentham's nephew George planned to study law at Lincoln's Inn. Bentham 'then asked, "What! you are not going to study the law for practice? ... there will be an end of all communication between us" ... he will not hear of my studying the law in any shape.' Lawyers were 'a class of persons against whom he certainly has a most inveterate hatred.' Bentham relented, since his nephew had to earn a living. *Lect. Juris.* 1118.

9 JA to Bentham, 20 July 1819, UCL; *Clarke's New Law List* (corrected to 6 February 1819) (London 1819) 16; *William Bodham Donne and His Friends* ed. Catherine B. Johnson (London 1905) 236; 'Sir John Patteson' *Law Magazine and Law Review* 12 (1862) 205-6. Like Patteson, Austin was a pupil in the chambers of Godfrey Sykes: *Encyclopaedia Britannica* (9th ed., 1875) III 102. The claim that he gave up his only brief because the case was unsound is not compatible with Henry Crabb Robinson's account: see p. 53 below. *Lect. Juris.* II 703, 1118. Austin probably shared the attitude of the other Benthamite radicals towards the legal profession; at the London Debating Society some years later they defended the proposition 'That the profession of a practical lawyer is morally and intellectually pernicious': Henry Cole, Diary, 24 April 1829, Victoria and Albert Museum.

10 Henry Reeve 'Autobiography of John Stuart Mill' *Edinburgh Review* 139 (January 1874) 99; SA *Characteristics of Goethe* (London 1833) II 257n; *Lect. Juris.* 1122

11 Mill *Autobiography* in *CW* I 69, 77, 79; John M. Robson *The Improvement of Mankind: The Social and Political Thought of John Stuart Mill* (Toronto 1968) 6; Henry Reeve to Janet Ross, 17 January 1873, Waterfield

12 Henry Crabb Robinson, Reminiscences, vol. 2, f. 100, Dr Williams's Library, London; JA to Bentham, 20 July 1819, UCL. Mill said that John Austin, unlike his brother Charles, was not an eager or extreme advocate of Benthamite principles, but Mill certainly was referring to a later period of Austin's life: *Autobiography* 49.

13 'Primogeniture' 512-14, 524, 526, 531, 536, 544, 546-8, 550-2. For evidence that SA shared her husband's politics, see her sympathetic review of a radical tract, 'Angeloni on Political Force' *London Magazine* n.s. 5 (June 1826) 231-42.

14 *TG* 67-71, 74; *Fragments* 312-13, 334; SA, Preface 5-6; SA to Brougham, 18 December 1826, UCL; *Köln und Bonn mit ihren Umgebungen* (Köln 1828); H. Hale Bellot *University College, London, 1826-1926* (London 1929) 96. It is difficult to establish precisely the period of residence in Germany. The Austins were in London in December 1826 and probably departed early in 1827. They returned to London during the summer of 1827 when the university appointment was formally made, and they returned to Bonn in early October and remained until the spring of 1828. Much later SA recalled visiting Heidelberg before settling in Bonn.

15 *TG* 67-9, 72; SA to Francis Lieber, 15 March 1834, Huntington Library

16 *Prov. Juris* 202n

17 *Prov. Juris* 109, 127, 137, 141; Henry Crabb Robinson, Reminiscences, vol. 2, f. 100, Dr Williams's Library, London. The records of the Political Economy Club show that on two occasions Austin (first name not indicated) visited the

club, on 5 May 1823 and 7 December 1829. At least on the earlier occasion it probably was John Austin (although his name was misspelt Austen). If it was John, he would have met Malthus and Ricardo at the 1823 meeting and McCulloch at the 1829 meeting: *Political Eonomy Club: Minutes of Proceedings, 1821-1882* (London 1882) IV 58, 95.

18 *Prov. Juris.* 126-8

19 Ibid. 129, 141. For an analysis of Austin's ideas about authority in relation to utilitarianism as a matter of philosophical theory rather than as a theory about institutions and political arrangements in which those ideas can be embodied, see Richard B. Friedman 'An Introduction to Mill's Theory of Authority' in *Mill: A Collecton of Critical Essays* ed. J.B. Schneewind (New York 1968) 379-419

20 *Prov. Juris.* 131, 136, 141

21 Ibid. 131-3, 135-6. For different interpretations of Austin's political ideas (as presented in this chapter and in chapters 8 and 9) see W.L. Morison *John Austin* (London 1982); Wilfried Löwenhaupt *Politischer Utilitarismus und bürgerliches Rechtsdenken: John Austin und die 'Philosophie des Positiven Rechts'* (Berlin 1972); and Eira Ruben 'John Austin's Political Pamphlets 1824-1859' in *Perspectives in Jurisprudence* ed. Elspeth Attwooll (Glasgow 1977). See also chap. 9, n. 11. Wilfred Rumble's recent articles focus not on Austin's politics but on his jurisprudence.

22 *TG* 423; 'National System of Education in France' *Cochrane's Foreign Quarterly Review* 1 (1835) 262, 279; 'Necessity and Practicability of a National System of Education' *Foreign Quarterly Review* 12 (October 1833) 290-1

23 *TG* 100. In contrast, before going to Bonn, she associated herself with 'female Radicals': SA to Place, 26 November 1825, BL, Add. 37949, f. 161. There was one, however, who recognized what she stood for. Recalling that in her preface to Cousin's *Report* she 'took the *compulsory* side ... I remember Lord Brougham seized me by the arm and shook me for being such "*a friend to despotism*"': *TG* 423.

24 SA, preface, v, viii-ix, in Victor Cousin *Report on the State of Public Instruction in Prussia* (London 1834)

25 Ibid. xvi-xvii; 'National System of Education in France' 277-8. In 1845 she still admired German education for making the people sober, tranquil, and governable: *Athenaeum* 19 July 1845, 717.

26 'National System of Education in France' 274, 282, 292, 297; JA 'List on the Principles of the German Customs-Union' *Edinburgh Review* 75 (July 1842) 527

27 'National System of Education in France' 263-6, 278, 292; 'Necessity and Practicability of a National System of Education' 292-5. SA praised Pestalozzi

as a leader of the movement 'in favour of the moral and mental culture of the people': *Fragments* 316.

28 'National System of Education in France' 301. SA's views did not escape criticism. William Howitt, for example, sharply criticized Cousin's celebration of Prussian education and the presentation of it in England. He thought the German system pernicious for encouraging passive support of a despotic regime: *German Experiences* (2nd ed., London 1844) 301-5, 308-9, 315, 331, 337-9.

29 *Prov. Juris.* 227, 243-4, 284, 304-5

30 Ibid. 124; JA 'Joint Stock Companies' *Parliamentary History and Review* (London 1826) 718. JA might also have been the author of two other articles in this issue of *Parliamentary History and Review*: 'Navigation Laws' 684-5 and 'Country Banks' 705-8. Grote's copy at the University of London Library includes a list of articles and authors in his handwriting. These articles appear to be associated with JA's name, but Grote's intention is uncertain.

31 *Law Magazine and Law Review* 9 (May 1860) 167

32 *Prov. Juris.* 143

33 Ibid. 248, 270, 283, 285; 'Centralization' 231n

34 *Prov. Juris.* 177, 182-9, 194, 238, 273-4

35 *The Principles of Moral and Political Philosophy* in *The Works of William Paley* ed. Robert Lynam (London 1825) I 43-6. On theological utilitarianism in eighteenth-century thought, see D.L. Le Mahieu *The Mind of William Paley* (Lincoln 1976) 115-17, 123-9; H.L.A. Hart 'Introduction' J.A. *Prov. Juris.* (London 1958) xvi. Austin thought Paley's theory of utility coherent but his explanation of motives inadequate; he greatly admired Paley but thought 'the book is unworthy of the man. For there is much ignoble truckling to the dominant and influential few': *Prov. Juris.* 138-9, 169. On the origin in Locke's *Essay* of JA's distinction between divine and other kinds of law, see *Prov. Juris.* 205-7.

36 *Prov. Juris.* 109, 113; see also lecture 2, passim and 147.

37 *TG* vii; Leslie Stephen *The Life of Sir James Fitzjames Stephen* (2nd ed., London 1895) 76; Henry Reeve 'Autobiography of John Stuart Mill' 115. Lucy confirmed Reeve's statements: 'Our house was much frequented by a certain set of young men, Sir Wm Molesworth, Charles Buller, Cornwall [sic] Lewis, and a good many others of the same set, all downright and avowed infidels and I heard all their discussions with my father and among themselves': Lucy Austin to Alice Spring-Rice, 15-21 September [1835], Bodleian Library, MS Eng. letters, d.8.

38 Lucy Austin to Alice Spring-Rice, 15-21 September [1835]. Lucy said her father regarded religion 'as the highest system of philosophy and morality';

she also reported that she had had no religious instruction. See also p. 170 below.

39 Mill said Austin was without prejudice, either for or against religion: *EL* 620. Charles Austin exemplified the unacknowledged agnosticism of many Benthamites; see his *The Argument for the Genuineness of the Sacred Volume, as Generally Received by Christians, Stated and Explained* (Cambridge 1823). Lucy called Charles Austin an infidel.

40 *Letters of GCL* 105-6. Cf. SA's phrase, 'that curse of England, the spirit of sect and party': 'National System of Education in France' 286

41 *Prov. Juris.* 121-4

42 Thomas B. Macaulay 'Mill's Essay on Government' (1829) *Miscellaneous Writings of Lord Macaulay* (London 1860) I 282, 301; *Prov. Juris.* 122-3, 248-9. Austin's opposition to doctrinairism was distantly connected with the formal, repetitious, unornamented, and generally unattractive style for which he is known. He thought felicity should be sacrificed if it led to the loss of 'exactness and coherency,' for he held that imprecise language promoted extremism, discouraged conciliation, and encouraged civil discord. He concluded plaintively on one ocassion that 'it really *is* important ... that men should think distinctly, and speak with a meaning': *Prov. Juris.* 123, 137, 140, 221, 248-9.

43 Mill *Autobiography* in *CW* I 185. Elie Halevy (*A History of the English People* [London 1927] III 5) claimed that as a 'raw Radical' John Austin accompanied J.S. Mill and John Roebuck on a pilgrimage to Paris during the Revolution of 1830; Austin was in Paris during the summer (SA to T. Coates, [c. 14 October 1830], UCL), but he no longer was a radical; the evidence Halevy cited does not support his claim.

44 *Prov. Juris.* 284-6; he also parodied language that was unmistakably that of Benthamite radicals and condemned it for causing obscurity: SA to 3rd Earl Grey, [1866], Durham; SA to Jane Welsh Carlyle, 25 December [1832], NLS. JA said, 'Even before the Reform of 1832, I had rejected [Bentham's] *radical* politics': *Plea* vi. Sarah said of Mill's new *London Review*: 'It is too Radical for my taste but ... well worth seeing': SA to Francis Lieber, 17 July 1835, Huntington Library. These statements make it unlikely that SA was the author of the moderate radical article 'D'Israeli's Vindication of the English Constitution' (*London Review* 2 [January 1836] 533-52). The article is identified as probably SA's in *Wellesley Index to Victorian Periodicals* III 586.

45 *TG* 381-3. The Austins had moved from Queen Square Place to Henrietta Street, Brunswick Square, by June 1824.

46 Austin, however, was left to determine which of Bentham's books were to go to Chadwick: JA to Chadwick, n.d.; Grote to JA, 19 January [1833], UCL.

47 JA to J.S. Mill, 25 December 1844, Yale

48 *TG* 382. In her translation of the first two (of three) volumes of Raumer's *England in 1835*, Sarah generally suppressed Raumer's unflattering and erroneous statements about Bentham. She 'had much cause to know the warmth, singleness and kindness of heart of the venerable man of whom Herr v. Raumer has conceived such erroneous impressions.' She added, however, that these suppressions were 'the effect of grateful and affectionate regard for the memory of a revered friend, and [had] no relation to speculative systems of politics and ethics, which it is quite beyond my objects and my province to affect to judge': translator's preface, in Frederick von Raumer *England in 1835* (London 1836) I xiii.

49 'Centralization' 257-8. Mill anticipated the Legislative Commission in 1834: 'The preparation of Bills for Parliament shall be the duty of a responsible Minister of Legislation, aided by a standing Commission of the first jurists in the nation': 'Notes on the Newspapers' *Monthly Repository* 8 (March 1834) 169. Austin described such an arrangement, although less elaborately, in *Lect. Juris.* 1134. That this passage had been included in London University lectures is indicated by SA at 1106.

50 Richard B. Friedman was the first, I believe, to emphasize Austin's contribution to the shaping of Mill's views on authority in relation to utilitarianism: 'An Introduction to Mill's Theory of Authority' 382, 388-9, 393-5, 419-25. Friedman's argument calls for qualifications to statements made about the St Simonian source of Mill's views about the 'instructed few' in Joseph Hamburger *Intellectuals in Politics: John Stuart Mill and the Philosophic Radicals* (New Haven 1966) 78-86. There were convergent themes in St Simonism and in JA's new outlook; Mill was exposed to both at about the same time; see *EL* 40 for a letter written 7 November 1829, very soon after Austin began his first course of lectures. See also *Prov. Juris.* 128 n 9.

51 'Austin's Lectures on Jurisprudence' *Tait's Edinburgh Magazine* 2 (December 1832) 347-8

52 *EL* 321-2, 527-8, 573; *LL* 5, 658. Reeve noted, 'although it has escaped Mr. John Mill's memory,' Sarah Austin 'had, from Mill's early years, been to him as a mother and a friend ... and that he owed to her the culture of the most amiable part of his character': 'Autobiography of John Stuart Mill' 116; see also 121-2.

53 *Prov. Juris.* 333-4 and 334n. This and similar passages cast doubt on Carlyle's observation that Austin 'set forth Utilitarianism *steeped* in German metaphysics, not dissolved therein': *CLC* V 397-8.

54 Andreas B. Schwarz in 'John Austin and the German Jurisprudence of His Time' *Politica* (August 1934) shares the view that 'German influence on Austin's *work* should not be regarded as too important' (180). In the *Province of*

Jurisprudence, he said, 'German influence is scarcely noticeable' (194). Schwarz, however, discerns the influence of German training in Roman and pandect law in what Austin wrote on pervading notions, sources, and purposes of law (195). Schwarz's analysis is especially valuable because he examined the marginal notations in Austin's German books in the Inner Temple Library before they (only Bentham's *Principles of Morals and Legislation* escaped) were destroyed by bombing in 1940. Austin, however, borrowed the phrase 'the philosophy of positive law' from Gustavus Hugo: *Prov. Juris.* 33. Pound noted that Austin was exposed to Kantian views on the separation of law and morals: Roscoe Pound *Interpretations of Legal History* (Cambridge 1930) 98-9; however, see *Lect. Juris.* 972.

55 *Autobiography* in *CW* I 185. Reeve confirmed Mill's observation: 'Autobiography of John Stuart Mill' 116.

56 *TG* 70; SA, translator's note, in [Pückler-Muskau] 'On the Recent Attempts to Revolutionize Germany' *New Monthly Magazine*, 2nd series 37 (1833) 42-3n. Raumer 'is [both] a Reformer and a loyal Monarchist, which I take to be the type of a good Prussian': SA to Whishaw, 28 December 1835, UCLA.

57 *Lect. Juris.* 1118. Cf. J.S. Mill's characterization of the government of Prussia as 'a most powerfully and skilfully organized aristocracy of all the most highly educated men in the kingdom': 'Rationale of Representation' (1835) *CW* XVIII 23.

58 Translator's note, in 'On the Recent Attempt to Revolutionize Germany' 42-3n; translator's note, in *Characteristics of Goethe* (London 1833) III 160-1. SA regarded Cousin's *Report on ... Prussia* as 'the noblest eulogy of the government of that country': ibid. 123.

59 *Autobiography* in *CW* I 185. SA said Prussia was a place 'where reform has so long been the exclusive business of the government': translator's preface, in *England in 1835* I xv.

60 SA, preface and translator's notes, in *Characteristics of Goethe* I viii-ix, 193; III 100; *TG* 72. See also *Fragments* 284-6, 357-8.

61 Translator's note, in 'On the Recent Attempt to Revolutionize Germany' 42-3n; *TG* 70; see also Pückler-Muskau *Tour in Germany, Holland, and England in the Years 1826, 1827, and 1828* (London 1832) III 186. In Prussia, according to SA, 'Freedom of thought is combined with obedience to, and respect for, authority, in a degree rarely, if ever, witnessed': *Fragments* 291.

62 *TG* 69, 79; *Autobiography* in *CW* I 185. Mill wrote to Sarah that 'the German people are much more to your taste (as to mine) than the English': *EL* 522.

63 See *Prov. Juris.* 288n for an example of John Austin's very high praise for Hobbes and Bentham combined with points about disagreements with Hobbes. He often disagreed with Bentham, for example, about judge-made

law; he disapproved of Bentham's criticism of it: *Prov. Juris.* 224. Mill said Austin's favourite writers were Hobbes and Locke: 'Austin's Lectures on Jurisprudence' 347. Austin acknowledged affinities with some of the ideas of the Physiocrats: *Prov. Juris.* 289-90n.

64 William Markby 'Austin' *Encyclopaedia Britannica* (11th ed., London 1910-11) II 940; JA to James Stephen, 27 May 1840, CO 158/118. J.S. Mill also described JA as 'untying the hard knots': 'Recent Writers on Reform' (1859) in *CW* XIX 344.

65 *Prov. Juris.* 90, 93, 206n, 223, 286; *Lect. Juris.* 374, 791. JA adapted his classification of laws as Divine, Civil, and reputational from Locke's *Essay*: *Prov. Juris.* 205-7.

66 [John Stuart Mill] 'Centralization' *Morning Chronicle* 6 February 1847, 4

67 *TG* 69-72; *Germany* 8-9; *Fragments* 334. Their acquaintances at Bonn also included Arndt, Brandes, Adele Schopenhauer, and Sibylle Mertens-Schaaffhausen.

68 'Mr. Charles Austin' *Pall Mall Budget* 2 January 1875, 21; SA, Preface 13; JA 'List' 556. By 1866 these views had changed; Sarah then regretted the 'destruction of dear old Germany who [sic] has given us so much that is beautiful and so many profound thoughts': *TG* 419.

69 *Autobiography* in *CW* I 185; *CLC* V 386. Lucy returned from Bonn 'transformed into a little German maiden, with long braids of hair down her back, and speaking German like her own language': Henry Reeve to Janet Ross, 17 January 1873, Waterfield. Carlyle in 1831 said 'Frau Austin ... was ... a true Germanized spiritual *screamikin*': *CLC* V 397.

70 *TG* 87, 96; SA to Lansdowne, 6 May [1835], Bowood. Very little is known about Austin's participation in the Criminal Law Commission. See Rupert Cross 'The Reports of the Criminal Law Commissioners (1833-1849) and the Abortive Bills of 1853' in *Reshaping the Criminal Law: Essays in Honour of Glanville Williams* ed P.R. Glazebrook (London 1978) 5-20. The notes in *Lect. Juris.* 1056-85 may have been written while JA was on the commission: SA to Murray, 22 December [1862], MA. Frederick Arnold, in commenting on Macaulay's appointment as Law Member of the Governor General's Council in India, said it was 'impossible not to regret, both for his own sake and the sake of the public, that the appointment was not offered to Mr. Austin': *The Public Life of Lord Macaulay* (London 1862) 184.

71 Mill said Austin was not, 'at this time, fundamentally opposed to Socialism in itself, as an ultimate result of improvement': *Autobiography* in *CW* I 185; see also *LL* 5. But there is considerable evidence that Austin did not approve of Socialism. In *Prov. Juris.* 132 he defended private property and inequality. See also p. 170 below.

72 *Prov. Juris.* 281-2. In 1834 SA said Francis Jeffrey was exceedingly kind to her, but 'he and I are at interminable warfare on all political questions. I could not attack the *Edinburgh* [*Review*] as I would': SA to Charles Wentworth Dilke, 1834, C.W. Dilke *The Papers of a Critic* (London 1875) I 35.

73 *Prov. Juris* 304-6; John Knox Laughton *Memoirs of the Life and Correspondence of Henry Reeve* (London 1898) I 94; *Letters of GCL* 108.

74 *EL* 620 (AT)

Chapter 3

1 SA, Preface 4; Henry Crabb Robinson, Reminiscences, vol. 2, ff. 100-1, Dr Williams's Library, London. Austin's encounter in the Norwich court was also described in *Suffolk Chronicle* 26 December 1874, 5. Presumably this was the brief Austin claimed to have given up: see p. 29 above.

2 *LDG* 28; Samuel Warren *A Popular and Practical Introduction to Law Studies* (2nd ed., London 1845) 559

3 *TG* 72, 68-9

4 JA to London University, 30 October 1828, UCL

5 JA to Thomas Coates, 19 May 1829, 26 October 1829, UCL

6 Robinson, Reminiscences, vol. 2, f. 101

7 Henry Cole, Diary, 17 and 24 November 1829, Victoria and Albert Museum, London

8 JA to Leonard Horner, 28 November 1829, UCL; H. Hale Bellot *University College London, 1826-1926* (London 1929) 187-8

9 SA, Preface 6; George Grote *Posthumous Papers* ed. Harriet Grote (London 1874) 35; SA to A.W. Schlegel, n.d. [c. 1830], Sächsiche Landesbibliothek, Dresden; *TG* 80

10 *EL* 52; SA to London University, 15 June 1830 and n.d.; JA to John A. Roebuck, 5 July 1830, UCL

11 *TG* 68; SA, Preface 7, 10, 24-5; Janet Ross *Early Days Recalled* (London 1891) 70; *LL* 1142. A contemporary referred to Austin's 'practice of writing his lectures for delivery': 'Austin's Lectures on Jurisprudence' *The Jurist, or Quarterly Journal of Jurisprudence and Legislation* 3 (April 1832) 122; *LL* 1143; C.R. Sanders *Carlyle's Friendships and Other Studies* (Durham, N.C., 1977) 17; *EL* 51

12 *TG* 470; *Selection from the Correspondence of the Late Macvey Napier* (London 1879) 399. On another occasion Stephen said Austin's 'mission in this world was to read and to meditate, and to talk for the benefit of his fellow-men, and if he fulfils that office, he will merit a biography quite as much as Sydney Smith': *The Right Honourable Sir James Stephen* ed. Caroline Emelia Stephen (London 1906) 211.

13 M.C.M. Simpson *Many Memories of Many People* (London 1898) 116; Stephen to Napier, 27 July and 21 May 1842, BL, Add. 34623, ff. 40, 571; Macaulay to Napier, 14 July 1842, BL, Add. 34623, f. 7; Journal entry of 25 August [1858], vol. 11, f. 364, Trinity College Library Cambridge; Senior to Lansdowne, 28 January 1843, Bowood: Senior made this observation about both SA and JA.

14 *EL* 51-3

15 *Legal Observer* 4 (August 1832) 216; *EL* 51-3. Yet a colleague of Austin's, Andrew Amos, who taught English law, which admittedly had more practical relevance than jurisprudence, attracted as many as a hundred students from all branches of the profession (including conveyancers, pleaders, solicitors, and articled clerks) at a time when Austin had only six: *London University Magazine* (1829-30) 359. Amos later explained to a select committee, 'My object was to give as much theory as I could, consistently with keeping alive the attention of my class': Report from the Select Committee in Legal Education, ques. 1254-5, *PP* 1846 (686) X.

16 JA to Leonard Horner, 5 November 1830, 23 November 1830, UCL; *TG* 82; Henry Cole, Diary, 21 March 1831, Victoria and Albert Museum, London

17 Subscription lists, 1832, 1833, UCL; *EL* 72

18 *Province of Jurisprudence Determined* eventually sold five hundred copies: JA to Murray, 8 January 1849, MA.

19 *EL* 107; SA to London University, 10 November 1831; JA to Coates, 27 November 1832, UCL; Henry Cole, Diary, 31 December 1832

20 *EL* 134; entries in Henry Cole's diary suggest that James Mill attended on 31 January, 12 February, and 20 June 1833, and perhaps on 5 February and 9 May.

21 Henry Cole recorded that Austin missed lectures on 22 and 24 January, 5 March, 2 and 28 May, and 4, 6, and 25 June 1833; in most instances illness was mentioned as the reason. On the death of Austin's mother, see Henry Cole, Diary, 19 March 1833.

22 Henry Cole, Diary, 8 January 1833; JA to Coates, 13 October 1833, UCL. He did not submit his resignation until 1835.

23 *EL* 169; *TG* 96; SA, Preface 11. The work of the commission has been described as part of 'the largest and most abortive codification enterprise yet seen in this country' and as having had next to no practical influence on the development of English criminal law: Rupert Cross 'The Reports of the Criminal Law Commissioners (1833-1849) and the Abortive Bills of 1853' in *Reshaping the Criminal Law: Essays in Honour of Glanville Williams* ed P.R. Glazebrook (London 1978) 5, 20. Austin signed the first two reports; he resigned in 1836 and was replaced by David Jardine: ibid. 6. According to H.B. Ker, who was also a commissioner, Austin resigned when he went to Malta: Ker to Brougham, n.d. [1854], UCL.

24 *TG* 107-8; *CLC* VI 439; SA to Brougham, 22 February [1835], UCL. The Inner Temple lectures were regarded as an experiment in legal education. Austin was no more unsuccessful than Starkie, who also lectured. 'The attendance at first was rather numerous, but rapidly declined, and at the close of the first course, the idea was abandoned': Warren *Introduction to Law Studies* 13-14.

25 SA to Guizot, n.d. [c. 1849], GP; SA to Carlyle, 1 July [1833], NLS; SA, Preface 9; JA to C. Comte, 18 March 1834, Institut de France, Archives. In Preface 16 Sarah was mistaken in giving 1844 as the date of his election to the Institut de France.

26 *TG* 469; *CLC* IX 52

27 *LDG* 13; Janet Ross *The Fourth Generation* (New York 1912) 22; *TG* 90

28 *LDG* 28; Sarah Taylor to Richard Taylor, 30 December 1814, St Bride

29 SA, Preface 3; *Early Draft of John Stuart Mill's Autobiography* in *CW* I 76; *LDG* 32; Grote *Posthumous Papers* 56; Austin's symptoms have led A.D.E. Lewis to speculate that he may have contracted malaria while in the army: 'John Austin, Pupil of Bentham' *Bentham Newsletter* (March 1979) 28, n. 42.

30 Grote to SA, 3 December 1831, St Bride; *CLC* VIII 47-8, 79; SA to [unknown correspondent, possibly Jane Carlyle], 1 June [1835], Historical Society of Pennsylvania, Philadelphia

31 *EL* 170; John Stuart Mill *Autobiography* in *CW* I 77; SA to Brougham, 22 February [1835], UCL; *TG* 78; Janet Ross 'Index of Family Characteristics (Suggested by Francis Galton, Esq.)' [1887?], MA; *TG* 67

32 *EL* 292-3; *TG* 174

33 He earned £3000 for his work in Malta (in addition, he received a portion of the £2224.1.3 paid for personal expenses incurred by himself and the other commissioner, George Cornewall Lewis [CO 158/115]); £800 at the Criminal Law Commission; £450 for the Inner Temple lectures; £300 per year for three years (1828-31) and £200 per year for two years (1831-3) at the University of London (he was paid for 1828-9 although he did not lecture). In the army he earned about £500 (6s. 3d. per day during four years as a lieutenant and somewhat less during one year as an ensign). In addition, there was his salary as a conveyancer and as an equity draftsman and fees for the few articles in the quarterlies. The emoluments for conveyancers were comparatively poor: Warren *Law Studies* 559. It is uncertain how much he was paid by the Criminal Law Commission; it was said that £800 were owed him, but since he served for about three years at £500 per year, he may have received more: *LDG* 48.

34 *EL* 169; *LDG* 48.

35 John Taylor to SA, 16 June 1824, Osborn Collection, Yale; John Neal *Wandering Recollections of a Somewhat Busy Life: An Autobiography* (Boston 1869)

299-300; Margaret C.W. Wicks *The Italian Exiles in London 1816-1848* (Manchester 1937) 252; Henry Reeve to Janet Ross, January 1873, Waterfield; Nassau Senior to JA, 15 May 1829, 10 April 1835, Wales.

36 John Taylor's will, PRO, Prob 11/1719, C03015. Before John Taylor's death Sarah received from him £100 per year. However, in view of these distributions he left her only £700 in addition to the £1000 in bond that had been set aside for her when she married, whereas £2000 appears to have been the amount he intended for each of his children. Consequently, her income from these funds after her father's death would have been £68 per year (assuming a 4% return).

37 *TG* 80, 83

38 JA to Bentham, 20 July 1819, UCL

39 *LDG* 27; *TG* 83

40 *EL* 335, 516; SA, Preface 10

41 SA to Carlyle, 1 July [1833], NLS; SA to Besser, 18 October [c. 1841], Staats-und Universitätsbibliothek, Hamburg; Philip Taylor to Brougham, 31 December 1859, UCL

42 A translation of Christoph Martin Wieland *The Graces: A Classical Allegory* (London 1823) has been attributed to Sarah Austin, perhaps because it was signed ST. The attribution is doubtful, for she was married by 1823 and did not use these initials as a signature. Wicks *Italian Exiles in London* 235 (AT); Alan Probert 'Italian Exiles in Mexican Mining' *Journal of the West* 14 (April 1975) 93-104; A. Probert kindly sent us information about the Vocabulary. SA translator 'Journal Description of the Route from New York to Real del Monte by Way of Tampico' *London Magazine* 5 (February 1826) 145-71 (for attribution, see Frank P. Riga and Claude A. Prance *Index to London Magazine* [New York 1978]). SA to Murray, 6 July 1825, MA; SA to Bentham, 17 December 1824, BL, Add. 33546, ff. 26, 30; SA to William Hepworth Dixon, 20 January [n.y.], UCLA; Edgar Taylor *Lays of the Minnesingers or German Troubadours of the Twelfth and Thirteenth Centuries* (London 1825); *Edinburgh Review* 43 (November 1825) 107-25; SA to Coates [21 October 1830], 15 October [1830], UCL.

43 *TG* 50, 63; SA to Foscolo, 17 November 1826, 9 January [n.y.], Biblioteca Labronica, Livorno; *TG* 307-8; E.R. Vincent *Ugo Foscolo: An Italian in Regency England* (Cambridge 1953) 202-3

44 *TG* 80-1; *EL* 10 n. 1; Anna Jean Mill, ed. *John Mill's Boyhood Visit to France* (Toronto 1960) 41 n. 74

45 SA to Murray, 18 October 1830, MA; Herman Merivale 'Mrs Austin's Characteristics of Goethe' *Edinburgh Review* 57 (July 1833) 372

46 *Selections from the Old Testament: or the Religion, Morality and Poetry of the Hebrew*

Scriptures, Arranged under Heads (London 1833). 'I never received one farthing for that laborious job': SA to Murray, 27 October 1857, MA.

47 *Spectator* 9 (23 January 1836) 89. The sixth thousandth copy of *Story without an End* was printed in 1836; SA to Coates [21 October 1830], [c. 14 October 1830], UCL; on Sismondi translations, private communications from H.O. Pappe; SA to Francis Lieber, 15 March 1834, 17 July 1835, Huntington Library.

48 SA to Gladstone, 22 January 1853, BL, Add. 44373, f. 323; *TG* 99; SA to Francis Lieber, 21 November 1835, University of South Carolina Library

49 Jean-Marie Carré '*The Characteristics of Goethe* de Sarah Austin et la collaboration de H.C. Robinson' *Archiv für das Studium der Neueren Sprachen und Literaturen* 131, 146

50 *CLC* IX 397, VI 273, 242

51 Herman Merivale 'Mrs Austin's *Characteristics of Goethe*' 377, 372, 402-3; *CLC* VII 143; SA to Francis Lieber, 15 March 1834, Huntington Library; *Briefwechsel zwischen Pückler und Varnhagen von Ense* ed. Ludmilla Assing-Grimelli (Berlin 1874) III 123; SA to 'gentleman,' 6 January 1834, Osborn Collection, Yale

52 *TG* 117; SA to Francis Lieber, 15 March 1834, Huntington Library

53 Dionysius Lardner to J.C.L. Sismondi, 23 November 1833, private communication from H.O. Pappe. In the dedication of his *Reminiscences of an Intercourse with George Barthold Niebuhr, the Historian of Rome* (London 1835), Francis Lieber wrote that Sarah had 'become the interpreter of German literature to the English nation and their brethren in the Western hemisphere.' Jean-Pierre Lefebvre 'Heine à Boulogne-sur-Mer' *Revue de Littérature Comparée* 47 (1973) 209; *TG* 101

54 *CLC* VII 175, VIII 92, 43, VII 203, VIII 43

55 SA to Francis Lieber, 15 March 1834, Huntington Library; CLC V 396; SA to Gladstone, 22 January 1853, BL, Add. 44373, f. 323; SA to Brougham, 22 February [1835], UCL

56 SA to Murray, [29 April 1834], 14 January 1836, MA; Miscellaneous Publication Expenses Ledger, A2, 1820-42, ff. 208-9, 219, 221, and Cabinet Cyclopaedia Ledger, ff. 25, 41, 46, 57, 324, 331, 335: Longman Archives, University of Reading. Later, in 1844, she was promised at least 200 guineas for the first two volumes of Ranke's *Reformation*: Murray to SA, 30 July 1844, copy, MA. The sum of five guineas was received for an article in the *Athenaeum*: SA to Dixon, 3 January 1856, UCLA. SA to Murray, 27 June 1835, MA.

57 SA to Lady William Russell, 23 December 1865, Blakiston; SA to Sismondi, 8 November 1834, private communication from H.O. Pappe

58 SA to Jane Welsh Carlyle, 25 December [1832], NLS; *EL* 170; *CLC* IX 397, 394

59 SA to Murray, [23 November 1835], n.d. [1836], n.d. [1830], MA

60 Werner Vordtriede 'Bettina's englische Wagnis' *Euphorion* 51 (1957) 271-94; Abraham Hayward to Ottilie von Goethe, 17 December [n.y.], Weimar; Bettina von Arnim to SA, 20 January [1835], Freies Deutsches Hochstift, Frankfurt am Main

61 SA *Characteristics of Goethe from the German of Falk, Von Müller etc.* (London 1833) II 316n; SA to Murray, [1836], 20 February 1836; 27 June [1835], n.d. [1836], MA

62 *Anna Jameson, Letters and Friendships (1812-1860)* ed. Beatrice [Mrs Steuart] Erskine (London 1915) 172; SA to Susan Reeve, 30 December 1814, St Bride; Grote *Posthumous Papers* 78; *EL* 522

63 SA *The Duchess of Orleans: A Memoir* (London 1859) xxviii; SA to Carlyle, 1 July [1833], NLS

64 *TG* 82, 83; *CLC* VI 320, 404, IX 394; SA to Francis Lieber, 15 March 1834, Huntington Library; *CLC* VIII 92.

65 Sarah was to resort to a similar intense social life, and probably for similar reasons, in 1839-40, before their 'exile' to Germany: *CLC* VIII 104, 9, 130, VI 323.

66 SA to Francis Lieber, 17 July 1835, Huntington Library; SA to Murray, 5 May [1835], MA; SA to Jane Welsh Carlyle, 20 July [1835], Harvard University Library

Chapter 4

1 The approximately one hundred manuscript letters from Sarah Austin to Prince Pückler and drafts of his letters to her were in the Varnhagen von Ensesche collection in Berlin. See Ludwig Stern *Die Varnhagen von Ensesche Sammlung in der Königlichen Bibliothek zu Berlin* (Berlin 1911). During World War II the letters removed to Silesia and are now reported as probable war losses by the Preussische Staatsbibliothek Berlin, in the D.D.R. The excerpts from the Sarah Austin – Pückler-Muskau correspondence have therefore been taken from published pre-war accounts: E.M. Butler *The Tempestuous Prince, Hermann Pückler-Muskau* (London 1929) and Gordon Waterfield *Lucie Duff Gordon in England, South Africa and Egypt* (New York 1937). For background information, see also *Briefwechsel und Tagebücher des Fürsten Hermann von Pückler-Muskau* ed. Ludmilla Assing-Grimelli (Berlin 1873-76); Ludmilla Assing-Grimelli *Fürst Hermann Pückler-Muskau: Eine Biographie* (Hamburg 1873); E.M. Butler, introduction to *A Regency Visitor: The*

English Tour of Prince Pckler-Muskau Described in His Letters, 1826-1828 (New York 1958).

2 *TP* 19, 151
3 Ibid. 151
4 Butler *Regency Visitor* 10; *Allgemeine Deutsche Biographie* (Berlin 1970) XXVI 692-5; *Briefwechsel* ed. Assing-Grimelli VI 386, 365 (AT); Assing-Grimelli *Fürst Hermann Pückler-Muskau* 193; *Biographisches Wörterbuch zur deutschen Geschichte* (Munich 1974) II 2224
5 SA to Murray, 25 December [1830], [22 March 1831], MA
6 *Edinburgh Review* 54 (December 1831) 385; SA to R.M. Bacon, 21 February 1832, Cambridge University Library; *Briefwechsel* ed. Assing-Grimelli III 156
7 Sarah's bowdlerizing continued to rankle in Pückler's mind. When he later passed through Malta he 'made his own works in the public library a curiosity by marginal-noting them from end to end in elucidation of many parts relating to England, which he averred, by way of excusing himself, were badly translated.' It was 'not *his* fault if Sarah Austin chooses to translate his books so beautifully, and he might add, so partially, for the translation conveys a feeble idea of the liberties he took *in German* with his English friends': Adolphus Slade *Turkey, Greece, and Malta* (London 1837) I 1832. E.M. Butler, who saw Pückler's letters before the disappearance of the collection, wrote: 'They were unparalleled in my experience in the expressiveness with which they disclosed the stark, unadulterated overpowering truth of his emotional life. Reticencies, discretions, inhibitions he had none when writing to Lucie. The *Letters from a Dead Man* are incomparably less interesting as human documents; and Sarah Austin's fig leaves have deprived the *Tour of a German Prince* of some of the author's cranks, quirks and quiddities as well as of some of his "indiscretions"': *A Regency Visitor* 27; *TP* 149-50.
8 SA to R.M. Bacon, 5 November 1831, Cambridge University Library; [Pückler-Muskau] *Tour in England, Ireland, and France in the Years 1828 and 1829 ... by a German Prince* (London 1832), translator's preface, I viii.
9 SA to R.M. Bacon, 21 February 1832, 5 November 1831, Cambridge University Library; [Pückler-Muskau] *Tour in Germany, Holland, and England ... by a German Prince*, translator's preface to III viii, ix
10 *Tour in Germany, Holland, and England*, translator's preface, III ix, x; Sarah Austin's public caution was also evident in an anonymous, favourable, but not uncritical review of Pückler's next book. See *Foreign Quarterly Review* 13 (May 1834) 380-97.
11 *TG* 85-6; *TP* 21; *LDG* 56
12 *LDG* 59, 53, 52
13 *TP* 22, 19

14 Gerhard F. Hering and Vita Huber *Ein grosser Herr: Das Leben des Fürsten Pückler* (Düsseldorf, Köln 1968) 245-6; *Briefwechsel* ed. Assing-Grimelli III 190 (AT); *LDG* 54

15 *LDG* 66, 54-5, 55, 58

16 *TP* 20

17 *LDG* 54

18 Butler *A Regency Visitor* 22; *LDG* 28-9

19 *LDG* 30

20 Margaret C. Wicks *The Italian Exiles in London, 1816-1848* (Manchester 1937) 233

21 *TG* 360; *LDG* 58; SA to Guizot, 3 December 1849, GP

22 *CLC* VII 175; *LDG* 57; *CLC* VII 83

23 Heinrich Heine *Briefe, 1850-1856* (Säkularausgabe, Berlin-Paris 1972) XXIII 333 (AT); *CLC* VII 174, VIII 291. Towards the end of his journey to England Pückler wrote to his wife that he was 'still a great libertine, a great jester, and a great child': *Briefwechsel* ed. Assing-Grimelli VI 444.

24 SA to Richard Taylor, n.d. [1834], St Bride

25 *LDG* 55

26 *LDG* 58, 74

27 *TP* 152; SA to Francis Lieber, 15 March 1834, Huntington Library

28 SA to Francis Lieber, 15 March 1834, Huntington Library; *LDG* 59; SA to Guizot, n.d., GP

29 SA to Murray, n.d. [1835], MA

30 *LDG* 60; SA to Brougham, 22 February [1835], UCL; SA to [Jane Welsh Carlyle(?)], 1 June [1835], from Hastings, Historical Society of Pennsylvania

31 SA to [Jane Welsh Carlyle(?)], 1 June [1835]. Some ambiguity remains as to whether the breakdown occurred in 1834 or 1835. E.M. Butler uses the phrase, 'after a nervous breakdown dramatically described,' but because Sarah's letters were probably undated, she gives no year. Assuming that the letter from Hastings signals Sarah's breakdown, its date would appear to be 1835, for at that time she was in Hastings (*CLC* VIII 130), whereas in early June 1834 she was in London (*CLC* VII 206). A letter from Richard Taylor to Brougham of 5 June 1835 corroborates this period for Sarah's depression; he explains that John Austin was still sick in Hastings at this time.

32 *CLC* VIII 104, 111

33 *TG* 199, 276. 'Please do not say that I am a Unitarian, because I am not at all sure that I am in any sense of the word understood here': SA to W.J. Fox, 18 November 1832, Richard Garnett *The Life of W.J. Fox* (London 1910) 125.

34 James Stephen to SA, 5 December 1854, copy, Cambridge University Library;

Heinrich Heine *Briefe an Heine, 1823-1836* (Berlin-Paris 1974) XXIV 373-4
(AT); SA to Anna Jameson, 26-8 September [1835], Osborn Collection, Yale
35 J.W. Croker 'Raumer's England in 1835' *Quarterly Review* 56 (July 1836) 540;
Tour in England, Ireland, and France, translator's preface I x-xii; *TG* 87
36 SA 'Cholera in Malta' *Fraser's Magazine* 73 (January 1866) 102
37 *TG* 355-6; *Fragments* 344; SA to Ottilie von Goethe, 9 August 1840, Weimar
38 SA to Kate Whittle, 4 February 1849, Waterfield
39 SA to Henry Crabb Robinson, 18 May 1855, Dr Williams's Library

Chapter 5

1 SA to Lansdowne, 6 May [1835], Bowood; *LDG* 67
2 *CLC* IX 52. Unlike his predecessors, however, 'here is all Britain to enforce for
Austin!' With his usual spleen, Carlyle forecast that the appointment would
not do Austin much good. See also p. 39 and the observation on p. 103 that he
was 'a thoroughly lamed man.'
3 *TG* 126-7; GCL to Thomas K. Lewis, 4 November 1836, Wales; *Malta
Government Gazette* 2 November 1836, 373. Sarah was 'glad [Lucy] is not here to
be surrounded and flattered by a whole fleet and garrison, abused by all the
English women and girls, worshipped by the poor despised Maltese (whose
part she would be sure to take with more zeal than discretion) – spoiled in
every way': SA to Mill, 3 March 1837, London School of Economics and
Political Science. Sydney Smith told her, 'Your reception ... was just what it
ought to be everywhere, for I have no doubt that all the Vivats were intended
for you, and not for the Philosophers. Doubtless the two disciples of Bentham
thought that the Maltese were hailing Liberal Principles ... whereas it was their
joy at seeing Donna Anabele Inglese': Smith to SA, 30 November 1836,
Waterfield.
4 GCL to Thomas K. Lewis, 4 November 1836, Wales; *TG* 127.
5 *TG* 134, 139; *Reports* pt II, 41-4, *PP*, 1837-38 (141-II), XXIX; Sarah S.
Bunbury *Life and Letters of Robert Clement Sconce* (London 1861) II 13; A.V.
Laferla *British Malta* (Valletta 1938) I 168-9; SA to J.S. Mill, 3 March 1837,
London School of Economics and Political Science; SA to Cousin, 25 April
1838, 31 December 1838; J. Barthélemy Saint-Hilaire *M. Victor Cousin: Sa Vie
et Sa Correspondance* (Paris 1895) III 140-3. SA did an abridged translation into
Italian of Cousin's *Report on the State of Public Instruction in Prussia*: *TG* 139-40.
Evidently Sarah visited Sicily at this time: see *Fragments* 276.
6 *TG* 129; Brougham said that Stephen suggested Austin: *Law Magazine* (1860)
168; *Letters of GCL* 56. *Greville Memoirs* ed. R. Fulford and L. Strachey (London
1938) III 88 (entry of 25 September 1834). Melbourne told Greville that

Benthamites 'were all fools [and Austin] a damned fool.' Melbourne, wrote Greville, had read all of Austin's jurisprudence and he found it 'the dullest book he ever read, and full of truisms elaborately set forth.'

7 Glenelg *Hansard* XLVII 656 (30 April 1839), XLII 807-8 (3 May 1838); George Mitrovich *The Claims of the Maltese: Founded upon the Principles of Justice* (London 1835) 3-8; Laferla *British Malta* I 146-52, 156; J.J. Cremona *The Malta Constitution of 1835 and Its Historical Background* (Malta 1959) 19-22, 27. The government announced its intention to send a commission of inquiry, but not its composition, on 7 June 1836, following the presentation of a petition by William Ewart, a radical who co-operated with Mitrovich and agreed to serve as spokesman for the Maltese in the House of Commons: *Hansard* XXXIV (7 June 1836) 161-5. The grievances were also stated in 'Maltese Claims,' a printed but not published statement presented to Austin and Lewis in Malta on 15 November 1836. The eighteenth and last complaint in the list was 'Misery!' We are grateful to Dr Albert Ganado for showing us a copy. On Mitrovich's activities in London, see Hector Mercieca 'The Political Career of George Mitrovich' B.A. (Hons)thesis, University of Malta, 1968, 32-5, 53-5, 95. Stephen acknowledged that it was in Mitrovich's 'complaints [that] the Commission in fact originated': Mitrovich to Normanby, 23 April 1839, endorsement, CO 158/109.

8 JA and GCL to Glenelg, 2 April 1837, CO 158/113, 8, 12-13, 14-15, 17; *Letters of GCL* 96. Mitrovich acknowledged that 'a general discontent prevails amongst [the Maltese], though they are patient, submissive, and quiet': *Claims of the Maltese* 6.

9 Commission, 10 September 1836, *Reports* pt I, 4, *PP*, 1837-38 (141), XXIX; pt III, 4-12, *PP*, 1839 (140), XVII; Glenelg to JA and GCL, 16 September 1836, CO 158/113

10 Stoddart to Bouverie, 30 November 1836, CO 158/92; JA and GCL to Glenelg, 6 November 1836, CO 158/113. Stoddart (1773-1856) wrote for *The Times* from 1810 and was editor from 1814 until his dismissal, because of disagreements with the proprietor, in 1817. He then founded and edited the rival *New Times* in 1817. He defended the French ultra-royalists. He was scurrilously known as Dr Slop, a name used by William Hone, in whose pamphlets he was caricatured by Cruikshank: *The History of The Times* (London 1935) I 157-63.

11 Stoddart to Bouverie, 30 November 1836, CO 158/92; Stodddart to JA and GCL, 4 January 1837, 'Papers Relative to the Compensation of the Chief Justice' 23-6, *PP*, 1839 (219), XVII; 'A Speech Delivered on the 5th of November 1836 ... ' MS in Ganado papers; JA and GCL to Glenelg, 6 November 1836, 14 January 1837, 5 February 1837, CO 158/113; *Letters of*

GCL 64, 70. The commissioners' account was confirmed by the governor, Sir Henry Bouverie, who described the speech as indiscreet and as 'a studied harangue': Bouverie to Glenelg, 3 December 1836, 5 December 1836, CO 158/92.

12 Glenelg to Bouverie, 1 December 1836, CO 158/91; 29 March 1837, CO 159/14; Col. Evans to Glenelg, 6 November 1836, CO 158/91; *Letters of GCL* 85; *Reports* pt III, 38-9, *PP*, 1839 (140), XVII; Stoddart to Brougham, 29 November 1838, UCL

13 JA and GCL to Glenelg, 14 January 1837, CO 158/113; Stoddart to JA and GCL, 4 January 1837, in 'Papers Relative to the Compensation' 13-14, *PP*, 1839 (219), XVII; Glenelg to Bouverie, 29 March 1837, CO 159/14

14 *Reports* pt III, 31-7, 47, 68, *PP*, 1839 (140), XVII. Although Stoddart knew quite early what was coming, he was not formally notified until November 1838. The report as printed includes amendments made after consultations with the Lord Chancellor, which took place soon after Austin's return to London. JA and GCL to Glenelg, 11 January 1838, CO 158/115; Glenelg to Bouverie, 10 November 1838, CO 159/17, ff. 317-18.

15 JA and GCL to Glenelg, 31 August 1837, in *Reports* pt I, 70, *PP*, 1837-38 (141), XXIX; Hilda I. Lee *Malta 1813-1914* (Valletta 1972), 27-9; Report on the Police of Malta, 10 January 1838, and confidential communication on report, CO 158/116; Bouverie to Glenelg, 26 October 1837, CO 158/97

16 *Reports* pt III, 58-60, *PP*, 1839 (140), XVII. The governor supported the commissioners' recommendations, as he regarded the offices of both chief justice and attorney general as 'entirely useless, or rather positively hurtful': Bouverie to Glenelg, 8 March 1838, CO 158/100. He also had a low opinion of Langslow's qualifications: Bouverie to Glenelg, 17 May 1838, CO 158/101.

17 JA and GCL to Glenelg, 14 January 1837, CO 158/113; 14 August 1837, CO 158/114; Glenelg to Bouverie, 30 September 1837, *Reports* pt I, 68-70, 73, *PP*, 1837-38 (141), XXIX; Bouverie to Glenelg, 17 August 1837, CO 158/97

18 *Reports* pt II, 21, *PP*, 1837-38 (141-II), XXIX

19 Glenelg to Bouverie, 6 July 1837, *Reports* pt I, 67-8, *PP*, 1837-38 (141), XXIX; *Reports* pt II, 21-5, *PP*, 1837-38 (141-II), XXIX. Sarah said, 'However unfit the poor Maltese are for the business of Govt. I am sure they are as fit morally and intellectually as the sort of refuse that (in many cases) was sent them from our shores': SA to Octavian Blewitt, 8 December 1838, Historical Society of Pennsylvania.

20 *The Harlequin* no. 1, 12 July 1838, 2; no. 45, 15 December 1838, 177; no. 46, 29 December 1838, 181; no. 69, 30 May 1839, 9-10; no. 71, 6 June 1839, 17; no. 76, 22 June 1839, 39; no. 77, 27 June 1839, 42; no. 81, 15 July 1839, 57; no. 85, 24 August 1839, 7; no. 113, 7 March 1840, 69. Sarah said, 'An attempt is always made to throw the odium of radicalism on all attempts to redress real

wrongs': SA to Octavian Blewitt, 8 December 1838, Historical Society of Pennsylvania. The *Malta Times*, which was the successor to *The Harlequin* in 1840, sounded the same theme. It condemned the 'whole scheme of the Radical and Chartist Commissioners,' and asked, 'Who but the most imbecile of Commissioners would have given out, by reports, and ordered to be printed in the Maltese journals, that the native mind was *only* capable of governing the island?': *Malta Times* no. 2, 10 April 1840, 60.

21 SA to Lansdowne, 13 December 1837, Bowood; *Letters of GCL* 67, 70, 86, 90; *The Harlequin* no. 31, 27 October 1838, 121; *TG* 128-9; Nassau William Senior *Conversations and Journals in Egypt and Malta* ed. M.C.M. Simpson (London 1882) II 240n, 259-60; JA and GCL to Glenelg, 2 April 1837, CO 158/113, ff. 17-18; SA to J.S. Mill, 3 March 1837, British Library of Political and Economic Science. Sarah 'observed that men's intolerance and contempt was in the inverse ratio of their right to any such airs of superiority. The most illiterate, insipid and silly of the officers there were the most full of scorn': SA to Octavian Blewitt, 8 December 1838, Historical Society of Pennsylvania. Years later she said, 'In Malta I was first awakened to the detestable state of mind and manners of the *large majority* of English men (and women) towards all whom it has pleased God to bring into the world under circumstances less favourable than [their own]': SA to 3rd Earl Grey, 7 July [1864], Durham. See also *Germany* 348-9. 'For nearly two years I have spoken, written and thought little except Italian': SA to Raumer, 1 September [1838], E. Petzetiana, V (Austin), Bayerische Staatsbibliothek, München.

22 Bouverie to Glenelg, 4 April 1838, CO 158/100; SA to Lansdowne, 13 December 1837, Bowood

23 'Report on the Expediency of Introducing into Malta a Liberty of Printing and Publishing' 10 March 1837, in *Reports* pt I, 8-13, *PP*, 1837-38 (141), XXIX; JA and GCL to Glenelg, 1 September 1837, CO 158/114; 'Remarks on the Objections to the Ordinances for Granting a Free Press to Malta, by the Commissioners of Inquiry' CO 158/115

24 JA and GCL to Glenelg, 1 September 1837, CO 158/114; Glenelg to Bouverie, 14 October 1837, CO 159/17

25 *Report* pt I, 13-18, *PP*, 1837-38 (141), XXIX; Glenelg to Bouverie, 1 June 1837, CO 158/113; JA and GCL to Glenelg, 1 September 1837, and draft dispatch, 28 September [1837], not sent, with Sir George Grey's minutes, CO 158/114; GCL to Thomas K. Lewis, 3 July 1837, Wales; Glenelg to JA and GCL, 22 August 1837, CO 158/114; Glenelg to Bouverie, 27 November 1837, in *Reports* pt I, 26, *PP*, 1837-38 (141), XXIX; James Stephen to SA, 1 July 1837, 28 October 1837, copies, Cambridge University Library, Add. 7888, I 107-9, 121-4

26 JA and GCL to Glenelg, 11 January 1838, CO 158/115. The governor, who

endorsed the commissioners' press law, shared their fear of Stoddart's opposition: 'I cannot answer for the effect which his legal subtlety and talent for quibble may have': Bouverie to Glenelg, 6 January 1838, CO 158/100; 5 February 1838, CO 159/17, ff. 130-4. The council consisted of the senior military officer in command, the chief justice, the archbishop, the chief secretary, and two Maltese landed proprietors and one British merchant residing in Malta, all appointed by the governor.

27 Stephen's minute, 6 January 1838, CO 158/100

28 Glenelg to Bouverie, 5 February 1838, CO 159/17, ff. 132-3. The draft of this letter makes it clear that Stoddart was the target of the proposed pressure; a deleted passages states, 'The Chief Justice should be privately informed of the views of HM's Govt ... you have my full authority to acquaint him that ... HM's Ministers are not prepared to assume the responsibility of any material deviation from the course recommended to them by yourself as Gov[erno]r and by the Commm[issione]rs of Enquiry; and that an endeavour to modify the Law ... though it might produce a serious temporary embarrassment, could not alter the determination which has been formed ... I am persuaded that Sir J. Stoddart will not under such circumstances embark in a controversial contest with you': CO 158/100.

29 JA and GCL to Glenelg, 21 March 1838, CO 158/115; Glenelg to JA and GCL, 22 August 1837, CO 159/16, ff. 65-8. A year earlier JA had evidently threatened to use means that went beyond persuasion, for in a private letter Stephen acknowledged receiving 'with dismay the intimation your [SA's] letter conveys of the purposes which Mr. Austin silently entertains in the event of the advice of the Commissioners on the subject of the Press not being followed,' and he tried to dissuade Austin: James Stephen to SA, 1 July 1837, copy, Cambridge University Library, Add. 7888 I ff. 107-9.

30 Glenelg to Bouverie, 31 March 1838, CO 159/17

31 JA to Glenelg, 3 May 1838; JA and GCL to Glenelg, 21 March 1838, CO 158/115; Glenelg to Bouverie, 31 March 1838, draft, CO 158/100; Bouverie to Glenelg, 19 April 1838, including minutes by Stephen and Vernon Smith, CO 158/100

32 Bouverie to Glenelg, 28 June 1838, CO 158/101

33 JA to Glenelg, 17 September 1838, CO 158/115. Two months later Austin felt defensive about the delay: 'I have so much esteem for Lord Glenelg, and I am so grateful for the confidence with which he has honoured me, that I shall be extremely sorry if he should be blamed for the delay. In truth, nobody is to blame for it ... But if blame be due to any body, it ought to fall upon myself': JA to Stephen, 24 November 1838, CO 158/115.

34 Bouverie to Glenelg, 28 June 1838. Earlier Glenelg urged prompt completion

of the press law: Glenelg to GCL, 31 July 1838, CO 158/101; Glenelg to JA, 18 September [1838], draft; Sir George Grey's endorsement, CO 158/115.

35 Campbell and Rolfe to Glenelg, 5 December 1838, 24 December 1838, CO 158/103. The letter of 24 December was much longer than the earlier one. After receiving the latter, Glenelg explained, 'It was certainly not my purpose to call on you for any Report as to the general expediency of adopting the law' and said that he wanted only legal comment: Glenelg to attorney-general and solicitor-general, 15 December 1838, CO 158/107. The commissioners also faced criticisms of their recommendations for changes in the appellate courts from the lord chancellor; after a meeting with him they made small changes in their proposals: JA to Glenelg, 17 September 1838, CO 158/115; Glenelg to Bouverie, 10 November 1838, CO 158/116. On Austin's authorship of the libel law: SA to J.S. Mill, 3 March 1837, British Library of Political and Economic Science.

36 JA and GCL to Glenelg, 28 December 1838, CO 158/115, especially ff. 3, 18, 40-1. This letter is ascribed to both Austin and Lewis in the CO records, but a twenty-six-page draft in Austin's hand (also in CO 158/115), apparently written in preparation of the formal letter, strongly suggests that the defence of the press law mainly came from Austin. In the draft Austin goes to great lengths to defend the law from the criticism that it was 'too restrictive': ff. 5, 8-10, 14-17. The commissioners were offered an opportunity to discuss their differences with the law officers; Lewis attended the meeting on 5 December, but Austin did not: Glenelg to Campbell, 4 December 1838; Rolfe to Glenelg, 5 December 1838, CO 158/115; Campbell and Rolfe to Glenelg, 5 December 1838, CO 158/103. This controversy seems to have been unnecesssary. The law officers at first approved the draft law; then, in response to a request from Glenelg, which they misunderstood, they objected, but only partly on legal grounds; when they were asked to justify their opposition on legal grounds, they sent the letter of 24 December listing their several objections, which were directed not 'to its general scope and policy, but to the structure and composition' of the draft. According to Stephen, the law officers' original report 'was made after a very slight and cursory reading of the Draft, and the second Report [of 24 December] after an examination stimulated by the anxiety to vindicate the general terms, somewhat hastily used, in the [first] Letter of remonstrance': Stephen to Labouchere, 10 April (endorsement on Bouverie to Normanby, 19 March 1839), CO 158/105.

37 Stephen to Labouchere, ibid.; Glenelg to Bouverie, 19 January 1839, *Reports* pt III, 73, *PP*, 1839 (140), XVII; 'Further Correspondence Relative to the Reports' 2, *PP*, 1839 (211), XVII. Austin's notes were not to be promulgated as part of the law, but they were to be published separately 'as with the sanction

of Government': Glenelg to Bouverie, private, 19 January 1839, CO 159/17, ff. 355-7. The law officers capitulated: Campbell and Rolfe to Glenelg, 4 January 1839; Campbell and Rolfe to Normanby, 26 April 1839, CO 158/108. Glenelg rejected a radically different alternative which would have had him support the crown lawyers and temporarily use English libel law in Malta: draft in CO 158/115. For evidence that this draft was not sent, see letter book for January 1839, where it is not entered: CO 159/17. This proposal had a curious history in Whitehall: it was sent by mistake (or conceivably, surreptitiously) for approval by the queen in council; it was passed on 29 November 1838, despite counter-directions having been sent; the approval had to be revoked later: Record of Queen in Council, 29 November 1838; Stephen's endorsement, 11 January [1839], CO 158/103. Austin's press law was sent to the privy council office on 30 November 1838, despite its not having received the law officers' approval: CO 158/115. Approval by the privy council had to wait until the law officers withdrew their objections.

38 Stoddart to Brougham, 13 March 1839, 29 November 1838, [March] 1839, UCL. Stoddart petitioned for appointment as assessor and vice-admiralty judge; Austin opposed the petition: JA to Glenelg, March 1839, ff. 25-6, CO 158/118.

39 *Hansard* XLVII 225 (18 April 1839), 311, 314-15 (19 April 1839), 641-4, 646, 650-1, 654 (30 April 1839); XLVIII 954, 956 (27 June 1839). *The Times*, 20 April 1839, 2-3; 1 May 1839, 3; 28 June 1839, 3-4. Stephen anticipated the end of the session, as 'Lord Brougham then also will be gone, and I shall not be compelled to be following his steps, which he takes every other day, with his seven leagued boots': Stephen to Napier, 10 August 1839, BL, Add. 34620, f. 329. There was almost no discussion in the House of Commons: see Hawes' comment in *Hansard* XLVII 548-9 (22 April 1839). William Ewart, who took an interest in Malta on behalf of Mitrovich and other Maltese radicals, had lost his seat in the 1837 election. The Parliamentary radicals may have had a dilemma. They were very critical of Glenelg's Canadian policy, but they may have been reluctant to oppose his Malta policy in view of their attachment to the Austins. Brougham's hostility was also evident in private conversation: the Austins '"would probably cease to be reformers, having experienced the practical difficulties of reform, and would retire disheartened from the cause." In making this remark, he obviously intended to allude to a supposed want of perseverance and resolution on the part of these persons. A dinner at Lansdowne House, he said, "was a great cure for radicalism"': Edward L. Pierce *Memoir and Letters of Charles Sumner* (Boston 1877) I 531.

40 *Hansard* XLII 799-803, 813-15, 818 (3 May 1838); XLVII 671-5 (30 April 1839); XLVIII 924-6, 929, 931-7, 944 (27 June 1839)

41 JA to Stephen, 18 July 1839, CO 158/118; *TG* 147-8

42 *Letters of GCL* 66; JA to Russell, 25 May 1840, ff. 2-4, 8-9, 11-12, 15; JA to Stephen, 27 May 1840; JA and GCL to Normanby, 19 July 1839, CO 158/118; JA and GCL to Glenelg, 21 March 1838, CO 158/115. The commissioners were criticized in Malta for their failure to consider the establishment of a representative council; and there was a petition of complaint about this, submitted 15 June 1839, which, according to Austin and Lewis, was '*got up* by the extreme and insignificant party who ... in their resentment at our refusal to comply with their unreasonable demand, naturally do all they can to throw discredit on our proceedings.' The petition may have been inspired by Stoddart: JA and GCL to Normanby, 19 July 1839, CO 158/118. See also Cremona *The Malta Constitution of 1835 and Its Historical Background* 31-2.

43 Glenelg to JA and GCL, 16 September 1836, CO 158/113; JA and GCL to Glenelg, 21 March 1838, f. 15, CO 158/115; JA and GCL to Russell, 28 October 1839, CO 158/118; Russell to JA and GCL, 30 September 1839, CO 159/18; Laferla *British Malta* I 154-5, 172-5

44 Glenelg to Treasury, 20 April 1836, CO 158/113; JA to Russell, 25 May 1840, ff. 1, 19-22; JA to Stephen, 27 May 1840, ff. 1-2, CO 158/118

45 Stephen to Vernon Smith, 2 June [1840]; Russell to JA, 8 June 1840; JA to Russell, 25 May 1840, ff. 1, 23, 25, minutes on f. [28], CO 158/118; Russell to JA, 2 June 1840, 13 June 1840, CO 159/16, ff. 84-7. Russell dealt with Austin in a rather peremptory manner. When Austin complained that the colonial secretary reportedly had said that the commissioners did not intend to make a final report, Russell explained that he had only said that 'they *had* not, and [that he] doubted the expediency of their doing so,' and he directed that they be asked 'if they wish [their statement of reasons, i.e., Austin's letter of 25 May 1840] to be laid before Parlt.': Stephen to Vernon Smith, 2 June [1840] and Russell's endorsement, CO 158/118. Sarah never forgave Russell; in 1860 she remembered him (incorrectly) as having ordered Austin home from Malta 'in the most abrupt and, I think, ungentlemanlike manner, – simply, as it appeared, that he might say in the House of Commons that the Comm[ission] was at an end': SA to Brougham, 13 February 1860, UCL. Glenelg resigned in February 1839 because of opposition to his Canadian policy.

46 'Summary of the Measures Introduced in Malta at the Recommendation of the Commissioners of Inquiry' CO 158/118; Lee *Malta 1813-1914* 104-5; Normanby to Russell, 2 September 1839, PRO 30/22, [vol.] 3rd, f. 5. Normanby did not mention, however, that the commissioners were criticized in the newly established Maltese press for not recommending an elected assembly. Opinion in Malta, as reflected in the non-English press, was divided about the commissioners; one paper supported them, the other was criticial: Mercieca 'Political Career of George Mitrovich' 107-8. See also Lee *Malta 1813-1914* 108.

47 Bouverie to Russell, 7 April 1840, CO 158/110; Russell to Bouverie, 1 May 1840, CO 159/19

48 Senior to SA, 31 July 1837, 13 January 1838, Wales; SA to Guizot, 22 December [1854?], GP. Stephen was not merely trying to prop up Austin's spirits. In another context he said Austin was 'a wise and good man, whom it is impossible to know without both affection and respect': Stephen to Napier, 13 June 1842, BL, Add. 34622, f. 604.

49 Stephen attempted but failed to arrange official employment for Austin in 1846. The criminal code was still under discussion, and the parliamentary under-secretary, Benjamin Hawes, suggested calling Stoddart out of retirement for help; but Stephen resisted this, saying he 'would rather suggest John Austin as an Adviser ... If he had but his brother's aptitude for affairs, he would (I think) be among the very first men of his age. For such an affair as this he is perfectly fitted, except that he is sure to be Slow. But *he* will not be prolix.' Hawes did not appreciate Austin's work, however; referring to an unidentified paper, he said, 'Few ever read such a useless and confused document as that of Mr. Austin's': Stephen to Hawes, 11 August 1846 and Hawes's endorsement, Hawes to Stephen, 6 August 1846, CO 323/61, ff. 474-6, 482. Reference to this correspondence was found in Paul Knapland *James Stephen and the British Colonial System 1813-1847* (Madison 1953) 241 n. 32. As early as 1839 Stephen had hoped that Austin would occasionally work for the Colonial Office, as it 'would afford him a quiet, useful and not un-lucrative employment': Stephen to SA, 23 October 1839, copy, Cambridge University Library, Add. 7888, II f. 2. In 1842 Lewis mentioned but did not explain Austin's rejection of a 'Malta project': *Letters of GCL* 125.

50 *Malta Government Gazette* 20 June 1838, 253; SA to Sibylle Mertens-Schaaff-hausen, n.d. [c. 1837], Universitätsbibliothek, Bonn; Laferla *British Malta* I 168; *TG* 145; the guard's conversation is in [Philip] Meadows Taylor *The Story of My Life* ed. A.M. Taylor (London 1877) I 156-7. The *Gazette* described Sarah's 'active exertions ... to ameliorate the social system, and to promote every object which might be conducive to the happiness of any class of the people ... By her perseverance the national industry has been excited, and resources have been brought to notice which formerly languished in obscurity.' She opened a bazaar for the sale of Maltese manufactures in Valletta, and helped establish government sponsored schools in rural districts.

Chapter 6

1 SA to Laura [Peyronnet] Russell, 1 January 1866, Blakiston

2 This portrait has not been located, and the description here is based on a

companion portrait painted by Linnell in 1840 (sold at Sotheby's, 18 October 1950, lot 152) and reproduced in Story's biography of Linnell. (One of these two portraits was owned by Maurice Duff Gordon, Sarah Austin's grandson.) A drawing, presumed to be a preliminary sketch for the 1835 Linnell portrait, is in the National Portrait Gallery. There are also two likenesses of Sarah, one drawn in 1835 and another in 1843, by Wilhelm Hensel in the Nationalgalerie, Berlin. A drawing of Sarah at fifteen or sixteen by Amelia Opie, which Janet Ross thought 'very characteristic,' was copied by Carlo Orsi for *Three Generations of English Women* (1888). Janet Ross thought 'the mouth too much accentuated, so that she looks like a "pouting beauty" (not at all her line)': Janet Ross to John Murray, 27 May 1888, MA. The National Portrait Gallery also has a portrait of Sarah Austin by Lady Arthur Russell, painted a year before Sarah's death, showing her as a melancholy, sick woman. Alfred T. Story *The Life of John Linnell* (London 1892) I, 294-5, II 128-9, 250, 297; Richard Ormond *Early Victorian Portraits* (London 1974) 19-20; Sebastian Hensel *Die Familie Mendelssohn, 1729-1847* (2nd ed., Berlin 1880) II 188.

3 Frances Arabella [Horsley] Thompson *Mendelssohn and His Friends in Kensington: Letters from Fanny and Sophy Horsley, Written in 1833-36* ed. Rosamund Brunel Gotch (London 1934) 202

4 Story *Linnell* II 128

5 *TG* 309; Edward L. Pierce *Memoir and Letters of Charles Sumner* (Boston 1877) 46; *CLC* VI 44, n. 3, V 387

6 *TG* 278; *The Letters of Sydney Smith* ed. Nowell C. Smith (Oxford 1953) II 624; Margaret C. Wicks *The Italian Exiles in London, 1816-1848* (Manchester 1937) 226

7 *CLC* V 386, 396, 387, 416; *The Early Draft of John Stuart Mill's Autobiography* in *CW* I 186

8 James Anthony Froude *Thomas Carlyle: A History of the First Forty Years of His Life, 1795-1835* (New York 1882) II 190; John Sterling to SA, n.d., University of Michigan; *Lettres d'Auguste Comte à John Stuart Mill, 1841-1846* (Paris 1877) 222, 278 (AT)

9 Lithograph by Weld Taylor of Henry P. Briggs' portrait, present location unknown.

10 *CLC* VI 44-5; Diary of 7th Earl of Carlisle, vol. 17, ff. 26-7, Castle Howard; Janet Ross *Early Days Recalled* (London 1891) 9-10

11 John Knox Laughton *Memoirs of the Life and Correspondence of Henry Reeve* (London 1898) I 100

12 PRO, ADM 1/1688; *The Standard* 3 September 1833, 3; 4 September 1833, 3; *The Sixtieth Annual Report of the Royal Humane Society* (London [1834]) 18-33; *The Standard* 10 September 1833, 3

13 *TG* 119; *L'Annotateur* (Boulogne) 5 September 1833, 459-61; Jean-Pierre Lefebvre 'Heine à Boulogne-sur-Mer' *Revue de Littérature Comparée* 47 (1973) 208; SA to Edward Taylor, 20 September 1833, St Bride

14 Heinrich Heine *Briefe (1831-1841)* ed. Fritz H. Eisner (Berlin, Paris 1970) XXI 63-4 (AT); *The Times* 4 September 1833, 3; 'Eyewitness Account' *The Sixtieth Annual Report of the Royal Humane Society* 18-33

15 *The Times* 16 October 1833, 5; 26 September 1833, 3; PRO, ADM 1/1688

16 Paul Cassar *Medical History of Malta* (London 1964) 192-8; Report of All Cholera Cases, 2 September 1837, CO 158/97; GCL to Thomas Frankland Lewis, 3 July 1837, Wales; SA 'The Cholera in Malta' *Fraser's Magazine* 73 (January 1866) 97; *TG* 133-4

17 *TG* 148

18 *TG* 83; SA to John Murray, [31 May 1833], MA

19 V.L. Saulnier *Lettres d'un Dernier Amour: Correspondance Inédite avec Augusta* (Geneva 1952) 107 (AT); *Germany* 335; Janet Ross *The Fourth Generation* (New York 1912) 18

20 SA to Lady William Russell, 23 December 1865, Blakiston; Wicks *Italian Exiles* 233; SA to Fanny Wright, 3 May 1827, University of South Carolina Library. These notes were added to *Fragments* (1841) 303 and were not in the earlier translations in the *New Monthly Magazine* (1830).

21 *Germany* 231

22 SA to Anna Jameson, 26-8 Septeember [1835], Osborn Collection, Yale

23 Ibid.

24 *Anna Jameson: Letters and Friendships (1812-1860)* ed. Beatrice [Mrs Steuart] Erskine (London 1915) 171; *TG* 147; Janet Ross *Three Generations of Englishwomen* (London 1888) I 138; SA to Ottilie von Goethe, 9 August 1840, Weimar; Sydney Smith to SA, 23 January 1840, Waterfield

25 JA to James Stephen, 27 May 1840, CO 158/118

26 SA to Gladstone, 4 January 1853, BL, Add. 44373, f. 230; *TG* 174

27 *EL* 486

28 SA to Thomas Carlyle, 17 July [1841], NLS; Sydney Smith to SA, 29 October 1841, Waterfield

29 SA to Guizot, [c. 1843], GP; SA to Carlyle, 17 July [1841], NLS

30 J. Barthélemy Saint-Hilaire *M. Victor Cousin: Sa Vie et Sa Correspondance* (Paris 1895) III 147 (AT); *TG* 178; *EL* 521

31 SA to Guizot, 20 December 1841, GP; *EL* 573

32 Barthélemy Saint-Hilaire *Cousin* III 147 (AT)

33 SA to Guizot, 20 April 1843, GP

34 *EL* 521; *TG* 177; Nassau Senior to Macvey Napier, 28 May 1841, BL, Add. 34621, f. 674

35 SA to Sieveking, 4 July 1843, letter in authors' possession; *TG* 192; George Grote *Posthumous Papers* ed. Harriet Grote (London 1874) 75; *Athenaeum* 10 June 1843, 550; 3 October 1846, 1020

36 *Henry Crabb Robinson und seine deutschen Freunde: Brücke zwischen England und Deutschland im Zeitalter der Romantik* ed. Hertha Marquardt and Kurt Schreinert (Göttingen 1967) II 170

37 Grote *Posthumous Papers* 75; Barthélemy Saint-Hilaire *Cousin* III 127 (AT); H.H. Houben *Gespräche mit Heine* (Frankfurt am Main 1926) 566-7; *TG* 202; SA to Ottilie von Goethe, 9 August 1840, Weimar

38 *EL* 611, 599-600

39 Lewis Melville [pseud., Lewis Saul Benjamin], ed. *The Berry Papers 1763-1852* (London 1914) 431; SA to Berry, 2 March [n.y.], BL, Add. 37726, ff. 256-8; SA to Macvey Napier, 24 October [n.y.], BL, Add. 34624, f. 174; 2 January 1845, BL, Add. 34625, f. 4; SA to Laura [Peyronnet] Russell, 12-13 June [1864], Blakiston; James Stephen to Henry Taylor, 21 November 1847, Cambridge University Library

40 SA to Macvey Napier, 18 June [1846], BL, Add. 34626, ff. 230

41 SA to Francis Lieber, 15 March 1834, Huntington Library; SA to Guizot, 1 November 1840, GP

42 Years after Madame Guizot's death, Guizot told Sarah that only she could write adequately about his mother: Guizot to SA, 12 May 1862, GP.

43 *TG* 202. Sarah disliked Guizot's mistress, Madame Lieven: see *TG* 324.

44 *TG* 196-7

45 SA to Lansdowne, 25 December [1846?], Bowood

46 *EL* 711. Under Jonathan Austin's will money was left in trust to four of his children; only Charles and Charlotte Austin received their inheritance outright. Each was left 10/62 of his estate, except John Austin, who received 12/62, which amounted to about £3900. In 1850 John Austin received £701, which represented interest on the annuities and part of the bequest. The will was dated 11 August 1846 and proved 22 September 1849: PRO, PROB 11/2098, IR 26/1827, 3237.

47 William M. Colles *Literature and the Pension List* (London 1889) 22; Charles Wentworth Dilke *The Papers of a Critic* (London 1875) I 35; Henry Hallam to SA, 12 August [1849], Waterfield; *TG* 235. Evidently Gladstone spoke on her behalf on the pension issue: SA to Gladstone, 4 January 1855, BL, Add. 44373, f. 229.

48 SA to William Stark [n.d.], UCLA; SA to Henry Taylor, 12 March [1848], Bodleian Library, Oxford. The Austins rented Nutfield, probably from Sir John Easthope; the 1863 rate returns show him as owner. Later the house was considerably altered, but it remained two dwellings under one roof. After

John Austin's death, and probably before, Sarah occupied only one part of the house. Mrs Avril Lansdell, curator of the Weybridge Museum, kindly supplied information about the house.

49 SA to Guizot, n.d. [1849], GP; SA to [unknown recipient], 11 June [n.y.], Harvard University

50 SA to Madame Baudrant, 28 May 1849, University of Iowa Library

51 SA to Blackwood, 12 November [1849], NLS; SA to Madame Friqueti, 6 May [1849], UCLA

52 SA to Madame Baudrant, 28 May [1849], University of Iowa Library

53 SA to Guizot, n.d. [1849], GP

54 Guizot to SA, 26 September 1849, GP. Subsequently there were changes in the plans, but Sarah went to France for the translation.

55 TG 242; SA to John Murray, n.d. [1850], MA

56 SA to G.C. Lewis, 23 October [1854], Wales. On contemporary criticism of Smith's irreverent wit, see Alan Bell Sydney Smith (Oxford 1980) 198.

57 SA to GCL, 23 October [1854], Wales

58 SA to GCL, 23 October [1854], Wales; TG 311

59 TG 244; SA to Murray, 22 October [1854], MA

60 TG 324-5

61 SA to Murray, 22 October [1855], MA; SA to Lansdowne, 18 October [n.y.], Bowood

62 TG 244; Philip Meadows Taylor A Memoir of the Family of Taylor of Norwich (privately printed 1886) 34

63 George Grote to GCL, 6 September [1853], Wales; SA to Guizot, 18 November [post 1848], GP; TG vii

64 SA to Gladstone, 1 April [n.y.]; BL, Add. 44356, f. 231; SA to Guizot, 31 December 1856, GP; Erskine, ed. Anna Jameson; Letters and Friendships 172

65 Grote Posthumous Papers 151

66 TG 361; SA to Adele Schopenhauer, n.d. [1842], Badische Landesbibliothek, Karlsruhe

67 SA to Macvey Napier, 1 July 1846, BL, Add. 34626, f. 260; SA to Lansdowne, 29 November [1835], Bowood; SA to Macvey Napier, 24 January 1847, BL, Add. 34626, f. 561

68 SA to Macvey Napier, 27 May [1846], 27 July [1846], BL, Add. 34626, ff. 216, 299

69 SA to Macvey Napier, 27 May [1846], 18 June [n.y.], 27 July [1846], BL, Add. 34626, ff. 216, 230, 299

70 SA to Murray, 22 January 1849, MA

71 SA to Lansdowne, 6 May [n.y.], Bowood

72 Ibid.; SA to Brougham, 23 February 1831, UCL. Sarah could be persistent in

promoting her family; for example, she secretly petitioned Gladstone on behalf of her son-in-law, and she suggested to G.C. Lewis, in his capacity as editor of the *Edinburgh Review*, that he encourage Lucy to undertake more work. In an understatement Janet Ross said of Sarah, 'The extraordinary vigour of her mind and body was occasionally almost overpowering:': *TG* iii.

73 SA to Brougham, 24 December 1857, UCL; Grote *Posthumous Papers* 68; SA to Guizot, 20 April 1843, GP

74 SA to Richard Taylor, n.d., St Bride

75 SA to Guizot, 21 February 1855, GP

76 Croker called her a 'clever Whig lady' and with justification accused her of suppressing some of Raumer's unflattering descriptions of whig notables, such as Brougham and Russell: J.W. Croker 'Raumer's England in 1835' *Quarterly Review* 56 (July 1836) 530-83; SA to J.W. Carlyle, 25 December [1832], NLS; SA to Macvey Napier, 18 June [1846], BL, Add. 34626, f. 230; A.R. Wheatley *Life and Work of Harriet Martineau* (Fairlawn 1957) 133

77 SA to Henry Taylor, 12 March [1848], Bodleian Library, Oxford; SA 'Souvenirs et Correspondance de Madame Récamier' *Edinburgh Review* 111 (January 1860) 233

78 JA to J.S. Mill, 25 December 1844, Yale; Grote *Posthumous Papers* 88; SA to Murray, 26 July [c. 1853], MA; Ross *Early Days Recalled* 107

79 *LDG* 48; Janet Ross to Murray, 12 February 1887, MA

80 Wicks *Italian Exiles* 236; SA to James Whittle, 24-5 December [n.y.], Waterfield; Grote *Posthumous Papers* 75-6; SA to Harriet Grote, 25 August 1865, UCL

81 SA to Guizot, n.d. [post 1848], n.d. [post 1848], GP; *TG* 325

82 SA to Henry Taylor, 12 March [1848], Bodleian Library, Oxford

83 SA, Commonplace book, Waterfield

84 Douglas Johnson *Guizot: Aspects of French History 1787-1874* (London 1963) 16-18; Melville *The Berry Papers* 434; SA to Guizot, 10 August 1861, GP; Guizot to SA, 29 October 1850, 8 August 1855, 23 March 1857, GP (AT)

85 *François Guizot et Madame Laure de Gasperin: Documents inédits, 1830-1864* ed. André Gayot (Paris 1934) 84 (AT); Guizot to SA, n.d. [March 1849], GP (AT)

86 *TG* 359

87 Guizot to SA, 1 May 1861, GP (AT)

88 SA to Guizot, 9 February 1850, GP; *Athenaeum* 19 July 1845, 717; SA to Lansdowne, n.d. [1847], Bowood

89 *TG* 360; M.C.M. Simpson *Many Memories of Many People* (London 1898) 117; *TG* 378

90 *TG* 326

91 George Eliot *Middlemarch* (New York, Signet edition 1964) 197, 355

Chapter 7

1 H. Mutschman 'Sarah Austin und die deutsche Literatur' *Die Neueren Sprachen* 27 (June-July 1919) 123, for example, wrote of Sarah's 'great fervour for women's emancipation.'
2 SA 'National System of Education in France' *Cochrane's Foreign Quarterly Review* 1 (1835) 277, 291
3 'Disposition of Property by Will – Primogeniture' *Westminster Review* 2 (October 1824) 544
4 *TG* 71
5 *Fragments* 324, 320; *Tour in England, Ireland, and France in the Years 1828 and 1829 ... by a German Prince* (London 1832) II 95n
6 *TG* 172-3
7 SA to Ottilie von Goethe, 9 August 1840, Weimar; *Germany* 28
8 Charles Wentworth Dilke *The Papers of a Critic* (London 1875) I 35; *Fragments* 270
9 SA 'Madame Récamier' *Fraser's Magazine* 40 (September 1849) 268-9
10 Ibid. 268-9, 274
11 SA, translator's preface, xv-xvii and appendix 192, in *The Duchess of Orleans: A Memoir [by Paule d'Harcourt] Translated from the French by Mrs. Austin* (London 1859)
12 SA to Lansdowne, [April 1851], Bowood
13 *TG* 343; *Germany* 414, 417; Sarah noted that Perthes was one of the ten Hamburgers who were declared enemies of the State.
14 *Fragments* 270
15 SA, preface, Lady Holland *A Memoir of the Reverend Sydney Smith* ed. Sarah Austin (New York 1855) II xii
16 *Fragments* 269
17 *Germany* 335
18 SA to Brougham, 19 October [1857], UCL
19 *Hansard* XXIX (17 July 1835) 679-80. Brougham later altered this view.
20 *Evening Mail* (London) 4-6 June 1862, 6
21 SA to Brougham, 16 September [1858], UCL
22 SA to Brougham, 20 October [1858], UCL
23 SA *Two Letters on Girls' Schools, and on the Training of Working Women* (London 1857) 26, 27
24 *Anna Jameson: Letters and Friendships (1812-1860)* ed. Beatrice [Mrs Steuart] Erskine (London 1915) 168
25 SA to Brougham, 12 October [1859], UCL

26 SA *Two Letters* 13-14, 10
27 SA to Hepworth Dixon, 18 December 1860, UCLA; *Two Letters* 28, 14
28 John Taylor to SA, 16 June 1824, Yale
29 SA to Edward Sieveking, 4 July 1834, in authors' possession; L.T. Markby *Memoir of Sir William Markby* (Oxford 1917) 18; SA to Laura [Peyronnet] Russell, 4 August [n.y.], Blakiston
30 *Germany* 230
31 SA to Ottilie von Goethe, 9 August 1840, Weimar
32 SA to Murray, 25 July [1844], MA
33 *Germany* 41, 38n
34 SA to Brougham, 19 October [1857], UCL
35 SA to Ottilie von Goethe, 9 August 1840, Weimar
36 SA to Hepworth Dixon, 4 May [n.y.], UCLA
37 SA to Ottilie von Goethe, 9 August 1840, Weimar
38 H.G. Fiedler 'A Letter from Ottilie von Goethe to Sarah Austin' *Modern Language Review* 14 (1919) 332
39 Sarah translated a few excerpts from *Wahlverwandschaften* in 'Specimens of German Genius,' *New Monthly Magazine* (1830); SA, preface *Letters from Egypt, 1863-65* (London 1865) ix; SA 'Goethe's Character and Moral Influence' *Edinburgh Review* 106 (July 1857) 225.
40 SA to Madame Baudrant, 28 May [1849], University of Iowa Library
41 *TG* 72
42 SA to Ottilie von Goethe, 9 August 1840, Weimar
43 Ibid.
44 *Die neue deutsche Biographie* (Berlin 1952) I 369-71; SA to Besser, 18 October [n.y.], SA to Speckter, 23 March [n.y.], Staats- und Universitätsbibliothek, Hamburg
45 *Germany* 32-3
46 Ibid. 236
47 Ibid. 236-7, 230
48 *Briefwechsel und Tagebücher des Fürsten Hermann von Pückler-Muskau* ed. Ludmilla Assing-Grimelli (Berlin 1873-6) III 122; SA, 'Goethe's Character and Moral Influence' 223-5.
49 Anne Ritchie 'Mrs. John Taylor of Norwich' *Macmillan's Magazine* 55 (December 1886) 115; SA to J.S. Mill, 3 March 1837, British Library of Political and Economic Science
50 F.A. Hayek *John Stuart Mill and Harriet Taylor* (London 1951) 89-90
51 Janet Ross *The Fourth Generation* (London 1912) 73
52 Ironically, in 1832 Harriet Taylor reviewed Sarah Austin's translation of

Pückler-Muskau most favourably: *Monthly Repository* 2nd ser. 6 (1832) 354; SA 'Madame Récamier' 264-74.

53 *EL* 621 (AT)

54 SA to Laura [Peyronnet] Russell, 4 August [c. 1864]; SA to Grey, 20 April [1866], Durham

55 'Amelia Alderson Opie: Worldling and Friend' *Smith College Studies in Modern Languages* 14 (1932-3) 27

56 Anna Letitia (Aikin) Le Breton *Memoir of Mrs. Barbauld, including Letters and Notices of Her Family and Friends* (London 1874) 87

Chapter 8

1 *TG* 265; Thomas Babington Macaulay *Journal* vol. 8, f. 106, 26 August [1854], Trinity College Library, Cambridge. Macaulay added, 'I remember when he was dumb and a Chartist or nearly so. However he is very clever and well informed.'

2 *Plea* vi; SA, Preface, 13

3 *Letters of GCL* 108; 'Centralization' 238, 249; SA to Macvey Napier, 1 July 1846, *Selection from the Correspondence of the Late Macvey Napier* ed. M. Napier (London 1879) 528; SA to Napier, 24 January 1847, BL, Add. 34626, f. 561; J.S. Mill to JA, 13 April 1847, *EL* 712. For SA's pre-1848 conservatism see her 'Ritter von Lang's Life and Times' *Edinburgh Review* 78 (October 1843) 346; and *Athenaeum* 15 March 1845, 263

4 JA to [?], [1848], fragment, Waterfield; *TG* 194; *The Times* 1 March 1848, 6; SA to Lansdowne, [1848], Bowood; Nassau Senior *Journals Kept in France and Italy from 1848 to 1852* ed. M.C.M. Simpson (London 1871) I 115-16; Frances Anne Kemble *Records of Later Life* (London 1882) III 421; *Athenaeum* 31 March 1849, 327-8

5 SA to 3rd Earl Grey, [1866], Durham; *TG* 283-4; SA to Guizot, n.d. [c. 1849], 5 December [c. 1856], GP; SA to Blackwoods, 12 November [1848], NLS. In another explanation Sarah said, 'Time, the example of France, and the manifest growth of democratical spirit in England converted his doubts into grave disapprobation of many of the doctrines held still by some of his early friends': SA to 3rd Earl Grey, n.d. [1865], Durham.

6 *Plea* 16, 18-19; *The Times* 1 March 1848, 6; *TG* 98; 'Centralization' 240. JA thought anarchical notions were easily spread in the absence of sound notions about political economy: SA to Lansdowne, n.d. [1848], Bowood. SA complained of 'the loud dissonances of our times ... the angry vociferations for an unattainable social equality': 'The Grave of Locke' *Athenaeum* 5 October 1850, 1046. See also *Napier Correspondence* 529; SA 'The Late Mr. Charles

Buller' *Fraser's Magazine* 39 (February 1849) 223. Since Mill referred to JA's disavowal of a letter in *The Times* (*EL* 734), it should be said that JA was the author of the letter signed 'J.A.' in *The Times* 1 March 1848, 6. The disavowal, which has not been located, probably repudiated a letter signed 'John Austin' in *The Times* 14 January 1848, 4. A passage also used in the 1 March letter was reproduced from a letter to Lucy in *TG* 98.

7 *Athenaeum* 16 September 1848, 924; SA to 3rd Earl Grey, 10 December [1863], Durham; *TG* 380, 387, 406; SA to Lansdowne [1859], Bowood; SA 'France' *Bentley's Quarterly Review* 1 (July 1859) 518

8 *Plea* 37-8; SA to Lansdowne, [c. 1846], Bowood; *TG* 248, 288, 290-1; SA to Guizot, 22 December [c. 1854], 27 September 1858, 31 December 1860, GP. In her correspondence with the editor of the *Edinburgh Review* Sarah claimed that John Austin was a Whig, but the circumstances of the correspondence gave her statements a self-serving character: SA to Napier, 1 July 1846, 24 January 1847, BL, Add. 34626, ff. 260, 561. Austin adopted the title from Bentham's *Plea for the Constitution* (1803); of course the resemblance between the two essays ends with the titles.

9 SA to Lansdowne, 17 April 1853, Bowood; *TG* 323; SA 'France' 518, 538; SA to 3rd Earl Grey, 3 June [1863], 10 March 1867, Durham; SA to GCL, 24 April 1855, Wales. Sarah spoke of 'the nonsense talked by such feather heads as the good-natured poet Milnes who quarrelled with me last March for not being enchanted and sanguine [about the revolution] – and he was far from being alone': SA to J. Blackwood, 12 November [1848], NLS.

10 Henry Reeve 'Autobiography of John Stuart Mill' *Edinburgh Review* 139 (January 1874) 117

11 James Stephen to SA, 3 September 1853, copy, Cambridge University Library, Add. 7888, II, ff. 90-1; J. Barthélemy Saint-Hilaire *M. Victor Cousin: Sa Vie et Sa Correspondance* (Paris 1895) II 452. See also *TG* vii.

12 Reeve to GCL, 5 January [1859], Wales. Reeve might have thought that Austin's opposition to reform would have been awkward if the Conservative government had introduced a bill for parliamentary reform; in fact the editor shared Austin's views but wanted more discussion of the politics of the day and editorial changes which Austin would not allow: Whitwell Elwin to John Murray, n.d., 21 December 1858, 24 January 1859; SA to Murray, 18 January 1859, MA; SA to 3rd Earl Grey, 2 February 1859, Durham. The pamphlet was the same as the proposed review except for the first few paragraphs. It went into three editions.

13 Notes by SA on Grey's *Parliamentary Government* [c. 1859], Durham; *Germany* 284, 405-6; *Plea* 37, 39-40; JA could have found similar phrases in George Grote *History of Greece* (London 1847, 1850) IV 205-6, VIII 56. Grote referred

to 'constitutional morality' and 'sentiment of constitutional duty.' We are grateful to Professor Frank Turner for directing our attention to Grote as a possible source of JA's usage.

14 SA, Preface 18; *Plea* 39-42; *Letters of GCL* 176-7. See also *Germany* 406.

15 *Plea* 42; *TG* 224, 245, 261; SA 'France' 523. Sarah's statements may be taken as evidence of Austin's opinions, for they spoke with one voice on politics. She claimed there was a 'community of thought and feeling' between them, and that their last eleven years (i.e., 1849-59) 'were spent in an almost unbroken *tête à tête.*' A comparison of their political opinions presented separately, in letters or publications, reveals no more than trivial discrepancies. SA to Dixon, 17 July [1860], UCLA; *TG* 360.

16 SA 'France' 514, 527; *TG* 229; notes by SA on Grey's *Parliamentary Government* [c. 1859]; SA to Grey, 26 December [1863], Durham. The Austins' disapproval of democracy, including the belief that it was linked to conflict and despotism, was shared with and may have been influenced by Guizot. With JA's assistance, SA translated his *Democracy in France* (London 1849). In a puzzling letter Mill suggested that Austin had depreciated Guizot's opinions: *LL* 5.

17 SA 'France' 511. France was destroyed in part by 'that feeling of impotence wh[ich] always cleaves to the mass, and drives them into the arms of despotism': SA to GCL, 21 February [1855], Wales. Sarah also deplored the influence of French revolutionary ideas in Germany and the Napoleonic conquest of the German states: *Germany* 198-9, 222, 294-378, 424.

18 SA 'France' 534-5; JA to SA, 21 April 1848, Waterfield; SA to Lansdowne, [c. March 1848], Bowood; SA to J. Blackwood, 12 November [1848], NLS. Sarah made the following statement in conversation with the Queen of Saxony: 'I think him [Louis Philippe] as odious and contemptible as you do, but I am persuaded we ought all to pray that he may remain where he is': SA to J. Blackwood, 12 November 1848, NLS. Austin thought that 'whatever may be [Louis Philippe's] demerits, his government is the only tolerable one ... which is now possible in that country': JA to [?], [1848], Waterfield.

19 DNB I 739; Lucy Duff Gordon to Lansdowne, 31 May [c. 1854], Bowood; Janet Ross *Early Days Recalled* (London 1891) 31; SA to GCL, 24 April [1855], Wales; SA to Dixon, 3 January 1856, UCLA; SA to 3rd Earl Grey, 20 December [c. 1863], Durham; SA 'France' 527, 539-40

20 SA 'France' 518, 521-2, 530, 539-40; *TG* 229, 238; M.C.M. Simpson *Many Memories of Many People* (London 1898) 117. *Contrasts of Foreign and English Society*, in two volumes, was advertised in 'Mr. Murray's List of Works in the Press' (April 1851) 2. Sarah was also deeply worried by the ignorance that made Chartism appealing: 'I *saw* the wretched crestfallen creatures on the 10th April, and I went home profoundly melancholy. Poor wretches, I

thought, you are silenced – thank God – but will nobody now try to teach you better? Are you for ever to be left to the teachings of the O'Connors etc.?': SA to J. Blackwood, 12 November [1848], NLS. On the need to educate the working classes, see also *Athenaeum* 1 February 1845, 109; 23 December 1848, 1289-90; 16 June 1849, 614.

21 JA to SA, 3 October 1846, BL, Add. 34626, ff. 420-2; *Plea* 11, 14, 27; JA to J.S. Mill, 25 December 1844, Yale; *TG* 218; SA 'France' 509; SA to GCL, 21 February [1855], Wales. For SA's criticism of aristocrats, see *Athenaeum* 18 October 1845, 1016; 16 June 1849, 614.

22 *Plea* 7, 12-14; SA to Grey, 25 November [1863], Durham; *Lect. Juris.* 1125

23 *EL* 734; *TG* 222; SA 'France' 538; see also her reference to 'enlightened Liberals' at 518-19.

24 'Recent Writers on Reform' (1859) in *CW* XIX 344; *The Early Draft of John Stuart Mill's Autobiography* in *CW* I 186, also 78n.; see also F.A. Hayek *John Stuart Mill and Harriet Taylor* (London 1951) 129, 156.

Chapter 9

1 *TG* 199, 325; *Letters of GCL* 132; JA to John Murray, 8 January 1849, MA; SA, Preface, 8-16; John Knox Laughton *Memoirs of the Life and Correspondence of Henry Reeve* (London 1898) II 36.

2 SA to Guizot, 7 September 1849, GP; *TG* 325. Also, 'he meditates and plans, but he does not write. The reason is stronger than the will': SA to Guizot, 3 December 1849, GP.

3 GCL to JA, 23 October 1843, *Letters of GCL* 132; J.S. Mill to SA, 18 January 1845, *EL* 655

4 *Edinburgh Review* 85 (January 1847), e.g., 222

5 John Murray to JA, 6 January 1849, copy; JA to John Murray, 8 January 1849; (in 1854 Murray, in response to SA's suggestion, again proposed reprinting: SA to John Murray, 22 October [1854]), MA; J.S. Mill to Harriet Taylor, 27 January [1849], *LL* 5. On antecedents of revolution project, see *EL* 711-12; *Selections from the Correspondence of the Late Macvey Napier* ed. M. Napier (London 1879) 528.

6 SA, Preface 16-18. In 1860 SA described the prospectus as the announcement of 'the more perfect and extended volume which my husband contemplated.' She had the only surviving copy, and she assumed it had been printed for Murray's quarterly announcements: SA to John Murray, 17 December [1860], MA. SA found a table that may have been drawn up in the planning of the new book: *Lect. Juris.* 1106, 1138. The prospectus or announcement is undated, but it was most probably composed in early 1849, for Murray advertised the book in October 1849. Murray used a truncated title, calling it

The Principles and Relations of Jurisprudence: 'Mr. Murray's List of Forthcoming Works' (October 1849) 5. Furthermore, the prospectus described the projected work in language Austin used in 1847 and 1849 but not earlier; also during much of the 1840s he was said to have been engaged on other projects, for example, on Prussia in 1842-3, on an advance copy of Mill's *Logic* in 1842, and on the province of government in 1847: *EL* 541, 622, 712; *TG* 191. Also, in 1849 SA told Murray that his proposal for a reprint had led JA to revive 'his long dormant projects of resuming his labours': SA to John Murray, 8 January [1849], MA. She later revealed, however, that he did not work on the book during most of the last twelve years of his life: Preface 20.

7 Mill *A System of Logic* book VI, chapter 10, sect. 5, in *CW* VIII 920-24; SA to J.S. Mill, 27 June 1842, British Library of Political and Economic Science; J. Barthélemy Saint-Hilaire *M. Victor Cousin: Sa Vie et Sa Correspondance* (Paris 1895) III 147; *EL* 712. Austin could have read the passage on conditions of permanent political society in Mill's 'Coleridge' (1840), from which it was reprinted in the *Logic*; but there is no evidence that he read it there.

8 SA to Grey, 25 November [c. 1863], Durham; *Plea* 11. The *Plea for the Constitution*, although published in 1859, may be taken as summarizing the conservatism that developed after about 1848.

9 *Plea* 37. Also, 'public utility (though not involving absurdities) leads to differences of opinion which are all but invincible': *Plea* 41. Cf. *Prov. Juris.* 301-3. In enlightened society habitual obedience 'would exclusively arise from reasons bottomed in the principle of utility'; and even in actual society where habitual obedience was partly the consequence of custom and prejudice, it also 'partly arises from a reason bottomed in the principle of utility,' and this reasoned judgment was made by the generality or bulk of the community. Thus in 1832 Austin thought reasoned judgment always contributed to shared belief that lent support to government.

10 *Plea* 37-8. Cf. *Prov. Juris.* 120: although calculation is the guide and not the antagonist of sentiment, 'sentiment without calculation were blind and capricious.'

11 John Stuart Mill *Autobiography* in *CW* I 185. Austin's doubts about the principle of utility are mentioned by Ruben but are incorrectly attributed to a belief that utilitarianism was a potentially radical doctrine which did not adequately 'defend the existence of a particular economic order.' This argument is part of Ruben's view that 'the unifying theme of [Austin's] political thought ... is his defence of the political ascendancy of the middle classes.' This view exaggerates the unity of Austin's thought and tendentiously attributes to him an ideological defence of the middle classes which is difficult to document and, if Austin's own words are used, easy to contradict: Eira Ruben 'John Austin's Political Pamphlets 1824-1859' in *Perspectives in Jurisprudence* ed. Elspeth

Attwooll (Glasgow 1977) 28, 38 (on utility); 21, 23, 24, 27, 29, 33, 37-8 (on middle classes). An explanation of some of Austin's political views as expressions of middle-class, bourgeois interests can also be found in Wilfried Löwenhaupt, *Politischer Utilitarismus und bürgerliches Rechtsdenken: John Austin und die 'Philosophie des positiven Rechts'* (Berlin 1972) 19-20, 32, 357.

12 *Prov. Juris.* 281-5; *Plea* vi, 15, 27

13 *Plea* 40-2

14 *TG* 238; SA 'France,' *Bentley's Quarterly Review* 1 (July 1859) 512. See also *Germany* 179.

15 'Disposition of Property by Will – Primogeniture' *Westminster Review* 2 (October 1824) 524; *Prov. Juris.* 130, 141, see also 565. Of course, in 1832 constitutional 'law' was regarded as positive morality and therefore not as law and not within the province of jurisprudence: *Prov. Juris.* 82; *Lect. Juris.* 771-2.

16 *Prov. Juris.* 131, 136, 142-3

17 Ibid. 143 n. 1

18 *TG* 284. 'Think of Saxony, the cradle of popular education, sending seven deputies to the Landtag who can neither read nor write. It is enough to make one doubt of everything': SA to Kate Whittle, 4 February 1849, Waterfield.

19 *TG* 171, 419-24: 'All the most perverse views on the relations of nations are put forth here as a sort of religion, and are called patriotism'; also, 'A nation is now to be an army': SA to 3rd Earl Grey, [1866], Durham. 'The absorption of Germany in Prussia, is, I am sure, a calamity for the country and the world': *TG* 424. Although she condemned intense and aggressive nationalism in Prussia, she applauded the national feeling that accompanied the reaction against Napoleon and the subsequent assertion of German independence: *Germany* 298, 322, 381, 399, 424-6, 437.

20 *Germany* 286; see *Athenaeum* 16 September 1848, 923: 'Searching for the clear rays of truth and wisdom that are to supersede authority ... can we in conscience say that the condition of the mass of men seems much more hopeful for it ... [than it was] under the unreasonable guidance of blind obedience and unquestioning subjection?'

21 'Centralization' 222-3, 236-7, 239-40, 244-50, 252-5; *Napier Correspondence* 529-30. Sarah welcomed centralized administration of a system of national education: 'National System of Education in France' *Cochrane's Foreign Quarterly Review* 1 (1835) 263. Austin planned another article on 'the legitimate province of the governing power': *Letters of GCL* 152. On contemporary discussion of centralization, see P.B.M. Blaas *Continuity and Anachronism* (The Hague 1978) 174-80.

22 'Centralization' 234-6. See also JA to Napier, 3 October 1846, BL, Add. 34626, ff. 420-2. Sarah also defended centralized administrative authority and used

the word 'centralization' as early as 1833: 'Necessity and Practicability of a National System of Education' *Foreign Quarterly Review* 12 (October 1833) 290-1, 295.

23 *TG* 229, 238-9; SA 'France' 511-12, 526, 536

24 *TG* 121-3; SA 'National System of Education in France' 301 n.; 'Centralization' 244. Sarah knew of Tocqueville's (and Beaumont's) penitentiary report as early as 1833: 'National System of Education' 273. Tocqueville was in London from 8 May to 24 June 1835; the Austins were then residing at Hastings, but SA (and perhaps JA) made journeys to London.

25 *Prov. Juris* 258-9, 264; 'Centralization' 223, 251-2

26 *The Greville Memoirs 1814-1860* ed. Lytton Strachey and Roger Fulford (London 1938) V 401 (entry [21 January] 1847); Georgiana Blakiston *Lord William Russell and His Wife 1815-1846* (London 1972) 497; Harriet Grote *Life of George Grote* 183-4; *Memoirs, Letters, and Remains of Alexis de Tocqueville* (London 1861) II 86. The Austins were critical of Tocqueville's pre-1848 politics: SA to 3rd Earl Grey, 16 March [1858], Durham.

27 SA to Guizot, 2 August [1858], GP

28 SA 'France' 510-12

29 SA, Preface 16

30 *TG* 343, 345

31 Paul Vinogradoff *Outlines of Historical Jurisprudence* (London 1920) I 117. See also Maine, who said of Austin's method, 'That which we reject in the process of abstraction by which the concept of Sovereignty is reached is the entire history of each community': Henry Sumner Maine *Lectures on the Early History of Institutions* (London 1880) 359-60.

32 *Plea* 41-2. Sarah said Austin owned a copy of Blackstone '*covered* with M.S. notes, which my Bro in law Alfred Austin thinks of the highest value. I am going to read them through not with the absurd project of judging them but in order to know of what they consist, and whether they could be arranged in any form for publication': SA to Brougham, n.d. [1860], UCL. This volume was in the Inner Temple Library and was destroyed in 1940. If these notes were made after 1848, one can be confident that they were in sharp contrast to the passage in his lectures where he ridiculed Blackstone for saying English liberty depended on customary common law: *Lect. Juris.* 558. See also 555-6, 565-7 on customary law; and *Outline of the Course of Lectures* (1831) in *Prov. Juris.* 71, where Austin depreciated Blackstone's *Commentaries*.

33 *Plea* vi, 16, 37, 40-2

34 On Savigny, see his *Of the Vocation of Our Age for Legislation and Jurisprudence* (1814; translated by Abraham Hayward; London 1828) and Hermann

Kantorowicz, 'Savigny and the Historical School of Law' *Law Quarterly Review* 53 (July 1937) 326-43.

35 *TG* 186-7, 190, 193; *Henry Crabb Robinson und seine deutschen Freunde:Brücke zwischen England und Deutschland im Zeitalter der Romantik* ed. Hertha Marquardt and Kurt Schreinert (Göttingen 1967) II 458; *Fragments* 329; SA, Preface 15. Sarah said that among the few Englishmen interested in Savigny's subject, those competent to judge admired him; of course, Austin shared with Savigny an interest in Roman law. At Bonn in 1827 Austin was assisted in his study of German by a Doctor of Law who had studied with Savigny: *TG* 69. One of Austin's reasons for being in Berlin was to prepare an article on Prussia: *TG* 180, 191. In his University of London lectures Austin expressed admiration for Savigny's scholarship while disagreeing with him, particularly with his *Vocation*, which was the work that contained his clearest statement as a spokesman for the historical school. Austin called this 'his specious but hollow treatise'; Savigny was called self-contradictory and his arguments fallacious, ridiculous, and absurd: *Prov. Juris.* 55; *Lect. Juris.* 689, 691, 700, 702-3, 773, 1072. Sarah Austin's favourable and conciliatory statements in the note at 1073-4 were written after her husband's death, and she attributed high esteem for Savigny to her husband in the posthumous Preface (p. 15). Austin's bizarre statement (*Lect. Juris.* 701-2) that Bentham belonged to the historical school was justified with the statement that Bentham, like those in the historical school, thought law should be based on experience and not on *a priori* principle. Of course, in this Austin ignored the differences between Bentham and the historical school regarding the definitions of law, the character of society, and the ways of changing law. Austin also said the historical school should be renamed the inductive and utilitarian school.

36 *Plea* e.g., 38-9, 41; William Markby 'Austin' *Encyclopaedia Britannica* (11th ed., London 1910-11) II 940; *EL* 707

37 SA, Preface 15. There is an indication in Sarah's editing of the essay 'On the Uses of the Study of Jurisprudence' that she did not appreciate the significance of the changes. This essay combined material from Austin's introductory lectures at the University of London and the Inner Temple with 'a few links from other sources.' One of these links, apparently, was an account of the aristocracy, 'whose stations and talents destine them to the patrician profession of practical politics,' even though such a statement would have been out of place in the lectures given in the early 1830s: *Lect. Juris.* 1106, 1125. Sarah was not the only one who did not realize that fundamental changes had taken place. Mill attributed Austin's failure to complete his work to character defects: *Autobiography* in *CW* I 77. Senior thought Austin's

problem was to have gone on 'extending and deepening his foundations till time failed for erecting his walls.' He also said, 'I have learned much from two or three great men, from Whately, from Stephen and from Macaulay, but I think from no one (except perhaps Whately) as from John Austin': Senior to Charles Austin, [December 1859].

38 *TG* 325; SA to John Murray, 22 October [1854], MA. Finally Sarah 'shrunk from asking what *might* be a reproachful question.' She reported that 'even the homage continually paid to his book in England and abroad seems to give him little pleasure.'

Chapter 10

1 SA to Dixon, 17 July [1860], UCLA; Harriet Grote to Lady William Russell, 13 July [1861?], Blakiston. Austin had been ill with bronchitis for seven weeks.

2 *TG* 358, 362; SA to 3rd Earl Grey, 20 April [1866], 4 September [1866], Durham; SA to Lansdowne, 15 February [1860], 18 February [1861], Bowood

3 *TG* 325, 394; SA to 3rd Earl Grey, 2 February [1859], Durham; SA to Lansdowne, 18 October [1858], Bowood; SA to Anna Jameson, 26-8 September [1835], Osborn Collection, Yale

4 SA to Laura [Peyronnet] Russell, 1 January 1866, Blakiston; SA to Lansdowne, 7 December [1860], Bowood; SA to Dixon, 30 June [1863], UCLA. Henry Reeve said, 'Nothing can equal her devotion to his memory': John Knox Laughton *Memoirs of the Life and Correspondence of Henry Reeve* (London 1898) II 36.

5 Laughton *Life of Henry Reeve* II 44; SA to Brougham, 4 May [1860], UCL; *Law Magazine and Law Review* 9 (May 1860) 164-70

6 SA to Lansdowne, 1 October [1849?], 15 February [1860], Bowood. Sarah told Brougham, '[Austin] begs me to offer to your Lordship the expression of his ardent admiration and sympathy'; and on another occasion 'Nobody is more able [than Austin] to estimate your Lordship's immense claims to the respect and gratitude of mankind, and nobody more constantly insists on them': SA to Brougham, 19 October [1857], [24?] December 1857, 13 February [1860], UCL. Sarah also told Elwin – and Elwin told Brougham – 'that her husband always said that the great name which would stand conspicuous above all others in the future histories of this generation would be that of Brougham.' Since on the same occasion she asked Elwin to send Brougham her regards, we may assume that she intended the flattery also to reach him: Whitwell Elwin to Brougham, 11 November 1856, UCL. In contrast to the obsequiousness of Sarah's letters, John, in the only extant letter to Brougham, was quite restrained; he thanked Brougham for allowing him to

read certain letters and expressed gratitude for Brougham's kind attentions to Mrs Austin: JA to Brougham, 10 October 1859, UCL.

7 SA to Dixon, 2 April [1862], UCLA; *TG* 372-3. The text of the 1861 edition is not quite the same as the 1832 edition. There were a few deletions and some additions of JA's manuscript notes, a table, and a few notes composed by Sarah.

8 *TG* 365-6, 372. Lewis and Romilly were 'my right hand and my left': SA to Arthur Russell, 17 August [c. 1862], Blakiston. Sarah was also aided by William Markby, a young barrister recommended by Erle, by a Mr Booth, and by Richard Quain (who had heard Austin lecture). Markby married Sarah's niece and later became a prolific writer on jurisprudence. James Fitzjames Stephen had proposed attending Austin's funeral, 'as there were few men,' he said, 'for whom I had more respect or who deserved it more': Leslie Stephen *Life of Sir James Fitzjames Stephen* (2nd ed., London 1895) 172; 'Austin's Jurisprudence' *Saturday Review* 11 (20 April 1861), 397-9.

9 SA to Brougham, 9 November [1862], 13 February [1860], UCL; SA to Guizot, 7 July 1861, GP; SA to Murray, n.d. [1861], MA; SA to Dixon, 18 December [1861?], UCLA; SA to Lansdowne, 22 January 1862, 9 January [1863], Bowood; *TG* 363-5, 400-1, 404; Janet Ross *Three Generations of Englishwomen* (1st ed., London 1888) II 135

10 SA to John Murray, 7 July [1860], MA. Sarah said with specific reference to the previously unpublished lectures that they would appear as 'they were delivered or nearly so. The work will be imperfect, but it will be *genuine*': SA to Dixon, 17 July [1862?], UCLA. See also SA, Preface 25, 27. Austin read his lectures from prepared texts, and Henry Reeve must have been referring to them when he reported that the manuscripts were 'in perfect order, and might be sent at once to the press': Reeve to Brougham, 7 August 1860, Laughton *Life of Henry Reeve* II 47. In his obituary Reeve contradicted this, for he said Sarah 'completed the imperfect edifice from the fragments that remained': *The Times* 12 August 1867. There may have been a few difficulties. For example, a lecture was missing, and notes made by John Stuart Mill filled the gap, but only after the 1863 edition appeared. And Sarah had to decide whether to publish notes that Austin made after the lectures were given. There also was a difficulty in integrating the Inner Temple lectures with those that had been given at the University of London, but it was removed when she discovered that Austin had indicated how this could be accomplished.

11 Sarah Austin's description of parts of the manuscript as confused and fragmentary (Preface 23-4) referred to the supplementary material, not the lectures. These parts included Tables and Notes, Essays on Interpretation and Analogy, Notes on Codification, Notes on Criminal Law, and an essay, which

she also published separately in 1863 in 250 copies, 'On the Uses of the Study of Jurisprudence.' One fragment on Analogy consisted of numerous scrawled scraps. She complained about the difficulty of deciphering, which, in view of Austin's large, legible, unhurried handwriting could only have been directed at the discontinuous and unordered character of this part of the manuscripts. In the essay 'On the Uses of the Study of Jurisprudence' she certainly exceeded normal editorial discretion, for she combined two lectures into one continuous essay, omitted repetitions, and supplied 'a few links from other sources.' She acknowledged that it was 'welded together out of scraps.' *TG* 366; SA to Brougham, 16 June [1863], 6 April 1863, UCL; SA to 3rd Earl Grey, 3 March 1863, Durham; SA to John Murray, incomplete [1862], MA; *Lect. Juris.* 1106, 1127.

12 *The Student's Edition: Lectures on Jurisprudence ... Abridged ...* ed. Robert Campbell (London 1875); Gordon Campbell *An Analysis of Austin's Lectures on Jurisprudence* (London 1877); Henry Sumner Maine *Lectures on the Early History of Institutions* (3rd ed., London 1880) 345; Albert Kocourek 'The Century of Analytic Jurisprudence since John Austin' in *Law: A Century of Progress 1835-1935* (New York 1937) II 202; Richard A. Cosgrove *The Rule of Law: Albert Venn Dicey, Victorian Jurist* (Chapel Hill 1980) 23-6

13 *TG* 401; SA to Lansdowne, 1 December [1864], Bowood. Sarah also said, 'My dear husband's fame and authority are constantly rising, and I have been permitted to assist in this! ... I am surprised to find myself *wishing to live*, but I do wish to last long enough to finish': SA to Guizot, 29 November 1865, GP. The book was also used in constructing the examination at the University of London in 1865, when Quain was the examiner: SA to Murray 15 February [1865], MA.

14 SA to Dixon, 30 June [1863], UCLA; SA to Arthur Russell, 17 August [c. 1862], Blakiston; 'Austin on Jurisprudence' *Edinburgh Review* 118 (October 1863) 439-40. Sarah said of Mill's review, 'It is the best of many which have appeared – all equally laudatory if not equally intelligent. This is, after all, my greatest earthly consolation': SA to Guizot, [1863 or 1864], GP. Mill ultimately found and sent his notes; Sarah acknowledged their value and used them to prepare the third edition, which appeared after her death.

15 SA to 3rd Earl Grey, 6 November 1863, Durham; *TG* 413, 418. Maine, despite being a spokesman for the historical school, contributed to Austin's reputation, and he may already have done so in the early sixties. William Markby suggested that in both public and private lectures Maine urged on his audiences the importance of Austin's analytical inquiries: *Encyclopaedia Britannica* (11th ed., London 1910-11) II 939. This perhaps explains why Sarah hoped to meet Maine: 'He is one of the persons in whom I take the

greatest interest': SA to John Murray, 5 May 1865, MA. Austin was heavily relied upon in *Thoughts on Government and Legislation* by Lord Wrottesley (London 1860).

16 *TG* 363, 371-2, 407, 413; Alexander Duff Gordon to GCL, [1861], Wales; SA to Guizot, 21 August 1861, 29 November 1865, GP; SA to Laura [Peyronnet] Russell, 1 January 1866, Blakiston; Lucy Duff Gordon *Letters from Egypt 1863-65* (London 1865); 'Letters from the Cape' in *Vacation Tourists and Notes of Travel in 1862-3* ed. Francis Galton (London 1864) 119-20

17 The inscription was in Latin, which was composed by Sarah with Hawtrey's help. We are grateful to the former rector of the parish church at Weybridge, the Reverend Michael R. Buckley, for sending the inscription and the translation from the parish records.

Index